THE QUEER POLITICS OF PRIDE

THE QUEER POLITICS OF PRIDE

Global LGBTQ+ Activism and Homocapitalism

Dr Daniel Conway

BLOOMSBURY ACADEMIC
LONDON • NEW YORK • OXFORD • NEW DELHI • SYDNEY

BLOOMSBURY ACADEMIC
Bloomsbury Publishing Plc, 50 Bedford Square, London, WC1B 3DP, UK
Bloomsbury Publishing Inc, 1359 Broadway, New York, NY 10018, USA
Bloomsbury Publishing Ireland, 29 Earlsfort Terrace, Dublin 2, D02 AY28, Ireland

BLOOMSBURY, BLOOMSBURY ACADEMIC and the Diana logo are trademarks of Bloomsbury Publishing Plc

First published in Great Britain 2025

Copyright © Daniel Conway, 2025

Daniel Conway has asserted his right under the Copyright, Designs and Patents Act, 1988, to be identified as Author of this work.

For legal purposes the Acknowledgements on pp. vii–viii constitute an extension of this copyright page.

Cover image: Queer Liberation March 2019, New York. Image © Daniel Conway.

All rights reserved. No part of this publication may be: i) reproduced or transmitted in any form, electronic or mechanical, including photocopying, recording or by means of any information storage or retrieval system without prior permission in writing from the publishers; or ii) used or reproduced in any way for the training, development or operation of artificial intelligence (AI) technologies, including generative AI technologies. The rights holders expressly reserve this publication from the text and data mining exception as per Article 4(3) of the Digital Single Market Directive (EU) 2019/790.

Bloomsbury Publishing Plc does not have any control over, or responsibility for, any third-party websites referred to or in this book. All internet addresses given in this book were correct at the time of going to press. The author and publisher regret any inconvenience caused if addresses have changed or sites have ceased to exist, but can accept no responsibility for any such changes.

A catalogue record for this book is available from the British Library.

Library of Congress Control Number: 2025942283

ISBN: HB: 978-1-3504-0227-0
PB: 978-1-3504-0226-3
ePDF: 978-1-3504-0229-4
eBook: 978-1-3504-0228-7

Typeset by Integra Software Services Pvt. Ltd.

For product safety related questions contact productsafety@bloomsbury.com.

To find out more about our authors and books visit www.bloomsbury.com and sign up for our newsletters.

CONTENTS

List of Figures	vi
Acknowledgements	vii

Chapter 1
THE QUEER POLITICS OF PRIDE: GLOBAL LGBTQ+
ACTIVISM AND HOMOCAPITALISM ... 1

Chapter 2
A QUEER CONCEPTUALIZATION OF PRIDE ... 23

Chapter 3
PRIDE AS A 'MIRROR', NOT A 'MICROCOSM', OF SOCIETY:
CONFLICTS OVER RACE, CLASS AND GENDER ... 59

Chapter 4
CORPORATE PRIDE, COMMERCIALIZATION AND THE GLOBAL
PRIDE CIRCUIT ... 83

Chapter 5
PRIDE, THE STATE AND RAINBOW DIPLOMACY ... 115

Chapter 6
RECLAIMING PRIDE: QUEER AND ALTERNATIVE PRIDE
ORGANIZING ... 141

Chapter 7
CONCLUSION: HOMOCAPITALISM AND THE QUEER POLITICS
OF PRIDE ... 165

References	176
Index	190

FIGURES

1	Brighton Pride parade, 2015	3
2	'Mobilize for Equality', Pride Luminaries Brunch, World Pride New York, 2018	7
3	Fundi Ndaba and Ntsupe Mohapi at London Pride's 'VIP Area', 2023	17
4	Soweto Pride 2018	25
5	'Death of Pride', London Pride protest. Permission granted by ACT UP London	36
6	Saks 5th Avenue, Stonewall Anniversary/Pride Month fashion range	56
7	'Move the Porsche Bitch Pride is here!', Johannesburg Pride parade 2018	69
8	Dion George MP, Roberto Quintas, Cape Town Executive Member, and the Democratic Alliance at Greenpoint Rainbow Crossing, Cape Town Pride 2024	76
9	TISS Queer Collective at Mumbai Pride 2019	78
10	IBM 'Legendary Pride', 2019	92
11	Out & Equal Asia Conference, Shanghai Pride 2018	97
12	Mac Stands with Inclusion by the refuse bin, Hong Kong Pride 2018	104
13	'Sweden Loves Equality', Cape Town Pride marshall 2024	116
14	Canada at Taiwan Pride 2018	121
15	Taiwan, First in Asia	131
16	New York Police with the Drag March	143
17	Kong and Vincent at Taiwan Pride	150
18	Hong Kong Migrants Pride 2018	155
19	Silent 'Die In', Soweto Pride, 2018	167
20	Jade Madingwane, Forum for the Empowerment of Women and organizer of Soweto Pride	167
21	Queer Liberation March, New York, 2019	173

ACKNOWLEDGEMENTS

The research for this book was supported by the Leverhulme Trust Fellowship (grant number RF-2018-440). The Fellowship enabled me to take twelve months of research leave and supported travel to different Pride events across the world and for that, I'm truly grateful. The thoughts, arguments and evidence presented in this book owe an enormous debt of gratitude to the activists, organizers, academics, journalists, diplomats and other attendees of Pride events that I encountered and who generously gave me their time. I am privileged that quite a few have become good friends. Thanks also to Jamie Martin at the Wits Centre for Diversity Studies, who helped with research assistance at Johannesburg Pride. Audiences at the University of Bristol, York University, Toronto, the University of British Columbia, the Chinese University of Hong Kong, and members of the Feminist Theory and Gender Studies Section and LGBTQA Caucus of the International Studies Association have also shaped my thinking. Different aspects of the argument and case studies were developed in articles published in the journals *Sociology, Sexualities, International Feminist Journal of Politics* and *International Affairs*. I am grateful to reviewers from these journals and to Emil Edenborg, with whom I co-wrote an article on Rainbow Diplomacy published in *International Affairs*.

Thanks to people who gave advice, shared contacts and facilitated introductions. In particular, thanks to Qingxuan Lin (Alfie) in Shanghai, Chi Ta-wei in Taipei, Suen Yiu Tung and Travis Kong in Hong Kong, Michael Lavers and Emily J. Kirk for their invaluable advice about the complexities of LGBTQ+ politics in Cuba and Richard Ballard in Johannesburg, and Jose Carlos Rivera and S. in Cape Town.

The project took an unexpected turn when I began exhibiting photographs of Pride in London, Johannesburg and the United States. Thanks go to Alex Green for helping with the technical and curatorial aspects of this and to Miriam Dwek and the University of Westminster for financially supporting these events. Thanks also to Antony Phillipson, the UK High Commissioner to South Africa, Adam Bye, Josh Reid and Louise Coskeran at the Foreign, Commonwealth and Development Office, Keval Harie and Linda Chernis at the GALA Queer Archive of South Africa, Axel Bayer at the German Embassy to South Africa, Joaquim A. Neto at Culthouse London, Phil Thurston at the Rand Club,

Johannesburg, Pliny Soocoormanee at the Peter Tatchell Foundation, Lord Jonny Oates at the All-Party Parliamentary Group on Global LGBT+ Rights, Christopher Joell-Deshields at London Pride, Roxanne Escobales, the staff at Chatham House, the Africa Centre, Newington Green Meeting House and Diane Price-Herndl at the Department of Women, Gender and Sexuality Studies, University of Southern Florida.

Thanks to my academic (and other!) friends for their advice, support and companionship: Ana Jordan, Olimpia Burchiellaro, How Wee Ng, Stijn van Kessel, Phillip Ayoub, Nicky Rehbok, Robert Gillis, Stephen Pentz, Matthew Clayton, Maria Holt, Ken Sable, Carla Tsampiras, Catherine Chiara Charrett, Ipshita Basu, Béatrice Châteauvert-Gagnon, Jutta Weldes, Martin Zebracki, Colin Yang and Lizzie Seal.

I dedicate this book to grassroots queer activists in South Africa: Ntsupe Mohapi of the Ekurhuleni Pride Organizing Committee, Jade Madingwane and the team at the Forum for the Empowerment of Women and Mpumi Mathabela at the One in Nine Campaign. They are the most courageous people I have met. Details of how to support Soweto Pride, Ekurhuleni Pride and other queer activists in South Africa can be obtained from the GALA Queer Archive in Johannesburg (gala.co.za).

Chapter 1

THE QUEER POLITICS OF PRIDE: GLOBAL LGBTQ+ ACTIVISM AND HOMOCAPITALISM

Pride is reclaiming our identity, claiming back the space. It's like taking back something that was taken from us, it's like coming out all over again, it's like, 'I'm here!' Pride, for me, symbolizes unity, symbolizes life, it symbolizes purity. If there was ever a God out there, I get to see a God on Pride because that's where love is shared. The LGBTI+ community is full of love. It's multi-coloured, it's a rainbow. So for me, Pride, it's reclaiming who we are, it's about the safe space, it's about getting the message out there to the people to say that LGBTI+ communities are there, they live in your very communities, they could be your neighbour, they could be your daughter ....So, for me, that is Pride, that's what Pride symbolizes, being out there and claiming back your identity and saying, 'I'm here whether you like it or not!'

– Zandile Matsoeneng, Soweto, South Africa
(interview with the author, 2018)

So, what is Pride? If we patterned it after the Western concept of Pride, then we're really fucked-up. You always go back to the model of what Pride is. It's not for the young alone. It's not for the beautiful alone, and in the West, it is in a way. For those, come on, it's like $11 for a beer! When you buy it outside it's $3 or $5, and then you go in the Pride area in LA, it becomes $11 for beer. Who benefits from that? That's not Pride, and do you give back the money to the community? No, they don't! So, what is Pride now?

– David, queer activist, Manila, the Philippines
(interview with the author, 2019)

In 2015, one float in the Brighton Pride parade with #ProudtobeaBrightonemployer emblazoned across the side caught my attention. On board, the financial service company's employees wore personalized t-shirts with #proudtobeScottish, #proudtobeaScouser[1] and a person with a ginger beard sported a #proudtobeginge t-shirt. Had the meanings and purposes of Pride really become this broad, meaningless and anodyne, I wondered? Did this symbolize Pride's total co-option by capitalism, its utility as a platform for corporate advertising and how Pride has become a feel-good party for corporate employees? I began to pay greater attention to criticisms of and protests at Pride in the UK and elsewhere, criticisms that focused on Pride's alleged over-commercialization, with the involvement of companies from banks, airlines and arms manufacturers being contested by queer and other social justice activists. The controversies over the involvement of state institutions, including the police and military at Pride became increasingly visible from the 2010s onwards, when Pride parades in North America and Europe were disrupted by Black Lives Matter and other anti-racist protestors. In June 2017, I went on a driving holiday from Vancouver to San Francisco. Unintentionally, and because it was 'Pride Month', I saw Pride parades on almost every stop on the trip. The difference in scale, aesthetics, and political and social issues highlighted by each Pride parade was striking. The friendly, community feel of Pride in the small city of Olympia, Washington state, contrasted with the massive scale, heavily securitized and ostentatious expense of San Francisco Pride. I thought about the different politics these events expressed, the purposes they performed and about whether the criticisms levelled against Pride are valid. I wondered if the same politics, criticisms and controversies happen at Pride events elsewhere in the world, particularly outside of Europe and North America, where new Prides continue to emerge and are marked as signs of progress for LGBTQ+ rights.

In this book, I focus on case studies of Pride to explore why, how (and if) Pride matters, what Pride is and means. What issues does it raise and what issues and communities it ignores. What forms of activism, protest and display take place at Pride events and what are the points of controversy and protest aimed at Pride. I aim to do this by focusing primarily, but not exclusively, on Pride events outside of Europe and North America, returning to my research background in South Africa and exploring Pride in selected territories in East and South Asia and North America, including Cuba and New York. As new Pride events continue to emerge across the world and are extolled as key moments in a country's LGBTQ+ rights progress (Ayoub et al., 2021), so have queer critiques of Pride in many of these contexts. In recent years,

1. Colloquial term for a resident of Liverpool.

Figure 1 Brighton Pride parade, 2015.

the organization of what can be considered as 'alternative', 'counter' or 'rival' Prides has occurred because of the perceived exclusions and marginalization of certain groups at official Pride events. These 'alternative' Prides include UK Black Pride, Trans Pride and the New York Queer Liberation March (McCartan and Nash, 2022). A key point of contention at these alternative Prides is the reclamation of queer protest, queer commitments to social justice and political radicalism. What constitutes 'queer' and 'queer activism' is complex. As this book will demonstrate, queer activists can also be Pride organizers, but their queerness is rooted in their desire to reject the 'respectability politics' (Ward, 2008) of the broader LGBT rights movement, and a wish to replace equal rights discourses with a 'celebration of difference and challenge to normative social relations' (Brown, 2015: 73). Queer activists who protest against mainstream Prides and/or organize alternative Prides essentially aim to 'return Pride to being active political protests against mainstream gender and sexual norms instead of merely celebrating "progress"' (McCartan and Nash, 2022: 775).

As Pride has grown in scale, tensions over the balance between protest and celebration, conformity or confrontation, have become acute. Queer criticism and protest against Pride have focused on a range of broad issues and specific controversies including opposition to the involvement of oppressive and violent state institutions, such as the police and military (Glass, 2020; Holmes, 2017; Rossdale, 2019), the use of Pride by foreign states to 'pinkwash' their international reputations either by sponsorship of Pride events, involvement in the parade or putting pressure on organizers to ban critics from marching (Schulman, 2012a), organizing Pride events that exclude people of colour, the disabled, immigrants or the economically marginalized and above all, the commercialization of Pride through corporate sponsorship and involvement in the parade is a key criticism (Glass, 2020; Schulman, 2012b; Ward, 2008). The LGBTQ+ activist Peter Tatchell summarizes broader queer criticisms of Pride in the Global North when he argues that 'Pride is now capitalism with a pink hue' and that Pride has retreated from the 'ideals and vision' of its pioneers (Tatchell, 2019). Tatchell believes that Pride embodies a majority of LGBTQ+ people's desire to 'no longer dissent' and 'happily settle for equal rights within the existing social order, often uncritically seeking what straights have' (Tatchell, 2019). Pride, from this perspective, has become part of the 'mainstreaming' of LGBTQ+ culture which has 'lost its critical edge' along with 'a huge loss of confidence and optimism' with Pride representing a 'depressing politics of conformism, respectability and moderation' (Tatchell, 2019). If this is the case, it poses the question of what purpose or utility Pride plays in contemporary LGBTQ+ organizing and campaigning, and casts doubt on its usefulness as an activist platform in other global contexts.

The commercialization of Pride has been the focus of sharp and ongoing queer criticism across the world, but the growing political and social backlash against LGBTQ+ rights in many regions of the world (Ayoub and Stoekl, 2024), along with the reversal of rights that has either happened or is threatened in countries including the United States, Hungary and Uganda have brought debates and controversies about the commercialization of Pride into sharp focus. The homophobic and transphobic backlash against LGBTQ+ rights and communities has led some corporations to step away from 'Pride Month' marketing and activities. For example, in 2023, the US chain store, Target, removed LGBTQ+ Pride branded products following a 'volatile' online anti-LGBTQ+ campaign that led to people physically threatening shop assistants and smashing rainbow-branded merchandise in stores (*The Guardian*, 2024). In the UK, a planned Pride exhibition at the department store John Lewis was cancelled following homophobic and transphobic online attacks (Fox, 2024). Following the advent of the second Trump Presidency in the United States, corporate withdrawal from Pride has significantly increased (Murray, 2025). Discussing these developments at the 2024 International Studies Association conference, some academics wondered whether the queer critique of 'homocapitalism' (Rao, 2015, 2020) is too purist and needs to be reframed in a world where LGBTQ+ rights progress has stalled and is subject to reversal. These are valid questions, and it is important to consider whether 'rainbow branding' and corporate involvement in Pride and LGBTQ+ advocacy, on balance, create positive social impacts from powerful allies, or whether it exists purely as a disingenuous smokescreen. Most of the world's population lives within capitalism and throughout this book, I emphasize the constraints and compromises these places on individual agency to leverage, contest and change social and political relations. For many queer critics of the commercialization of Pride, the withdrawal of corporations from LGBTQ+ spaces and causes in times of threat demonstrates business's lack of commitment to LGBTQ+ communities and rights in the first place. These alternative perspectives draw from contrasting ideological paradigms and divergent beliefs in either the ability of capitalism to adapt and deliver progressive change, or capitalism's ability to adapt to co-opt protest and to perpetuate and conceal injustice, exploitation and inequality.

Exploring Pride internationally

The research journey for this book began at Shanghai Pride in 2018, held on the tenth anniversary of Pride in the city and continued on an ethnographic exploration of Pride events in South Africa, China, Hong Kong, Taiwan, India, Cuba and World Pride in New York. In Shanghai, Pride took place without a parade and largely behind the closed doors of Western chain hotels, in diplomatic missions and cultural centres, and at some local LGBTQ+-friendly bars, galleries and restaurants. Wei, one of the organizers of Shanghai Pride, told me that Shanghai Pride adopted what was a 'soft, not hard, sell' approach to advocating LGBTQ+ rights. This 'soft sell' was also framed around the belief that, as Wei also said, 'money talks' in Chinese society. As a result, Shanghai Pride co-hosted an event with the US-based LGBTQ+ business advocacy group Out & Equal and repeatedly highlighted their international corporate sponsors, clearly wanting to show that tolerance and inclusion of LGBTQ+ communities made 'good business sense'. Despite this politically cautious approach, the organizers of Pride in Shanghai took a collective decision to stop the event in 2021 because harassment and intimidation from the local authorities had become so significant (see Bernot and Davies, 2024; Bernot et al., 2024). One member of the organizing committee, a Malaysian citizen but long-standing resident of Shanghai, had the renewal of his work visa denied and was forced to leave. The clampdown on LGBTQ+ organizing has continued, and, as will be discussed later in this book, this raises serious questions about the argument that to premise the value of LGBTQ+ people and rights in economic terms is a pragmatic and effective strategy for advancing rights.

The first phase of the research journey ended at World Pride in New York in 2019 that took place on the fiftieth anniversary of the Stonewall Riots. With a budget of $12 million, the World Pride parade was over nine hours long and included a two-week series of parties, conferences, exclusive VIP receptions and a concert headlined by Madonna. As I will describe in greater detail in Chapter 4, one of the first events I attended at World Pride was the 'Pride Luminaries Brunch' at an outside bar atop a skyscraper with views over Manhattan. It was clear from the photo release notice at the entrance and the professional photographers and camera people present that the event's sponsors viewed the occasion as an ideal marketing opportunity. The 'Pride Luminary' awardees were something of an afterthought and attendees talked loudly over their speeches as they drank at the Skyy Vodka and Barefoot Wine's free bars. The collision of the worlds of privileged consumers and the precarious and oppressed continued at the World Pride parade, with its large floats sponsored by corporations, embassies and TV shows. A few streets away, the Queer Liberation March held an 'alternative' anti-corporate and intersectional Pride parade that attracted over 45,000 attendees protesting the politics of the US government and values and approach of World Pride.

The criticisms about Pride having been co-opted by and a tool for capitalism, of being sites for racist and elitist exclusion, or as having morphed from what was a defiant protest march to commemorate a riot, to a complacent street party, have been openly debated in activist circles in Europe and North America (see Glass, 2020). Yet, these criticisms and open protests are largely absent in the academic and popular literature on Pride, most of which uncritically celebrates Pride, makes bold claims about its political and social impacts and either ignores or minimizes queer activist critiques. As I will argue in this book, I think this is partly because these authors consider Pride only as social movement and study it as such. While a particular Pride event can be part of a broader social movement for LGBTQ+ rights, social justice and protest, it can equally be none of these things and can exist only for a day. Pride can be organized as a music festival or a pop-up alcohol-fuelled street party and has no broader political intent. Pride events in major cities across the world are increasingly organized by professional

Figure 2 'Mobilize for Equality', Pride Luminaries Brunch, World Pride New York, 2018.

teams and are formally registered corporate or charity entities. Many and sometimes none of Pride's organizers have backgrounds in activist or social justice movements, and no desire or need to be. It is unwise to rely solely on the accounts Pride organizers give about the purposes and impacts of their events. This is because professional organizers who run large-scale Prides, with big budgets and close links with political and corporate elites can be unreliable narrators, they have a vested interest to present a positive impression about their event. This also explains why studies premised on accounts given by Pride organizers, sometimes without the researcher even having attended the Pride events they are discussing, tend to be positive, but these are flawed methods for the study of Pride and the resulting analysis is inevitably unreliable and inadequate.

Pride plays an important part in many LGBTQ+ people's 'coming out' journey of self-discovery and affirmation. This is, of course, a meaningful role Pride can play in people's lives. Pride, as a celebratory and fun party, can also play an important part for LGBTQ+ people, who are marginalized or isolated, in discovering that there is a wider community, forging relations and developing an affirmatory sense of self, developing Pride in place of shame at being an LGBTQ+ person. Yet personal investment in Pride for these reasons should not lead us to forget about who is not included, and who may not feel affirmed and celebrated by Pride. It is important to consider the ideological effects Pride has, particularly when commercial and state institutions are involved. Similarly, relying only on the accounts of those who attend Pride and who presumably enjoy it, as much existing work on Pride does, inevitably overlooks those who are not, or cannot be, at Pride. As I will discuss throughout this book, Pride in different societies across the world too often acts as a lightning rod for pre-existing social, political and economic divisions in that society, highlighting and reinforcing these divisions and being the focus for protest from queer social justice activists.

Pride and capitalism

There is a broader feminist and queer literature that draws from activist critiques of the injustices of capitalism and traces and considers changes in popular culture that and growth of rainbow hued and celebratory corporate 'diversity politics' (Ahmed, 2012) and what has been termed as 'global homocapitalism' (Rao, 2015, 2020). This book builds on this literature and the theoretical lenses that it provides to analyse Pride and what it does in the world, whom it empowers, considers and who it excludes and ignores. In the 1990s and 2000s, feminists began to discuss the significance of corporations ostensibly encouraging and celebrating women as professional employees and the shifts in advertising aimed at women in Western societies, which had hitherto addressed women as housewives and mothers, to women as empowered, career focused and independent. Angela McRobbie (2008) identified these shifts as the development of a neoliberal 'post-feminism' that addressed women in the Global North as empowered, individual subjects who had no need of the feminist struggles of the past. These 'post-feminist' discourses beguile, particularly younger, women who believe they can have equal opportunities and will get their just rewards from a competitive marketplace that values their contribution. Yet as McRobbie argues, late-capitalism remains rigged in racial, gendered and class terms and reinforces the same anxieties in women to conform with normative standards of beauty, material success, marriage and fertility.

Following feminist critiques of late-capitalism's ostensible embrace of 'diversity politics' (Ahmed, 2012), queer scholars have identified and conceptualized the expansion of capitalism to address and include LGBTQ+ communities. As is the case with 'post-feminist' discourses, 'folding queers into capitalism' (Rao, 2015) includes a significant expansion of LGBTQ+ representation in advertising and popular culture. In the Global North, these representations have transformed LGBTQ+ identities and 'lifestyles' from being pejorative and repudiated, to desirable and aspirational, with transnationally broadcast programmes such as *Queer Eye for the Straight Guy* and *RuPaul's Drag Race* framing particular gay and queer identities as being 'one more brand name to buy' (Bell and Binnie, 2000: 99). For corporate institutions, a combination of these shifts in societal discourses and advances in employment laws and rights protections in Europe, North America and elsewhere have led to institutions being presented as welcoming and rewarding, where LGBTQ+ employees can achieve success by 'bringing their whole selves' to work (Burchiellaro, 2023; Rao, 2020). Major transnational corporations, including Disney, EY, IBM and HSBC, now present themselves as being at the vanguard of LGBTQ+ rights progress internationally (Rao, 2020).

Pride's rationale for creating public visibility, occupying space in the centre of cities and towns, its colourful carnivalesque and positive emotional tenor make Pride a highly flexible and perfect platform for the expression of 'global homocapitalism', allowing for the (literal) parading of corporate rainbow colours which demonstrates an ostensible commitment to LGBTQ+ communities and progress, as well as delivering lucrative branding and advertising opportunities, alongside the presentation of transnational business as being progressive, modern and just. These shifts and Pride's place in corporate capitalism are not linear and all encompassing, however. As will be discussed in this book, Pride is also the location for the contestation of these discourses and practices, with queer activists protesting at and organizing 'alternative' Prides that are premised in a desire to highlight the precarity of marginalized LGBTQ+ communities and use Pride as a platform to advance social justice.

The professionalization of Pride organizing in many parts of the world corresponds with the growth of the 'NGO-ization' of activism and the rise of an educated, professional class of what have been termed 'career queers' (Rodriguez, 2022). The NGO-ization of LGBTQ+ activism has been in response to the codification of LGBTQ+ rights laws by national governments, formal commitments to LGBTQ+ advocacy as part of human rights foreign policies and the growth of LGBTQ+ advocacy and institutional capacity by international institutions, such as the UN and EU. Transnational membership organizations, such as the International Lesbian and Gay Association (ILGA), colloquially known as the 'Gay UN', hold major conferences that connect 'career queers' with government, business and, to a lesser extent, grassroots activists. For Pride organizers, there are the membership organizations InterPride and EuroPride, which organize World Pride and EuroPride, respectively. Few 'grassroots' or 'alternative' Prides discussed in the book are members of these organizations, one reason being they cannot afford the membership fees. While the growth of an elite tier of LGBTQ+ policy advocates has helped bring LGBTQ+ rights onto the international policy agenda, Rodriguez's (2022) analysis of international 'career queers' and the marginalization of grassroots LGBTQ+ activists in Uganda really struck a chord while I researched Pride events. Like Rodriguez, I became concerned about the role and impacts of the professionalization of LGBTQ+ activism and how a relatively small group of international LGBTQ+ advocates travel the world, repeatedly meeting each other at various major Pride events and LGBTQ+ rights forums often discuss LGBTQ+ rights without any obvious connection to, and sometimes even apparent interest, in grassroots activism, or smaller, alternative Prides.

The growth of 'career queers' and the institutionalization of activism has been a factor in fostering Pride as a high-budget, major event. Writing about the professionalization of LGBTQ+ advocacy in Los Angeles in the 1990s and the displacement of the Latinx working-class organizers of Pride, by a white, university-educated professional class of organizers, Ward states that Pride has become:

> Many seemingly contradictory things at once: disco parties; arts and crafts fairs; drug dens; health expos; high security cages (many events are surrounded by chain-link fence or other barriers); sites of mourning; sites of protest; ecstatic fun; and utter boredom.
>
> (2003: 88)

As a consequence, Ward (2003: 89) argues that there has been a 'disconnection between [Pride] and any sort of well-articulated political ideology, particularly a radical, grassroots ideology' and as a consequence there is little need for Pride organizers to engage with LGBTQ+ identities or movement building. Schulman adds to this claim by arguing that the co-optation of LGBTQ+ activism and advocacy by elites and corporate interests is not so much an absence of ideology than a 'gentrification' of activism and imaginaries of LGBTQ+ identities; one that supplants consideration of marginalized communities and questions of social justice and liberation, with neoliberal, individualized logics and a politics of whiteness (Schulman, 2012b).

Pride has been hailed as the most significant and effective transnational movement to help forge LGBTQ+ collective identities, raise visibility and change social and political attitudes towards LGBTQ+ rights (Bruce, 2016; Peterson, Wahlström and Wennerhag, 2018). Since the 1970s, Pride has been an example, in Butler's (2010) terms, of where making LGBTQ+ lives visible has made them matter. Yet Pride is not the only example of an LGBTQ+ movement that has aimed and delivered this transformational politics. Few academic or popular accounts of Pride mention the AIDS Coalition to Unleash Power (ACT UP) established in the New York in the 1980s and then in London, Paris and elsewhere. Sarah Schulman writes that ACT UP's combination of radical street protest, including mass 'die ins', public AIDS funerals, use of artistic expression alongside detailed engagement and lobbying of medical professionals, government and pharmaceutical industry achieved 'incredible success' in that it 'forced our country to change against its will, permanently impacting future movements of people with AIDS throughout the world and saving incalculable numbers of future lives' (Schulman, 2021: 9). ACT UP made HIV positive people and AIDS deaths visible, whereas they had been either invisible and/or despised by broader society (Butler, 2010; Schulman, 2021). Schulman (2021) argues that although ACT UP activists did understand and critique how capitalism underpinned the lack of interest in researching, access and price of early HIV medications, members of the group underestimated the power of capitalism to perpetuate these inequalities and they remain today.

The organizers of Reclaim Pride in New York and queer activists critical of Pride in London, Toronto and elsewhere are either members of ACT UP, or argue that ACT UP represents the original radical purpose of the Stonewall Riots. While there is a relationship between the kinds of organizing and communities ACT UP encompassed and Pride, particularly for the grassroots Prides discussed later in this book, there are also clear differences between ACT UP and many large-scale, mainstream Pride events, particularly in the Global North. Indeed, it is telling that ACT UP rarely features in histories of Pride and was absent from official accounts of the history of Pride and LGBTQ+ activism at World Pride New York on the fiftieth anniversary of the Stonewall Riots. The queer activists discussed in this book, like ACT UP activists before them, combine the focus on sexuality with anti-capitalist critiques of big business, intersectional demands for social justice and an open celebration of sex and sexuality (Brown, 2007: 268; Highleyman, 2002; Schulman, 2021). The overarching critique of Pride worldwide by queer activists is its utility for and complicity with global capitalism. The involvement of corporate sponsors and attendees is marked as deradicalizing Pride's political purpose, conforming to homonormative and 'respectable' modes of LGBTQ+ identity including same-sex marriage and relentless positivity about the inevitability and/or celebrating the achievement of progress for LGBTQ+ communities.

Researching this book

Conducting ethnographic fieldwork, particularly when the researcher is an 'insider' to the group being studied, requires self-reflection and consideration of the complexities when researching a community and social phenomenon we are familiar with and have participated in before. Amanda Chisholm writes that fieldwork 'is always a social enterprise. We, as researchers, create our stories through the stories we are told … Our own personal stories of how we come to be researchers who are curious about the topics we choose also matter' (Chisholm, 2022: 13). Like many LGBTQ+ people in the Global North, I come to the topic of Pride with a set of experiences, attitudes and assumptions that inevitably play a role in the research and my analysis. As described above, I had been thinking about Pride some time before embarking on academic research on Pride.

As a gay man, I have my own history and experiences at Pride events, although Pride does not play a significant role in my 'coming out' story unlike it does for many others. Nor do I look forward to Pride like it is a 'Gay Christmas' as some do. In 2006 and 2023, I marched in London Pride first with the LGBT Section of the University College Union and then with Ntsupe Mohapi, an organizer of Ekurhuleni Pride, Fundi Ndaba, from the Forum for the Empowerment of Women (FEW) and organizer of Soweto Pride and the LGBTQ+ activist Peter Tatchell. In 2024, my employer, the University of Westminster, sponsored the staff LGBTQ+ group to be part of the London Pride parade. I did not participate in this and have been reluctant to be involved with the staff LGBTQ+ group, because I agreed along with a number of my other colleagues that the university, while enthusiastically flying the rainbow flag on its Regent Street building during Pride Month and LGBTQ+ History Month, has also taken a punitive and uncompromising stance in the University College Union strikes over pay and working conditions and has adopted a definition of anti-Semitism that prevents free speech about Israel's domestic and regional policies. A group of us believed that participating in London Pride would aid the 'pinkwashing' of the university's treatment of its staff and students. This work-based experience reveals the complex politics of Pride and before embarking on the fieldwork, I was very conscious of how the complex relationship and role my personal history, identities and attitude would play in the research process and how I would navigate such a large, multi-sited ethnographic research process with its many logistical, ethical and ideological considerations.

While it is not always possible to conduct fieldwork and participate in the social and political phenomena we research, I believe it is particularly important to do so when researching Pride. A key principle of ethnographic research is to understand people 'in terms of what they actually do, i.e. as material agents working with a material world, and not merely what they say they do', and this requires 'to be in the presence of the people one is studying, not just the texts or objects they produce' (Miller, 1997: 16). It is particularly important to be present, observe and experience Pride events as a researcher, and not simply rely on media accounts, pictures or accounts given by organizers. Given Pride's contentious politics and mainstream Pride's intersection with political and economic elites, the accounts given by Pride organizers, corporate sponsors and potentially other activists may have ulterior motives. This was borne out on several occasions. For example, when I interviewed an official from InterPride at World Pride in New York, I did so with his deputy whom I had had numerous private conversations, yet in the interview his deputy was reticent, which I found strange since we had chatted well before the interview. Afterwards, I asked why he had not contributed to the recorded interview. He replied that his boss had told him to 'keep quiet' during the interview and let him do the talking. We both agreed that this was probably because the InterPride official was aware of the criticisms of Pride by queer activists and academics and wanted to control the narrative. I also sensed I was being given a 'boiler plate' line about the purposes and impacts of Pride from the organizers of New York, Cape Town, Mumbai and Johannesburg

Pride, aspects of which were contradicted and disputed by other queer activists in those contexts. Had I relied on talking to Pride organizers and not attended the Pride events, participating, observing and talking to other attendees and activists, I would only have had a partial story and have been presented with a potentially disingenuous understanding of what purpose, politics and impacts Pride has. Alongside conducting interviews with organizers, activists, diplomats, journalists and NGO staff, I took photographs and videos of Pride events, wrote field notes and collected a large volume of free, and paid for, Pride merchandise including t-shirts, flags, flyers, leaflets and some placards.

I conducted fieldwork in Shanghai, Johannesburg, Cape Town, Hong Kong, Taipei, Manilla, Mumbai, Havana and New York combining attendance at Pride parades or marches, afterparties, associated conferences, receptions, corporate and diplomatic events, protests, interviews with Pride organizers, activists, diplomats, journalists, academics, and corporate diversity and inclusion professionals. There were several reasons for why some locations and case studies were chosen over others. I decided that I would only visit territories where homosexuality was lawful. This was for ethical and safety reasons; both for those I was likely to speak to and myself. I also decided that I wanted to choose locations that had potentially more complex political and social dynamics that would feed through and be expressed by Pride and/or that they had been less extensively researched. For this reason, I decided not to attend Pride in Tel Aviv because the 'pinkwashing' politics of this event has been well documented and analysed (Franke, 2012; Schulman, 2012a). As previously discussed, I have extensive experience of researching, living and working in South Africa and I was aware that the country's complex racial and class politics played through and were reinforced by Pride. I attended Taipei Pride because it is the largest Pride in East Asia, also the tenth anniversary of Shanghai Pride in 2018, 2019 Mumbai Pride, the largest Pride in India and the first after the decriminalization of homosexuality in the country, 2018 Hong Kong Pride and Hong Kong Migrants Pride, and also spoke to LGBTQ+ activists and Pride organizers in the Philippines. I attended the Cuban equivalent of Pride, the Conga for the day against homophobia, biphobia and transphobia, because it was led by Senator Dr Mariela Castro-Espín, niece of Fidel Castro and the daughter of Raul Castro and the feminist activist Wilma Espín and World Pride in New York upon the fiftieth anniversary of the Stonewall Riots in 2019. In 2023, I participated in Ekurhuleni Pride in the township of Wattville near Johannesburg and in 2024, I attended Cape Town Pride. I attended other events attached to Pride, such as the Out Leadership Summit in Hong Kong, the Out and Equal Asia Conference and PFLAG China convention in Shanghai, along with countless other diplomatic, NGO and commercial receptions, workshops, events and meetings that were often serendipitous happenchance and deeply enriched the research.

Ethnographic research, qualitative interviewing and the ethics of research conducted by academics from the Global North and in the Global South have become the subject of considerable debate, feminist, queer and postcolonial critique in recent decades (O'Reilly, 2008; Rooke, 2009: 150; Sherman Heyl, 2007: 373). Conducting research across eight territories in three continents with all the complexities, histories, challenges and politics that this entails requires careful reflection on my subjectivities and responsibilities as a researcher. I was aware from the outset that I could be accused on embarking on a colonial and extractive research project and of flying into (and out of) contexts, some of which I had not visited before. I agree with Marsha Henry that the research 'field' is 'a place of complex power structures', where the identities of the researcher and researched have 'different meanings in different contexts' (Henry, 2003: 230). I found the framing of the research sites around the Global North and South, or East and West, to be unsatisfactory and that the typology used by Mohanty (2003) of 'One Third/Two-Thirds World' that exists in and across the same geographical locations captured the complex hierarchies and processes of marginalization that did not always easily map onto race, class or geographical location. Henry's experiences as a researcher in the field resonated with my own: 'not only was my identity a complicated thing to represent, but my participants had multiple, and sometimes unrepresentable identities' (Henry, 2003: 237). Amanda Chisholm writes that 'being reflective and thinking about positionalities in the field is not just a methodological issue; it is a theoretical one as well' (2022: 17). Feminist researchers have long argued that challenging the hierarchies between researcher and researched, considering those we speak to and study as active participants and agents in the research process and reflecting on our own identities is ethically, methodologically and theoretically important (Henry, 2003: 239; Taylor, 1998: 372). Similarly, researching LGBTQ+ lives and engaging with queer theory also advocates and develops these feminist approaches. As Rooke explains:

> An intellectual commitment to queer theory *and* queer methodology requires an epistemological openness and attention to one's own sexual subjectivity and the performativity of the self in the research

process. It depends that the ethnographer work from an honest sense of oneself that is open and reflexive, rather than ontologically holding on to a sense of self that provides a stable place to enter into the fieldwork and subsequently leave from.

(Rooke, 2009: 154)

I often found myself at ideological odds with LGBTQ+ elites and mainstream Pride organizers, even if we resembled each other in national, class or racial terms, and in agreement with and more comfortable in the company of marginalized, grassroots activists, even though there were racial and class differences between us.

As many other ethnographic researchers have found, there was not always a clear boundary between 'entering' the field and 'leaving' it. I have kept in contact with many of the research participants I met, and some have become friends. As I will discuss in Chapter 4, I intervened in the politics of Pride in Johannesburg to try and change it, forming long-standing partnerships with grassroots activists, NGOs, embassies and other LGBTQ+ advocates in the city and region. I invited the organizers of Soweto and Ekurhuleni Pride to London, funded by the University of Westminster and as explained above, we participated in London Pride as well as meeting with the members of the All-Party Parliamentary Group on Global LGBT+ Rights. I used some of the photographs I took to curate a travelling photo exhibition titled 'Pride Belongs to the People: Images of Soweto and Ekurhuleni Pride' that has been held at various locations in London, the United States and South Africa. The lines between being a researcher, participant, activist, friend and critic are blurred. I often found attending the glamourized and corporate LGBTQ+ or Pride receptions and events daunting. For example, feeling (and probably looking) out of place at an Out Leadership reception high up in HSBC's skyscraper in Hong Kong, or being a cynical observer of the official speeches that offered 'boiler plate' celebrations of diversity and inclusion at the Mayor of London's Pride reception, at the ILGA World Conference and at the World Pride Human Rights Conference. Like Olimpia Burchiellaro, who studied the world of corporate LGBTQ+ diversity and inclusion, I ended up 'mimicking but not mastering ... the art of queer networking' and often wondered if not being fully open about my emotional and intellectual responses to those events and the ideological differences with those I spoke to and connected with was a 'form of deception' (Burchiellaro, 2023: 20).

My previous research on white South Africans who were actively opposed to apartheid and with white British-born immigrants living in South Africa had made me well aware of the sometimes partial,

1. *The Queer Politics of Pride*   17

Figure 3 Fundi Ndaba and Ntsupe Mohapi at London Pride's 'VIP Area', 2023.

contradictory and even completely untrue accounts research participants can give and also the expectations placed on me as the researcher and writer to 'tell' the 'truth' as my research participants see it (Conway, 2016; Conway and Leonard, 2014). I have also been at the sharp end of a 'backlash' from research participants when I have not complied with their wish to be presented in entirely positive and celebratory ways exactly on their terms (Conway, 2016). While it is unsurprising that researching white people in contemporary South Africa would come with a fraught politics and I have no ideological, racial or personal difficulty in opposing discourses and positions I view to be problematic when expressed by other white people, writing about LGBTQ+ actors with whom I disagree or find problematic, particularly if they are people of colour and living in the Global South, comes with complex questions and dilemmas. Blee writes that qualitative researchers can approach interviews with mistakenly 'romantic assumptions about the subjects of history from the bottom up' (Blee, 1993: 597) and Power (2004: 859) is correct to caution that there are 'multiple, localized, contextual truths' rather than one definitive account. I disagreed with Kaye Ally, the organizer of Johannesburg Pride, whose criticisms of Soweto Pride I considered to be class and race based, even though Ally is a person of colour. Hearing the casually dismissive and contemptuous attitudes expressed by the South Asian LGBTQ+ attendees of a Pride reception in Mumbai about the poorer residents of the city and conditions in which they live reminded of the kinds of 'white talk' (Steyn, 2001) that is expressed by many white South Africans about the Black majority in the country they live in. The organizers of Mumbai Pride are right-wing Hindu Nationalists and their hostility towards the queer activists who wanted to raise broader questions of social justice troubled me.

There are several responses to the challenges of writing critically about people we have researched. In my previous work on white people in South Africa, I had always tried to situate research participants in their social, discursive and material context: to situate them in contexts where their words and actions might seem normal or make sense to them and this would locate what, on the page, might seem shockingly ignorant and racist to a reader living outside of South Africa. This draws from Bourdieu's (1992) argument that individuals have a 'logic of practice' that is situated in their material, spatial and social context. Similarly, the anthropologist Daniel Miller argues that people's 'behaviours be considered within the larger framework of people's lives and cosmologies' (1997: 19). Critical discourse analysis approaches are also premised on situating any 'text' in the material, social and discursive 'context' in which it is framed, influenced and bound by (Fairclough, 1995). In this project, as a white researcher based in the United Kingdom and researching mainly people of colour outside of Europe presents further dilemmas. Kiran Grewal's (Grewal, 2012) discussion of how to engage with and represent right-wing and regressive voices from marginalized communities in the Global South is useful when considering how to frame feminist, queer and decolonial critiques of social and political actors. Grewal, focusing on the right-wing and Islamophobic self-narratives and politics offered by the activist, politician and commentator Hirsi Ali, cautions that researchers should not fall 'into the trap of celebrating "authenticity"' (Grewal, 2012: 572), when this voice can provide 'a reinforcement of the dominant order through the "authentic" voice of the victim' (Grewal, 2012: 582). Like Rao (2020), who argues that locating and rationalizing homophobia as the product of the colonial past obscures postcolonial elites' agency and willingness to enact homophobia on their own terms, and also that 'racial capitalism' can intersect with new LGBTQ+ elites in postcolonial contexts (Rao, 2024), Grewal finds that openly debating the views of right-wing people of colour is important for feminist postcolonial studies, but also 'reinforces and expands the argument that the legacies of colonial structures of power live on in very meaningful ways' (Grewal,

2012: 572). As Chapter 2 will explore, the politics of neoliberalism plays a profoundly important role in encouraging and rewarding certain actors and marginalizing, disciplining and disempowering others.

Ultimately, as a researcher, all I have is myself and my existing set of social skills, ability to emote, connect and interact with people I have never met before and to gain, understand and represent their truths and my interpretation of it as best I can. In considering the complex dynamics of race, gender and location, Marsha Henry wryly notes that feminist researchers can spend too much time 'reflecting on these issues, perhaps at the expense of actually doing and completing feminist research' and that 'in an era of rampant reflexivity, just getting on with it may be the most radical action one can take' (2003: 239). I also agree with Skeggs (2007: 437) that from a feminist (and queer) perspective it is important to ask in whose interests are we researching, and that we should have a commitment to social justice and progressive activism in our writing. As Taylor argues, our purpose is to 'explain, and thereby to solve, social problems' (Taylor, 1998: 374).

I hope that this book can be read and be useful to LGBTQ+ activists and advocates, LGBTQ+ people and anyone interested in advancing social justice in the world today. Bevington and Dixon (2005) argue that academics focused on protest and social movements have not paid sufficient attention to the actual experiences, interests or needs of activists. As a result, activists themselves seldom read, or find useful, contemporary academic theorizing about activism. The constraints on academic researchers are considerable, in terms of ability to fund research, have time to do it and then if we have gathered research data, the pressure to publish can encourage (and reward) arguments and analyses that oversimplify the complexities of social and political life and/or write in levels of abstraction that make the text inscrutable. As I will argue throughout this book, it is important to think through the ideological effects Pride has and use social and political theory to do this. Yet as the pioneering feminist international relations scholar, Cynthia Enloe has long argued, we should 'write as we speak' and that we should always be 'curious', question accepted 'common sense' understandings and uncover the realities of power that exist in the every day and the mundane (Enloe, 2004). Enloe adapts the feminist adage that the 'personal is political' to argue that the personal is also international (Enloe, 2014). Adopting a feminist 'curiosity' about the lives, experiences and contexts of the people present in this book is important for understanding how, why and with what effects people become involved in activism and try to effect social change. Adopting a 'queer' approach to research is also premised on the desire to question and deconstruct traditional boundaries and hierarchies between the researcher and researched, think through what it is to research and write in ways that encourage and support social justice and to be honest, reflective and accessible to others who wish to change the world for the better.

While this book does not seek to provide a comprehensive history of the Pride 'movement', nor does it make universal claims about the roles and impacts of Pride everywhere, and I dispute that this is possible, it does seek to understand and analyse Pride from a queer perspective. Chapter 2 explores how queer theory emerged from subcultural spaces and artistic production in the 1970s and 1980s and how gentrification, as a set of economic, spatial, cultural and political processes of late-capitalism, radically alters and inhibits subculture and the possibility of a radical queer politics. Pride sits at the nexus of these processes of gentrification, serving as the perfect platform for consumption, advertising and a blithe, celebratory diversity politics. Chapter 2 discusses how Gilbert Baker's encouragement of corporate institutions to freely adopt the rainbow in their branding has, perhaps unwittingly, been key to Prides utility for global homocapitalism. Existing academic analyses of Pride tend to use a contentious politics model to assess Pride's impacts as a transnational social movement. I argue that this mischaracterises, overdetermines and simplifies Pride and overlooks Pride's ideological significance. Adopting feminist and queer approaches to social organizing and activism is a more useful and meaningful way to conceptualize Pride and understand its significance.

Queer activism, epitomized by the HIV/AIDS advocacy, support and activist group ACT UP, emerged from New York's radical subcultures and in response to an existential crisis and health emergency. Queer activism is utopic, envisioning and creating different, better worlds and new ways of being. Yet as Chapter 3 documents, Pride all too often acts as a 'mirror', rather than a utopic 'microcosm', to existing socio-political, spatial, economic and historical divisions in each society. This is evident in the sharpest of terms in South Africa where 'rival Prides' exist vividly illustrating the country's ongoing racial, class and political divides. In India, Mumbai Pride is mostly organized by right-wing, Hindu Nationalist men, with an attendant elite of wealthy, internationally mobile and rewarded 'homocapitalists' being highly visible at and benefitting from Pride. Queer activists have challenged and disrupted 'mainstream' Prides in both these contexts and in South Africa, rival, queer, grassroots Prides exist with the aim to include and highlight the precarious lives, deaths and challenges faced by the Black majority.

The commercialization of Pride and the co-option of LGBTQ+ human rights and activist discourses by corporations are the latest in a long lineage of developments in global capitalism. Chapter 4 explores how corporate discourses adapted to include some of the demands made by the women's and civil rights movements of the 1960s and 1970s and by the later 1980s and 1990s, corporate capital began to present itself as the natural home for women and diverse communities. The development of the 'business case' of LGBTQ+ equality, diversity and inclusion in the workplace sits in the same trajectory but goes further in that, unlike for women and people of colour, business now often situates itself as activists for change for LGBTQ+ communities. The claim that corporate capital acts as a social, political and moral good in the world underpins the logics of 'homocapitalism'. Chapter 4 traces and locates the history of corporate 'social responsibility' and 'ethical codes of conduct' in Western business operations in apartheid-era South Africa in the 1970s and 1980s. The development of ostensibly non-racial and ethical business practices enabled business to sidestep calls for economic sanctions and boycotts, and to present itself as being at the vanguard of positive change in South Africa. The presentation of business as a moral actor for progressive social and political change was difficult to accurately assess, had multiple contradictions, split the anti-apartheid movement and crucially, enabled Western capital to profit from doing business in South Africa's exploitative and lucrative market. Contemporary claims that business is a positive, inclusive good for LGBTQ+ and one that tackles the 'social/cultural' problem of homophobia deploys the same rationale as earlier corporate social responsibility discourses and has divided LGBTQ+ communities in the similar ways. Homocapitalism disavows the material and historical basis of homophobia and precarity for LGBTQ+ communities across the world and presents progress as an inevitable outflow from capitalist development, and where activism for social justice is unnecessary and naïve.

At almost every Pride event I attended, I saw members of the international diplomatic community participating in the march and supporting film screenings, receptions, discussion and social events. This participation was often deeply felt by the diplomats involved and diplomatic support, whether it be in kind, or financial, can make a significant difference. However, in Chapter 5, I discuss whether the rainbow branding of national flags and the positive messaging about the LGBTQ+ rights stances of countries such as the UK, Canada, Sweden and Taiwan are doing the same illusory and misleading 'non-performative' 'diversity politics' (Ahmed, 2012) work as corporations who adopt rainbow branding at Pride. While diplomatic involvement can make a positive difference to Pride events, they can also reward elite 'career queers' at the expense of grassroots queer activists and, as with corporate support, financial backing for LGBTQ+ rights causes is a fraction of already limited international development and human rights budgets. They are also subject to quick reversal, as has been the case at various times for the United States, the United Kingdom, Germany and Brazil. Pride can all too easily provide a platform that overemphasizes international support for LGBTQ+ rights, in much the same terms as it provides a flexible platform for the disingenuous presentation of corporate allyship.

The corporate co-optation of Pride and its pivotal role in signifying and advancing global homocapitalism raise the question of whether Pride can play any useful or meaningful role in grassroots and queer activist struggles, particularly in Global South locations. In every place I researched, I saw resistance to corporate, elitist, racist and homonormative iterations of Pride, whether by queer activists at the mainstream Pride event itself and/or by queer activist organized 'alternative' Prides. Chapter 6 explores these queer disruptions and alternative queer Pride organizing and argues that it is possible to 'Reclaim Pride' for queer, social justice and radical politics. These 'alternative Prides', from the Reclaim Pride in New York, Soweto, Ekurhuleni and Khumbulani Prides in South Africa, Hong Kong Migrants Pride, Taiwan Pride, or the 'unofficial' Pride march in Havana, are open for anyone to participate in the march, ban or have restrictions on corporate and political party involvement and seek to combine activism with education, socializing and partying. They also all build on and evoke local traditions of subversive, queer and radical politics and articulate a queer utopic vision of a different, more just, future.

'Pride holds people's lives in it' said the feminist and queer South African activist, Mpumi Mathabela when I met her in Johannesburg, and as I argue, the full complexity and precarity of queer lives should be included at Pride. 'Pride belongs to the people', continued Mpumi, and while this book provides evidence from across the world that this can be and is sometimes the case, Pride is too often beholden to the exclusive, exploitative, elitism of homocapitalism.

Chapter 2

A QUEER CONCEPTUALIZATION OF PRIDE

For me, Pride means not only one thing. It's political in the way that we're challenging the government, the powers in our community, political power. We're saying, 'We're here! These are our challenges. Fix this. Help us with this.' And also, it's about the LGBTI person. It's about our diversity. It's about showcasing who we are and telling the community that we are different, although we are all homosexuals, but we are different, we're not the same.

I think it's awareness. I think when we march, and we have our posters up, we are saying something to the community. I think it's that one-day where we can share our lives with the community. I think for me, also, it's important to invite them and they see what Pride is all about, spend time with us from morning until late, because we cannot have Pride on our own.

– Ntsupe Mohapi, organizer of Ekurhuleni Pride, South Africa (interview with the author, 2018)

At the 2024 Mighty Hoopla music festival in London's Brockwell park, many US performers shouted 'Happy Pride' from the stage. It was evidently unclear to them what the difference was between a Pride event and a music festival marketed at and attended by many LGBTQ+ people, but entirely unconnected with Pride. At the festival, the avant-garde queer performance artist David Hoyle performed on a small stage in between two bars, or 'on a shelf' in 'a glorified bus stop' as he called it. Known for his anti-capitalist, confronting and surrealist political comedy, Hoyle gave one of his regular catch phrases, calling on the small audience to 'kill all in authority!', adding immediately afterwards 'and that's why they didn't invite me to perform on the main stage!'. At a performance a few months later, Hoyle recalled that the festival organizers had not allowed him or any of the other queer performance artists 'anywhere near' the main performers at the festival. Hoyle had clearly felt marginalized and renamed the Mighty Hoopla festival 'the gaping shitter!' In a monologue to an audience at the Barbican in London, 2024, the trans musician and performance artist Anohni reflected on the remarkable queer subculture of 1980s and early 1990s Manhattan, where people who had 'slipped through the cracks and crevices of society' gathered to 'dream about different worlds' and produce a radically new culture. This queer subcultural moment had gone by the 2000s, and its disappearance was the product of the AIDS crisis and the gentrification of New York that disabled the ability of precarious subcultures to survive. Anohni would later recall that 'the door had slammed shut' on queer artists following AIDS and every US record label had turned down her first album. It was only upon the insistence of established artist, Lou Reed, that Anohni had secured a record deal.

These anecdotes may seem tenuous and tangential to Pride, but they are at the heart of the debates over the marginalization and cannibalization of queer culture, activism and the commercialization of Pride. The anodyne, glitzy and expensive Mighty Hoopla festival did indeed resemble a contemporary Pride event in many major cities, and this included the marginalization of queer critics of capitalism and those likely to cause offence. The gentrification of cityscapes has had radical impacts on cultural production and the ability of subcultures to create transgressive art. This, in turn, has profoundly conservative and conformist political impacts, changing the ways in which and limiting the scope of what LGBTQ+ advocates consider what is possible, desirable and achievable.

There was an enormous sense of energy and excitement as the Ekurhuleni Pride march weaved through the streets of the township of Wattville on the southern edges of Johannesburg. The marchers carried protest banners and rainbow flags and sang songs from the South African liberation struggle. At one point marchers held a silent 'die in' to commemorate LGBTQ+ people who had been killed in homophobic attacks in Ekurhuleni and the broader region. Few people had come to watch the march, and I observed residents suspiciously peering at us from above walls and fences and from around gates and doorways. At one point, a group of drunken men shouted homophobic abuse at the marchers. The march ended at a park in the centre of Wattville where there were stalls from NGOs, government, health services, food and music. There was a friendly and celebratory atmosphere. A few residents asked me what was happening and then stayed to talk to the other attendees at the afterparty. The march and afternoon event in the park, with their combination of protest, celebration, disruption and conviviality, were exactly what Pride should be.

2. A Queer Conceptualization of Pride

Figure 4 Soweto Pride 2018.

By contrast, the World Pride parade in New York had lasted over nine hours and some groups in the parade found themselves marching in the early hours of the morning. To me, at least, it felt like a joyless affair dominated by multinational corporations, diplomatic missions and reality TV stars. There had been numerous exclusive VIP receptions and ticketed events in the lead up to the parade. Manhattan was festooned with rainbows and shops had produced rainbow-branded fashion ranges and accessories. The Human Rights conference, which is a mandated part of every World Pride, had been organized at a New York Law School and seemed like an afterthought. There was no full programme printed, no room numbers or speakers listed, and the focus on LGBTQ+ rights was often lost in place of corporate motivational speakers and panels that centred corporate EDI speakers in place of grassroots activism. While there were more interesting conversations around race, trans and some focus on the Global South on the margins of the conference, the event functioned more as a networking session for international LGBTQ+ advocacy elites and was predominantly focused on panels discussing the value of corporate social responsibility. As will be discussed in Chapter 7, these were not the only Pride events in New York that week, with other Pride marches directly critiquing World Pride and seeking to 'reclaim' Pride's radical roots. These two Pride events in South Africa and New York demonstrate not only Pride's success as a globalized platform for LGBTQ+ activism and community building, but also the many contradictions, contrasts and controversies that Pride encompasses.

This chapter explores the existing academic literature on Pride in greater depth, placing them alongside activist critiques and popular debates about Pride. In particular, the chapter will question mainstream social movement studies, or contentious politics, analyses of Pride arguing that these approaches overdetermine the coherence of Pride as a social movement and overstate its transnational reach. As this chapter will argue, the complexities and contradictions of Pride are seldom considered or adequately conceptualized by the existing academic literature on Pride, much of which adopts liberal social movement studies analyses that minimize, or ignore, critiques of Pride from marginalized communities, relies exclusively on accounts of Pride from attendees and organizers, without using social, political and international theory to analyse the ideologies Pride is co-opted by and creates. Overall the existing literature discusses Pride based on Europe and North America, rather than considering the different effects and examples of Pride in contexts outside of the West.

The chapter will apply feminist and queer critiques of social movement studies approaches and argue that Pride can be better understood as playing an important ideological role in constructing understandings of who LGBTQ+ people and communities are, the lives they lead and the issues that matter to them. Drawing from a Foucauldian 'regime of truth' or 'politics of truth' (Foucault, 2001) perspective and its feminist (Macleod and Durrheim, 2002) and queer (Butler, 2010) applications, the chapter argues that Pride should be considered as a loose assemblage of people, events and practices that can manifest as a useful and important platform for movement building, activism, mutual support and affirmation for LGBTQ+ people, or it can be co-opted by neoliberal/corporate, nationalist and partisan constructions that marginalize and obscure the challenges, precarity and inequalities that LGBTQ+ people face, communicating liberal conceptions of inevitable progress and creating LGBTQ+ elites complicit with racial, class and global privilege.

Whereas the complete dismissal of Pride as little more than an event, akin to organizing a music festival or trade show, can overlook the significance of Pride to many of the individuals and communities featured in this book, the final section of this chapter explores Pride in relation to conceptions of radical queer activism and its manifestation in other LGBTQ+ groups, such as ACT UP. Sarah Schulman's (2012b,

2021) important work on ACT UP New York and the 'gentrification of the mind' – the class, race and spatial processes that have influenced LGBTQ+ cultural politics and advocacy – will be discussed in relation to the use of Pride by states, corporations and other institutions to 'pinkwash' their international image and provide states and corporate institutions with the 'happy smiling face' of diversity politics (Ahmed, 2012): one that belies any meaningful commitment to social justice.

The chapter begins by exploring the bold and positive claims made about Pride's utility and impacts and argues that universal claims about Pride should be avoided and nuanced by examples from outside the West and by listening to the perspectives of queer critics of Pride. The chapter then analyses the history of tension in Pride and critiques the social movement studies approaches to analysing Pride for being too reductive, simplistic and creates the basis for sweeping and inaccurate generalizations about Pride. The chapter then conceptualizes queer and queering as being located and emerging from subcultural spaces and artistic practice, outside of mainstream capitalist production. Queer activism, as expressed by radical movements such as ACT UP, emerged from these subcultures, but developments in late-capitalism including gentrification and 'homocapitalism' seek to incorporate, commodify and deradicalize queer politics. Pride sits at the intersection of these processes of gentrification and the lives, realities and communities it includes and excludes should be analysed from a Foucauldian and queer perspective to understand the ideological and real-world impacts Pride has.

Pride

Since the first Pride march in New York in 1970, LGBTQ+ Pride parades and associated events have spread across the world and have become a defining feature of LGBTQ+ campaigning, visibility and community building. Ayoub and colleagues argue that even in socially conservative societies 'Prides represent powerful tools for mobilizing the recognition of political elites, who are then faced with the responsibility of addressing movement claims in the halls of government', and that 'Pride can legitimate a local context's movement by drawing international attention to the surrounding status of LGBT+ politics' (Ayoub et al., 2021: 469). Pride has been described as 'foundational rituals for LGBT movements across the globe', which 'act as collective responses to oppression, encourage redefinition of the self, and express collective identity' (Peterson, Wahlström and Wennerhag, 2018: 17). Pride has become part of broader international political and commercial processes, used by states as evidence for worthiness for European Union membership (Franke, 2012; Paternotte, 2014; Slootmaeckers, 2017); as major tourist events, such as Sydney Mardi Gras; and as public relations strategies for cities and states, such as Tel Aviv and Israel (Johnston, 2005; Puar, 2002; Schulman, 2012a).

Discussing Pride in the United States, Bruce argues that 'Pride parades are loud, colourful, and joyful celebrations of LGBT identity' (2016: 3) and that 'Pride gives casual participants a central role and focuses on changing culture instead of state laws and policies … Pride really belongs to the marcher and spectators that participate' (Bruce, 2016: 7). While numerous authors also argue that by creating visibility, collectively 'coming out', occupying and queering urban space Pride plays an important role in changing cultural and attitudes (Ammaturo, 2016; Browne, 2007; Bruce, 2016; Peterson, Wahlström and Wennerhag, 2018), it is also true that Pride parades and marches can and do make specific political and legal demands, particularly in the global contexts documented in this book. Pride is enacted and shaped by participants and spectators, but there are considerable variations in how much control Pride organizers have over who and how people can participate in the parade and after events, what kind of displays and messages are allowed, and considered appropriate and inappropriate. Furthermore, the involvement of businesses, political parties and state institutions, including the police and military, and the role of sponsors in shaping expectations and restrictions can have a significant impact on how much LGBTQ+ individuals and communities can freely shape and participate in Pride.

In many contexts, Pride parades, with their carnivalesque and colourful displays, glittery and flamboyant costumes, camp humour and transgressive sexualized bodily displays treat the 'street as a stage' (Ammaturo, 2016: 20) and demonstrate that 'streets can be queered, and, as a result, heteronormativity becomes denaturalized' (Johnston, 2005: 55). Bruce conceptualizes the 'defiant visibility' that Pride parades demonstrate, reclaiming Pride in the from the shame that homophobia seeks to impose, and 'educational visibility' that visually communicates who LGBTQ+ people are and what issues and causes matter to LGBTQ+ communities (Bruce, 2016: 107–11). Ammaturo (2016) analyses how the street performances and dress of participants in Pride parades enact a queering of space (Ammaturo, 2016) and Browne (2007) explores what the celebratory nature of Pride means in personal, social and political terms for participants. However, these accounts are overly voluntaristic in that they rely entirely on the appearance, behaviour and attitudes of Pride participants and assume that social and political impacts inevitably flow from these individual aims and perspectives. Johnston (2005) cautions that the multiple roles the audience of Pride parades can play in changing, negating or emphasizing the intended impact of Pride. Audiences, whether onlookers at the time, media commentators, politicians and other elites, can welcome and celebrate LGBTQ+ communities, respond with disgust and repudiation, or completely ignore Pride parades. Locating and analysing Pride within its ideological context and impacts is important to avoid simplifying and overstating its political and social effects.

The choice of the Pride parade route 'often leads to public debate about which space they may occupy and what kind if displays are deemed appropriate' (Johnston, 2005: 1). Johnston discusses how a conservative mayor of Auckland in 1990s New Zealand banned Pride from marching in the centre of the city because this is where he considered 'national heroes' from the military and national rugby team should march and not LGBTQ+ people in a Pride parade (Johnston, 2005). Auckland Pride therefore marched in the 'gay district' of the city, which Johnston (2005) argued minimized its political impact. As will be discussed below, in some societies it is unlawful and/or dangerous to organize a Pride parade. In Shanghai, holding a march or parade was illegal, so the organizers of Pride held a 'rainbow bike ride' and 'rainbow fun run' in public with no banners or placards on display, and multiple events behind the doors of hotels, restaurants, consulates and bars. I was told by the organizing committee of Hong Kong Pride that at their first meeting to obtain official permission to hold a parade, the police had produced pictures from Pride parades in Europe and North American showing naked bodies, sex toys and fetish wear. The police asked worriedly, 'You're not going to do this in Hong Kong are you?' and reminded the organizers that public indecency laws prohibit nudity and lewd behaviour. As will be discussed in Chapters 3 and 7, the spaces and places Pride takes place assume major significance and are the points of contestation in societies where space and place reflect racial and class inequalities, such as in South Africa and India.

Laws, regulations and political authorities can limit the spaces Pride takes place in, the extent to which Pride can protest or make political statements and the kind of bodily displays allowed, but Pride organizers and activists can also self-censor. Santos (2012), discussing Pride in Lisbon in the 1990s and 2000s, documents how the focus of the Portuguese media on drag queens and glittery costumes in the parade had caused frustration for some LGBTQ+ activists who felt this hindered their ability to communicate demands for legal and political change and also justified homophobic social prejudices that argued 'those [LGBTQ+] people are not normal' (2012: 134–5). In 1992, the Montreal Pride Committee tried to impose a dress code for the parade stipulating that there should be no cross dressing, no exposure of breasts or buttocks, no displays that were 'too vulgar' or 'too erotic' and no flags. They recommended that participants wear blue jeans and t-shirts (Bell and Valentine, 1995: 14; Johnston, 2005: 105). As will be discussed in Chapter 7, the New York Drag March was started in 1994 in response to the ruling by the organizers of New York Pride that participants should not be dressed in drag or fetish wear. At World Pride in Rome in 2000, organizers had discouraged any costumes that could be viewed as religious parody and therefore provoke hostility from the Vatican (Johnston, 2005: 119). I also heard from Pride organizers and activists in Shanghai and Manila how they had discouraged participants from revealing their torsos, not just to comply with local laws, but also to avoid causing broader social offence. In Cape Town, I was told that one year a sponsor had been concerned to ensure the 'attractiveness' of people wearing their Pride merchandise and subsequent ability to use the pictures for marketing.

In 2018, London Pride told the director of an LGBTQ+ homeless charity that their bus, with its blacked-out windows to allow participants anonymity if they wished it, would be 'a dull uncreative coach in the middle of a sea of colour' and that the group of homeless LGBTQ+ people 'would stand out for all the wrong reasons'. The Pride committee advised that if any of the group were concerned about being photographed, they should walk in the parade wearing masks, hats and face paints and wear 'standard t-shirts'. Pride in London continues to regulate the bodily displays in the parade and afterparty requiring 'swimsuit coverage' and prohibiting 'nudity, obscenity, indecent exposure or sexual acts in public'. Closer relationships with city authorities and the police have also changed the nature and appearance of Pride parades. At Los Angeles Pride in 1970, the police were pushed by the crowd using a giant Chinese dragon puppet shaped as a penis (Ward, 2008: 72). Today, LA Pride organizers work closely with the police and allow them to march in the parade. These attempts to 'straight jacket' the Pride parade harked back to the respectable dress codes of the pre-Pride 'Annual Days of Remembrance' in the United States where LGBT activists would wear suits and ties (Bruce, 2016) and have all led to significant backlashes from queer activists, but they are not the only examples of attempts by organizers to regulate the displays and appearance of the parade. While these examples of self-censorship and efforts to conform to heteronormative codes of 'respectability' and 'normality' may, in some circumstances, be short-lived and not representative of all Pride parades, they do caution against some of the bolder claims made by academics about the transgressive bodily displays Pride parades enact and the universal claims that Pride always queers public space.

The claim that holding a Pride parade, collectively 'coming out' and using 'defiant' and 'educational' visibility in urban and rural spaces to change attitudes towards LGBTQ+ communities are a universal possibility and social good is also not always true. For example, in China it is illegal to hold a public parade or march, and, as will be discussed in Chapter 4, the extensive efforts of the organizers of Shanghai Pride to negotiate Pride in various spaces and places across the city were ultimately unsuccessful as police harassment increased. In other contexts, where homosexuality is illegal and/or the threat of physical violence against LGBTQ+ communities is high, it can be counterproductive and dangerous to hold public Pride events, or to use individual or collective 'coming out' as a basis for campaigning (Currier, 2011; Rodriguez, 2022). Rodriguez believes that the Western assumption that 'coming out' is a final achievement and causal, linear route to progress is a 'fallacy' (Rodriguez, 2022: 45). Rodriguez argues that 'we need to think of the 'wheres, hows, and whys of staying hidden' (2022: 45). Writing about LGBTQ+ campaigning in the 1990s and 2000s Namibia, Currier documents how 'invisibility' offered activists 'a modicum of safety' and was used as a strategic tactic to safely work for change (Currier, 2011). For these reasons, officials at Pan Africa ILGA and ILGA Asia told me that unlike in Europe and North America, these regional umbrella groups do not consider Pride as a priority for advocacy. In many African and Asian contexts, to attempt Pride based on a 'collective coming out' would place communities and individuals at greater physical risk and may provoke damaging political and legal backlashes. The previous example of the LGBTQ+ homeless group wishing to have a bus with blacked-out windows in 2018 London Pride also demonstrates that 'visibility' is not always a universal good, even in Global North contexts. The 'defiant' and 'educational' visibility of Pride is not always possible, or desirable, and we should not assume that the collective visibility of 'coming out' is always a universal good, or even possible, everywhere in the world.

Pride and political and social controversy

There have always been tensions and disagreements about what the purposes, messages and enactment of Pride should be. In the early 1970s, many lesbian groups argued that Pride should focus on protest to achieve legal and political rights and were critical of gay men's emphasis on partying and celebration of sexuality at Pride (Bruce, 2016). Browne's study of Pride in Brighton and Dublin identifies 'the serious politics of Pride and queer playfulness' (2007: 65) and therefore argues that Pride can be a 'party with politics' that overcomes the tensions in the 1970s. At the time of Browne's study, Brighton Pride was free to attend, and this was a significant positive factor mentioned by the participants in her study. Today, participation in Brighton Pride parade, the afterparty and even to access the streets of the 'Gay Village' where Browne's study took place is securitized and ticketed. These developments have rendered Browne's argument anachronistic, because Brighton Pride enacts an exclusive party with capitalist politics. As will be discussed about Pride in South Africa, India, New York and elsewhere, accessing the 'party' aspects of Pride has its own politics related to class, race, safety, transport, food, drink and cost. Considering Pride in global terms requires continual engagement with these factors and catch-all claims about the impacts, politics and role of Pride are best avoided.

There were tensions about the role of business and commercial involvement in Pride as early as 1972, when the New York Pride parade route changed from ending in Central Park, where there had been a free afterparty and stage with speeches, to ending in Greenwich Village, where mafia-run street bars and stalls were erected (Eisenbach, 2006). Marsha P. Johnson and Sylvia Rivera, key figures in the 1969 Stonewall Riots that led to the first Pride in 1970, criticized the Gay Liberation Front and the Gay Activists Alliance who were involved in Pride organizing for being a 'middle-class, white club' who 'refused to challenge the police and neglected the needs of impoverished and homeless queer and trans sex workers' (Danewid, 2023: 144–5). Johnson and Rivera had established Street Transvestites Action Revolutionaries (STAR) organization and ran a hostel for homeless LGBTQ+ people, particularly those who had been in prison. 'Y'all better quiet down', Rivera told a braying crowd from the stage at the 1973 New York Pride, 'your gay brothers and sisters in jail ask for your help and y'all don't do nothing!' Rivera later recalled, 'I had to fight my way up on that stage and literally, people that I called my comrades in the movement, literally beat the shit out of me' (Gan, 2007: 133). Rivera and Johnson faced racism and transphobia from the early Pride attendees, but they also identified the precarity and injustice of capitalism as the source of LGBTQ+ oppression and argued that Pride was complicit in this injustice. 'I have been to jail. I have been raped and beaten many times by heterosexual men. I have lost my job. I have lost my apartment for gay liberation,' Rivera told the crowd at 1973 New York Pride. As will be discussed below, the intersectional relationship between race, class, precarity and the social injustices of capitalism is a perpetual and fundamental theme of queer activist critiques of Pride. It is also a key criticism that can be made of literature about Pride that fails to consider the impacts of capitalism on the lives of LGBTQ+ communities, the intersections with race, class and gender and whether Pride is genuinely inclusive, or whether it remains essentially the 'middle class, white club' that Rivera criticized.

Pride, a social movement?

The global expansion of Pride, the establishment of international umbrella Pride membership groups, such as InterPride and EuroPride, and the high-profile significance of Pride in LGBTQ+ popular culture and history have led many to refer to a transnational 'Pride movement' on a par with other global social and political movements, such as the environmental, women's, anti-globalization and other movements for social justice. It is true that Pride has been taken up as an easily recognizable platform in at least parts of every continent and analysing specific Pride events from a social movement studies perspective can help to document, analyse and understand its impacts on public opinion and effects on political and legal change (see Ayoub, Page and Whitt, 2021). However, using a social movement studies, or contentious politics, framework to frame and analyse all Pride events can also limit our understanding of Pride and obscures the ideological role that Pride plays. There is also a feminist and queer critique of contentious politics analyses that argues these frameworks reduce all activism to protest, assume activists are rational actors with clear goals and target audiences and that this overlooks the emotional, supportive and mutually empowering aspects of being involved in activism, aspects that also occur outside moments of protest or public visibility (Conway, 2022; Eschle and Maiguishca, 2009; Maiguashca, 2011; Taylor and Dyke, 2004). Analysing Pride transnationally using contentious politics social movement theory downplays the debates about the co-option by Pride by global capitalism and the roles of social and political elites in LGBTQ+ advocacy and overstates the relationship and similarity between different Pride events in different parts of the world.

Contentious politics approaches primarily consider activists as both highly committed and rational actors, with clear and identifiable aims, leaders and audiences (McAdam, Tarrow and Tilly, 2001; Tarrow, 1998). Saunders (2022) summarizes the main criticisms of the contentious politics model, namely that it lacks conceptual clarity, is difficult to apply to real-world protest movements and that it is disinterested in what happens outside the period between contentious public protests. Adopting this rationalist framework can simplify and overstate the purposes and impacts of Pride. For example, Petersen and colleagues refer to the participants of their study of Pride in five European cities and Mexico as 'demonstrators', but Pride is not just a demonstration or protest and sometimes is not a demonstration or protest at all. Attendees of Pride are not necessarily committed activists and may have no political motivation or goal. Contentious politics approaches focus on the dynamics of the movement itself and conceptualizes activism as a practice influenced and bound by these movements. Taylor and Dyke also caution that traditional social movement studies rely too heavily on secondary media accounts of protest and lack a nuanced ethnographic approach to understanding social movements (Taylor and Dyke, 2004). This prioritizes an exclusive focus on the attitudes and intentions of participants in and organizers of these movements, as recent accounts of Pride have also done (Bruce, 2016; Peterson, Wahlström and Wennerhag, 2018). Ward (2008), quoted in the introduction chapter, argues that contemporary Pride events in North America have little to no relation to LGBTQ+ social movements, grassroots activism and are more redolent of music festival or trade fair, than an event with broader political, social or legal goals. While this is not true of every Pride event that takes place, it is important to accept that Pride events can be entirely undirected and unintentional, and/or, they can be directed purely for commercial, 'non-political' event-based ends, akin to a music or community festival. Ultimately, Pride can also be just a day, with no other political or social activity beyond that day. Academic analyses that impose contentious politics frameworks on Pride events often fail to adequately consider this.

Adopting contentious politics approaches to understanding Pride can also be too invested in liberal representative politics perspectives to understanding which, and how, communities should be represented at Pride. This can overlook the ideological importance of social justice and can lead to some problematic arguments. For example, Petersen and colleagues (2018) discuss the controversy at London Pride about the proposed participation of the right-wing populist, anti-European and anti-immigrant political party the United Kingdom Independence Party (UKIP), in the Pride parade. UKIP had proposed a ban on HIV+ migrants from entering the UK and ACT UP London and other queer activists protested this by carrying a coffin in the London Pride Parade and with the banner 'Death of Pride' (see Glass, 2020). Peterson and colleagues argue that despite the anti-human rights, xenophobic, homophobic and transphobic policy positions and pronouncements of UKIP, the members of London Pride's organizing committee who had supported UKIP's participation had 'a more inclusive attitude' than the queer protestors at London Pride. These queer protesters, conclude Petersen and colleagues, were 'perhaps not so broadminded as some of the Pride organizers' (2018: 159–60). Adopting this liberal approach to inclusion and political participation leads to a simplistic belief that all are welcome at Pride, even if they are critical of LGBTQ+ rights. Adopting a queer theoretical lens would point to how this distorts understandings of the issues and intersectional struggles LGBTQ+ communities face and removes the ability of Pride to be a useful platform that reveals the reality of LGBTQ+ lives and is a basis for campaigning. It is better to adopt queer and feminist approaches to understand how Pride can, does, or does not advance social justice, than neutral, liberal lenses.

Feminist and queer theory broadens our understanding of activism from being just an antagonistic and oppositional practice, with rational strategies and target audiences, to one that can include self-affirmation, mutual support, cultural practice and visibility, and playful and joyful social, cultural and political actions. Maiguashca (2011) argues that the loose and different elements that make up the transnational feminist anti-globalization movement play an important role in lives and identities of the people involved. Providing mutual emotional support and care, consciousness raising and individual and collective empowerment is an integral part of these feminist groups and this takes place outside and beyond moments of public protest. These affective and empowering aspects of activism are key aspects of queer activist movements. Schulman (2021) writes how ACT UP gradually emerged from Monday evening meetings at a community centre in New York. These were not exclusively political meetings discussing strategy; they were social events where friendships, support and relationships developed. The Monday evening meetings became a focal point for

Figure 5 'Death of Pride', London Pride protest. Permission granted by ACT UP London.

HIV+ people, but also for a broader community of LGBTQ+ people in New York. The combination of mutual support, empowerment and care was as important as the political actions and protests that ACT UP undertook. As discussed above, Pride is not always a protest and does not always prioritize activism, but Pride can and should be a space where these supportive and empowering affective elements can flourish. Pride should also be a platform where activists can gather, raise important issues and other attendees can be made aware of these issues and drawn into activism if they wish. Using feminist and queer approaches to understanding activism and the role that social movements play in people's lives, identities and beliefs is an important means by which to assess the role Pride plays in these terms.

Making universal claims about the Pride and its social and political value from the vantage point of the Global North and particularly, when only examples Pride in Europe and North America are used, can also lead to parochial and problematic claims. Focusing only on Pride in the Global North and not engaging with grassroots critics or considering LGBTQ+ communities who are not or cannot engage with Pride, can reproduce white epistemology (Mills, 2007; Toole, 2021). Petersen and colleagues claim Pride parades are 'rituals' akin to May Day parades. This claim assumes that Pride parades are enacted in the same ways across the world and that May Day parades also exist and are understood in the same ways internationally. Christensen and colleagues (Christensen, Just and Schwarzkopf, 2024) develop the 'Pride as a ritual' argument by claiming that Pride has become a 'viable civil religion' involving 'collective transcendence', 'sacred spaces', the equivalent of Catholic 'liturgical dress' and 'pageant wagons' in the parade. While some participants at Pride in Europe and North America do refer to it as a 'Gay Christmas' (Bruce, 2016), arguing that Pride has become civil religion decontextualizes Pride from its broader social, political and economic relations. There is also an epistemological whiteness inherent to this consideration of Pride: white authors in the Global North, who focus only on Pride in the Global North and choose to ignore the experiences, lives and critiques of Pride by LGBTQ+ activists not only in the Global South, but also marginalized LGBTQ+ communities and grassroots queer activists in the Global North.

The original purpose of Pride was to open transformative sociopolitical spaces, envisioning new social realities as well as campaigning for rights. Discussing Pride in the United States, Bruce (2016) argues that Pride has led to broader cultural and social attitude changes that have laid the groundwork for political and legal changes for LGBT communities. Bruce (2016) writes that criticisms about Pride's over-commercialization are not a significant concern for the Pride participants whom she interviewed, because such sponsorship enables Pride parades to occur and does not define Pride's social purpose. While there is merit in the argument that Pride has had cultural and social impacts leading to change, Bruce, alongside several other academic researchers (Browne, 2007; Bruce, 2016; Peterson, Wahlström and Wennerhag, 2018) rely on the accounts and attitudes of the attendees of Pride to analyse the impact and politics of these events. It is unsurprising that these studies found that attendees who have chosen to attend Pride enjoyed themselves and were unconcerned with accusations of racism or over-commercialization from queer activists who were either not in attendance, or at the margins of these events. These studies therefore either ignore such concerns or conclude that accusations are secondary to the importance of delivering an event that attendees enjoy. Basing analyses on the attitudes of participants of Pride is also shaped by which attendees' researchers spoke to. Lewis and colleagues' (Lewis, Chandra and Markwell, 2023) study of queer people of colour's perception of Pride in Sydney found that these participants felt alienated by the whiteness of Sydney's Mardi Gras and that the organizers had not done enough to engage and include queer people of colour. These findings contrast with other studies of Sydney's Mardi Gras who did not focus specifically on queer people of colour's responses (Markwell and Waitt, 2009). While it is understandable that Pride, like any social, political or commercial event, will want to create positive emotional responses from its attendees, relying on the accounts of attendees of events and not considering the levels of racial and class privilege of these attendees, or engaging with critics, leads to partial and misleading conclusions about the purposes and impacts of Pride. Following this, I would also caution against relying on the accounts of Pride organizers as a premise for understanding and analysing Pride. It is important to consider the nexus of corporate, political and celebrity power relations that many mainstream Pride organizers inhabit and how this may frame their accounts in positive and partial ways.

Pride and the queer politics of truth

I am primarily interested in exploring how Pride events represent, enact and reveal the truth of LGBTQ+ lives, needs, circumstances, identities and demands. This goes further than simply noting that Pride celebrates and engenders *pride* in LGBTQ+ people and requires analysing how Pride includes and represents the complexity of LGBTQ+ lives in intersectional terms that include how race, gender, class, age, physical ability and economic circumstance impact on LGBTQ+ lives, needs, circumstances, identities and demands. Pride can and should still be a utopic space where celebration, fun, irreverence and community can transcend broader socio-political challenges and participants feel *pride* in place of the shame of homophobia, even if for only a day. There is a 'politics of truth' (Foucault, 2001) to this utopic purpose, where Pride can serve as a platform and articulate a vision of a different, alternative social reality, a better world, one where LGBTQ+ individuals are seen and equally validated. This articulation of an 'alternative truth' and one that contrasts with existing socio-political order reveals, contests and can help lead to change. Pride can and should do this, however, as much of this book documents and argues, Pride all too often does not provide an 'alternative truth' or include and represent the complexity and precarity of many LGBTQ+ lives. The reasons for this include Pride's co-option by capitalism, the rise of an LGBTQ+ elite of Pride organizers and advocates and a disengagement from broader social justice movements.

2. A Queer Conceptualization of Pride

The need to make marginalized and oppressed lives visible and to *matter* is a common desire across progressive movements from feminist, anti/de-colonial, queer and other social justice activism (Butler, 2010; Eschle and Maiguashka, 2009; Mohanty, 2003; Roy, 2022). Obscuring marginalized and oppressed groups lives enables and legitimates unjust political and social attitudes and behaviour. Judith Butler (2010) gives the example of the US public's fixation with deaths of US soldiers in the Iraq War and their general disregard of the deaths that US soldiers cause in the Middle East. Butler is interested in 'whose lives are considered valuable, whose lives are mourned, and whose lives are considered ungrievable?' and defines an 'ungrievable life' as 'one that cannot be mourned because it has never lived, that is, has never counted as a life at all' (2010: 38). Similarly, Sarah Schulman compares the over 80,000 'rarely mentioned' AIDS deaths in New York with 'the highly individuated' deaths of almost 3,000 New Yorkers in 9/11. For Schulman, the individuals who died of AIDS 'were abandoned … did not have rights or representation' and 'died because of the neglect of their government and families', and have 'been ignored ….The replacement of deaths that don't matter with deaths that do' (Schulman, 2012b: 42). Butler (2010: 7) is clear that to make lives 'count', matter and therefore 'grievable' 'a life has to be intelligible as a life, has to conform to certain conceptions of what life is, in order to become recognisable'. The desire to make 'ungrievable' lives visible, understood and matter lies at the heart of social justice activism from the women's movement of the 1960s and 1970s (Rowbotham, 1993), by indigenous communities of North America and Oceania (Estes, 2023; Hokowhitu et al., 2020) and by critical race theory and the Black Lives Matter movement (Lowery, 2017; Mbembe, 2019). While Pride in North America and Europe has broadly been an example, in Butler's (2010) terms, of where making LGBTQ+ lives visible has made them matter, the criticisms of Pride by queer activists about the marginalization of precarious queer lives including Black lives, working-class lives and migrant lives, point to the risks of Pride obscuring the reality of the lives (and deaths) of LGBTQ+ individuals and communities.

Making sure everyone's life matters requires not just making everyone's life equally visible, but that representations are accurate in their portrayal of precarity, prejudice and inequality. Butler (2010: 7) argues that to make precarious lives 'matter', the conditions that underpin precarity must be fully considered and incorporated into 'the very terms of recognizability'. Butler and Schulman give the examples of the ACT UP HIV rights movement as examples of activism that has articulated the truths and complexities of marginalized HIV positive people and therefore made these lives visible, understood and matter. Schulman's (2021) detailed history of ACT UP New York demonstrates how ACT UP emerged from radical queer community building and the histories, practices and lessons of the feminist, civil rights, labour and anti-Vietnam War movements. Schulman documents how a coalition of activists, including HIV positive men, women, people of colour, sex workers, drug users and allies, 'united in anger to end the AIDS crisis'. As discussed above, these activists gathered at weekly meetings in a community centre, planned creative and often confrontational direct or 'zap' actions including 'die ins' and disruptions at church, government and pharmaceutical institutions, developed a nuanced media strategy, a sophisticated and well-evidenced expertise about HIV/AIDS and the research, medical and policy needs of HIV positive people and combined radical grassroots protest with high-level engagement with government and the pharmaceutical industry. As discussed in the introduction, Schulman argues that ACT UP achieved 'incredible success' in forcing HIV onto the US government's agenda, transforming medical research and treatment, and that ACT UP serves as a model for future social justice activism (2021: 9). While there is a relationship between the kinds of organizing and communities ACT UP incorporated and Pride, particularly in grassroots Prides discussed later in this book, there is also a clear difference and divide between ACT UP and many large-scale, mainstream Pride events, particularly in the Global North. Indeed, it is telling that ACT UP rarely features in histories of Pride and was absent from official accounts of the history of Pride and LGBTQ+ activism at World Pride New York on the fitieth anniversary of the Stonewall Riots.

While there is a clear differentiation between Pride in the Global North and the histories and politics of queer activism, such as expressed by ACT UP, it is certainly possible to discern the same creativity, anger and urgency in the immediate aftermath of the Stonewall riots and the early Pride parades. This urgency and dedication can also be found in grassroots queer activism in many parts of the world. As Schulman notes, 'people who are desperate are much more effective than people who have time to waste' (2021: 8). While most ACT UP activists in the 1980s were HIV positive, had no effective treatment options and were likely to die, today's Pride organizers in many contexts lack this urgent focus, sense of purpose or even desire to effect political and legal change. The roots of this difference also lie in Schulman's observation that while ACT UP was 'in a sense, able to beat HIV, they could not beat capitalism' (2021: 10). Access to HIV treatment is still structured by the inequalities of capitalism where cost, health provision and global location mean preventable AIDS deaths still occur. The individuals and communities vulnerable to HIV infection are also more likely to be either in areas of relative global poverty, or in economically precarious positions in wealthier global locations. By contrast, the advance of LGBTQ+ rights in many parts of the world has corresponded with the development of corporate equality and diversity policies that ostensibly celebrate LGBTQ+ employees and consumers. Today, the pharmaceutical companies that were once the focus of ACT UP's hostile protests now march at and sponsor Pride parades across the world and continue to structure access to, and profit from, HIV medication. In contrast to the ACT UP activists of the 1980s and 1990s, who were reviled and criminalized, contemporary Pride organizers in North America, Europe and elsewhere are often celebrated and rewarded by governments and big businesses. The changing dynamics and effects of global capitalism have dampened and, in some places, eradicated the anger and urgency of LGBTQ+ activists of the 1970s and 1980s. This expansion of 'global homocapitalism' (Rao, 2015, 2020) has profoundly changed the nature, tenor and content of Pride.

Queer subcultures, activism and gentrification

As queer has become an increasingly ubiquitous term across culture, business and academia, it is important to explore what, if anything, differentiates queer from LGBTQ+ and from other progressive politics. Queer remains an 'unresolved' (Ward, 2008: 3) term and has become a ubiquitous term in academic theorizing used loosely and widely in popular culture, by institutions, businesses and at Pride events. Burchiellaro (2023: 9) writes, 'analytically, queerness can be deployed as a verb (for example, to queer, queering) and as a mode of being in the world that resists normative definition and categorization' and evokes Ahmed's (2006: 566) definition of queer as 'wonky ... out of line, on a slant, the odd and the strange'. ACT UP has been widely identified as a trail blazer in defining and deploying queer activism (Ahmed, 2006: 566; Brown, 2015; Gamson, 1995; Stein and Plummer, 1994). Schulman is right to emphasize the influence of broader leftist, feminist and antiracist movements' influence on ACT UP's 'challenge [to] frames of power' (2021: 8), but the movement was also queer in its departure from the broader 'respectability politics' of other LGBTQ+ advocacy that had been premised on conformity and using existing channels of political influence to try and leverage change. ACT UP's confrontational direct action caused discomfort and shock and combined anger, art, humour, vulgarity, transgression and a 'celebration of difference and challenge to normative social relations' (Brown, 2015: 73). The distinction between LGBTQ+ activism and advocacy and queer activism is also evident in activists who protest at and against 'mainstream' Pride parades for being too conformist with dominant heteronormative, white, state and capitalist institutions and culture. Queer activists who protest against mainstream Prides and/or organize alternative Prides aim to reclaim Pride as a political protest against injustice, inequality and normative understandings of gender and sexuality (McCartan and Nash, 2022: 775). In a cultural moment where some multi-millionaire celebrities, elite institutions and even London property developers are comfortable adopting and deploying queer as an identifier, it is important to continually engage with queer's disruptive and discomforting roots to resist the neat application of this term by the privileged and powerful.

Analysing the roles and importance of cultural and particularly subcultural production is crucial when thinking through the differences and tensions between queer culture, queer activism and its co-optation by dominant frames of power. Queer theory emerged from social and cultural practice: art, music, fashion, literature, rather than originating from abstract academic theorizing or elite institutional spaces. Sarah Schulman (2012b) argues that the rackety, multiracial, working-class, low-rent and hedonistic subcultures of the 1970s and 1980s Manhattan were fundamental to the development of the transgressive and radical queer politics that generated ACT UP. Schulman documents the scale of deaths from AIDS in the districts of lower Manhattan, such as Greenwich Village and Chelsea, and connects this to the gentrification of those areas'. The eradication by AIDS deaths and the socio-economic gentrification that followed has had profoundly troubling political consequences. Other queer theorists have also been inspired by cultural, artistic and subcultural movements: Judith Butler conceptualized queer understandings of fluid gender performativity drawing from the drag subcultures in the late-1980s United States (Butler, 1999); José Esteban Muñoz (Muñoz, 2019) situates queerness in the utopic aesthetics, queer performance spaces and sexual subcultures of Manhattan; Rahul Rao explored the queer and decolonial imaginaries in literary works of fiction and film (2015, 2020); Halberstam exalted the importance of mass-media and subcultural artforms from children's cartoons to Punk music to enacting the messy, non-conformity that forms queer challenges to mainstream culture (Halberstam, 2011); and Burchiellaro (2023) located queer politics in the multiracial, working-class, eccentric community that coalesced at a queer bar in London's East End. Linking these different cultural spaces and artforms is an alter-capitalist politics, one that sits outside of and in tension with capitalist norms of production, success, fame and monetary value. While queer politics is anti-capitalist, there is a porous boundary between queer subculture and mainstream, marketized culture where conformity and profit define success. Queer critics have argued that Pride has helped engender the co-option and marketization of queer subcultures.

The importance of subculture lies not just in its potential to transgress, trouble and queer, but in its ability to imagine, create spaces and dream and articulate alternative visions, futures and truths about a different world: 'The social worlds we inhabit ... are not inevitable, they were not always bound to turn out this way, and what's more, in the process of producing this reality, many other realities, and ways of being have been discarded' (Halberstam, 2011: 146). José Esteban Muñoz maps New York's queer subcultures and artistic production of the 1970s and 1980s and writes 'Queerness is that thing that lets us feel that this world is not enough, that indeed something is missing. Often we can glimpse the worlds proposed and promised in the realm of the aesthetic' (2019: 1). Subcultures are spaces where different ways of being, thinking and acting are realized and this becomes the basis for radical activism and transgressive politics: 'Queerness is essentially about the rejection of a here and now and an insistence on potentially or concrete possibility for another world' (Muñoz, 2019: 1). In the 1980s London, queer subcultures were sustained by social housing, welfare and student grants and this enabled people to live, socialize, think, experiment, rebel, fail, start again and create. 'The genius of the human race lies in its freaks,' wrote the Punk fashion designer Vivienne Westwood, 'If you didn't have freaks then nothing would happen, nothing would develop.' Figures such as Leigh Bowery, whose club nights saw him dress in gender-bending avant-garde dress and whose performance art was 'brutal, visceral, gruesome, at best tasteless, at worst horrific', posed 'a radical challenge to the usual order of things' (Bancroft, 2012: 72; Green and Stevenson, 2024; Moran, 2025; Tilley, 2025) and has had long-lasting influence on queer culture and gender expression.

Subcultural figures from this era had expressly political aims: 'How to change the system!', wrote Vivienne Westwood, 'subversion lies in ideas' (Westwood, 2016: 2). Westwood believed in the power of art to articulate alternative truths about society and history. Engaging with and creating art was for Westwood, political because enabled the viewer to gain 'a perspective from which to form his own opinions and to act' (2016: 2). Indeed, Westwood often urged employees, students and interlocutors to regularly attend art galleries so they could independently form and understand their own tastes, thoughts and convictions. Westwood believed that the artist 'is responsible to the truth of things' and argued that it was important to 'see the world for what it is'. The visions of alternative ways of being come from society's margins. From this, transgressive politics and activism is generated and sustained. Alongside Westwood, who became a noted political and environmental campaigner, often scrawling political messages and manifestos on her fashion, other artists have played an integral role in radical political activism, including David Hoyle and Anohni discussed at the beginning of this chapter. Keith Haring designed the ACT UP symbol, used graffiti to communicate queer activist messages and channelled the profits of his commercial success to ACT UP. Zanele Muholi, the internationally renowned South African photographer, began their activist career with the Forum for the Empowerment of Women (FEW) and helped organize Soweto Pride. The 2024 retrospective of Muholi's work at the Tate Modern London included images of the impact of homophobic violence against Black lesbians in Johannesburg, pictures that evoked the complex politics of racism and gender injustice in South Africa and documents from the early years of FEW activism and Soweto Pride (Dlungwana et al., 2024). As Halberstam (2011) and Schulman (2012b) discuss and the above artists evidence, 'success' for queer artists is measured in mainstream cultural recognition and often in economic terms. The commodification of queer art and artists creates tensions and contradictions, but it is still possible to identify the queer politics of these cultural producers and their activist intent.

The gentrification of Pride

There has always been a symbiotic relationship between Pride and queer subculture, but also a tension around whether Pride includes, generates and validates these communities, or excludes, devalues and sits outside of queer subculture. A key tension has been around the gentrification and commodification of queer subculture and the areas that were once enclaves for queer and other marginalized communities. The areas where the first Pride parades took place in New

York, San Francisco and London are now among the most expensive and exclusive districts in the world. More recent Pride parades in cities including Sydney, Cape Town, Johannesburg and Tel Aviv also take place in gentrified, wealthy and tourist-friendly locations. Schulman argues that the process of urban gentrification that has priced the artists, immigrants, working class and students out of these areas has also removed an essential pre-condition for subcultural space, artistic thought and creation to take place (2012b: 81). Queer artists themselves, for example, Andrew Logan and Boy George, have commented on the impossibility of being a queer subcultural artist without access to subsidized public housing or communal squats (*Tramps!*, 2022). These opportunities have almost entirely gone in today's extortionate and competitive London, a reality that has a major de-radicalizing effect on British, and global, culture and society. Thus, Schulman argues that gentrification is not just a process that affects an area's property prices and business rates, but that there is a 'gentrification of the mind' in a fundamental re-ordering and valorization of values, people and communities. Out of this 'conformity of aesthetics and values' come 'conventional bourgeois behaviour', bland homogenization and suburban values that lead to conservative attitudes and ways of being (Schulman, 2012b: 81). The replacement of the marginalized, deprived and underground, with the privileged, glamorized and mainstream has profound political implications.

For Schulman (2012b) LGBTQ+ activism has been subject to forms of spatial, cultural and political 'gentrification', reproducing norms of respectability that are framed by capitalism, class privilege and whiteness. This process of gentrification erases knowledge of previous queer activist struggles, and the communities they served, and prevents consideration of inequality and social injustice in LGBTQ+ advocacy. Schulman ponders why the newly arrived younger, educated, wealthy and white residents of lower Manhattan never seem to complain, or organize to demand better services or improvements in the, now-expensive, Manhattan apartments they live in, whereas the older, working-class residents regularly do organize to protest. Schulman concludes that 'there's a weird passivity that accompanies gentrification', because gentrified people 'do not have a culture of protest' and they have 'a hypnotic identification with authority … they do not want to ask authority to be accountable' (Schulman, 2012b: 33–4). Schulman, like other critics of neoliberal politics (see Burchiellaro, 2023; Conway, 2023), writes that gentrification is predicated on a version of reality where struggles for social justice have been fully realized and there is no place for political grievance, or protest, for LGBTQ+, racial or class rights:

> Gentrification is dependent on telling us that things are better than they are – and this is supposed to make us feel happy. It's a strange concept of happiness as something that requires the denial of many other people's experiences. For some of us, on the other hand, the pursuit of reality is essential to happiness. Even if the process gets us into trouble.
>
> (Schulman, 2012b: 14)

Writing about LGBTQ+ employees and queer activism in London, Burchiellaro (2023) captures the complexity and contradictions of the 'all encompassing' commercialization of LGBTQ+ lives and politics by gentrification. After a London Borough endorsed the replacement of social housing and a racially and class diverse queer pub with luxury flats, queer activists who opposed the development found themselves at odds but also, ostensibly, in agreement with the authorities and property developers, because all sides of the dispute claimed to be supportive of LGBTQ+ communities. Burchiellaro concludes that 'neoliberal promises of LGBTQ+ inclusion engender forms of gentrification – both of queer activism and of queer spaces – that are ultimately at odds with a genuinely transformative vision for queer leftist politics' (2023: 8). Gentrification as an economic, social and cultural process has profound political consequences. As the case studies of Pride in this book will demonstrate, there are many parts of the world where queer activists find themselves at odds, but also in ostensible agreement with Pride organizers, who claim to want to advance LGBTQ+ belonging and rights. These tensions may be expressed in racial, gender and class terms, but they are all essentially tensions over the gentrification of LGBTQ+ activism, which itself has a racial, gendered and class logics.

The spatial, economic and cultural processes of gentrification have framed the progress and understanding of LGBTQ+ rights. The advance of LGBTQ+ rights in many countries has led to change not only in legal rights and employment policy, but in cultural and media representations of LGBTQ+ 'lifestyles' from being morally corrupt and deviant, to positive and normative (McRobbie, 2008). Duggan (2004) analyses how the creation of a new 'gay normality' is part of a broader neoliberal process of dismantling radical queer, anti-racist and feminist politics and replacing it with a 'homonormativity' that reproduces neoliberal norms of market-based equality. This defines LGBTQ+ subjects as consumers in markets for advertising and consumption, where new legal rights and protections, such as same-sex marriage, deliver these market opportunities (Duggan, 2004). There are numerous examples of 'commodified gayness' (Rushbrook, 2002) in popular culture. Sender (2006) argues that television programmes such as *Queer Eye for the Straight Guy*, where gay men are represented in positive terms and aim to help heterosexual men improve their masculinities and lives, mark not just shifts in masculinities, but are integral to the neoliberal project of developing new and profitable markets and addressing specifically the 'problem' of the male consumer who traditionally was expected to be disinterested in fashion, cosmetics and home furnishings. Ward notes that on *Queer Eye for the Straight Guy* 'queer refers to a glossy and marketable form of connoisseurship, one in which homosexuality is linked to other "excesses", such as consumption of high fashion and gourmet foods. Fine tastes are, it seems, also queer' (Ward, 2008, 3). The 'mass-mediated queer lifestyle' (Eng, 2010: 3) evident across many aspects of popular culture in the Global North, and in LGBTQ+-focused advertising, constructs and privileges particular LGBTQ+ 'homonormative' lifestyles over others (Butler, 2002; Conway, 2022; Duggan, 2004; Ward, 2008). This 'lifestylization' (Bell and Binnie, 2000: 99; Conway, 2022) of LGBTQ+ identities, where being gay becomes 'one more brand name to buy' (Bell, 2000: 99), is clearly evident at Pride in major cities, where Pride is part of a desirable 'lifestyle' leisure activity and/or tourist attraction (Conway, 2022). For queer critics of the 'lifestylization' of LGBTQ+ identities and of Pride, the framing of correct, or desirable, LGBTQ+ lifestyles is problematic in restricting identities to categories that are acceptable in heteronormative and capitalist terms.

Writing about the development and changes in LGBTQ+ advocacy and activism in the United States from the 1980s until the 2000s, Jane Ward documents the gentrification of Los Angeles Pride as its original working-class people of colour organizers were edged out and replaced educated middle-class white organizers 'people with professional diversity skills, multicultural connections, a mastery of diversity speak and their "finger on the pulse" of diverse communities' (Ward, 2008: 6). As Pride became more dependent on corporate sponsorship and involvement, Ward argues that their political motivations, understanding of LGBTQ+ history and connection with LGBTQ+ communities become redundant to their ability to be professional event organizers. Like Ward, I also heard 'mainstream' Pride organizers say they seldom discussed the political purposes and history of Pride, or how Pride might contribute to or advance queer politics. Large-scale mainstream Pride organizers often seemed reluctant, or unwilling, to self-identify as activists at all. Rather, organizing committees of large Pride events focused on the logistics and provision of security fences, guards, ticketing platforms and relations with corporate sponsors and local officials. The organizer of 2019 New York and World Pride parade told me he aimed to provide 'life experiences' that could be captured and communicated on attendees on social media, and in previous years, Johannesburg's Pride parade has stopped for the opportunity to take and record social media posts. For Schulman, the LGBTQ+ community has 'doomed' itself by believing state, or corporate, funding is essential in order to deliver large-scale Pride events with security personnel, fences, professional organizers and afterparties, all factors that were 'choices' made by Pride organizers (Schulman, 2012b: 119). These choices, according to Schulman, are rooted in the gentrified mindsets of organizers and the repudiation of the queer politics of their forebears. For Rao (2015: 44), considering 'choices' made by LGBTQ+ activists overplays the agency activists have in the structural conditions of neoliberalism. Essentially, these 'choices' take place within the commercial massification of Pride that reflects the LGBTQ+ community's 'folding into capitalism' (Rao, 2015: 43).

Pride and homocapitalism

Pride events in New York, London, Toronto, Sydney, Johannesburg, Cape Town and elsewhere have been heavily criticized by queer activists for being overly commercialized and/or excluding marginalized LGBTQ+ communities and their issues and needs (Conway, 2024; Glass, 2020; Holmes, 2017; Lewis, Chandra and Markwell, 2023). The involvement of businesses in Pride as sponsors, participants in the parade and the branding of corporate logos and consumer products in rainbow colours for 'Pride month' reflects broader, and controversial, shifts in global capitalism. In the 1990s, as equality laws and regulations incorporated LGBTQ+ rights, LGBTQ+ employees were protected in corporate employment policies, presented as model employees and as a lucrative consumer group. As two leading LGBTQ+ executives argue, 'Rainbow capitalism translates into an enhanced ability to recruit and retain top talent and access a wider marketplace' (Hewlett and Sears, 2024). This 'business case' (Burchiellaro, 2023; Rao, 2024) for LGBTQ+

inclusion and celebration by companies is reflected in internal employee organizing, such as the development of staff LGBTQ+ groups, transnational business advocacy groups such as Out Leadership, Out & Equal, Pride Circle and Open for Business, LGBTQ+-focused corporate advertising and of course, by the participation of corporate sponsorship and employees at Pride.

Many authors have detailed how LGBTQ+ advocacy has been co-opted in the reproduction of global capitalism (Ahmed, 2012; Burchiellaro, 2023; Duggan, 2004; Rao, 2020; Rodriguez, 2022; Roy, 2022; Liu, 2023; Tian, 2020; Ward, 2008). Rao defines 'homocapitalism' as building on concepts of homonormativity (Duggan, 2004) and 'homonationalism' (Puar, 2017),

> To signify the folding into capitalism of some queers and the disavowal of others, through a liberal politics of recognition that obviates the need for redistribution. Productivity, measured in terms of potential or actual contribution to economic growth, becomes the marker on the basis of which queer inclusion is premised. Selective inclusion widens rifts between queers deemed productive and unproductive, while also threatening to evacuate the anti-capitalist potential of queer movements themselves.
>
> (Rao, 2020)

Homocapitalism, expressed by corporate LGBTQ+ 'allies' and by some (arguably many) LGBTQ+ actors, fundamentally undermines the radical potential of queer politics and any alliance with broader transgressive, radical social justice politics: 'the dovetailing of queer progressiveness with discourses of rampant capitalism portrays queer commitments to anticapitalism and degrowth as counterproductive, unnecessary and unimaginable' (Rao, 2024: 82). This argument builds on Foucauldian perspectives of how we understand the world to be and how the possibilities of and need for change are framed. For Foucault, 'regimes of truth' are framed by, and have reproduced, the logics of capitalism, including market-based competition, individualism and the predication of personal value on productive labour (Foucault, 2001). This constitutes a 'political rationality' that renders the political economic, rather than radical, and the social individual, rather than collective (Lemke, 2001: 191). As Berlant (2011) and Burchiellaro (2023) argue, there is a 'cruel optimism' in the articulation of the freedom 'just around the corner' in the neoliberal marketplace, a freedom that will never be fully realized for the majority because of the inequality, authoritarianism and violence that are inherent to neoliberal capitalism.

As will be discussed below, Pride is a site where multiple aspects of capitalist governmentality can come together at once, providing an ideal platform for commercial advertising, expanding market reach, celebrating commercial and state institutions as models of diversity and inclusion, articulating understandings of LGBTQ+ rights and progress in capitalist terms and erasing more complex and messy politics that focus on poverty, injustice and radical politics. I contend that the commercialization of Pride is one aspect in the broader reframing of LGBTQ+ subjectivities, rights and political activism along neoliberal lines, and this raises significant implications for the possibilities for intersectional understandings of oppression, the erasure of histories of queer protest and the ability for activism to challenge inequality. However, Pride's co-option is not inevitable, nor is it a seamless, or always successful, process.

As discussed above, previous research on Pride has argued that attendees of Pride are unconcerned by the involvement of business and/or commercialization of Pride (Bruce, 2016; Kates and Belk, 2001), and even that focusing on concerns about the commercialization of Pride is 'shortsighted' (Christensen, Just and Schwarzkopf, 2024). While I believe that this argument is wrong and that analyses should focus on the ideological effects commercial involvement has, it is important to acknowledge the varying levels of agency and reward and that commercialization should not simply be considered as a process simply and uniformly imposed onto 'dupes'. As Srila Roy writes, capitalist 'governmentality' involves a complex 'micropolitics of the self' that depends not just on 'how one is governed' but also on how 'one lets oneself be governed' (2022: 9). Capitalism is not simply imposed on individuals, they can embrace it, believing it is in their best interests and that it offers meaningful rewards. Burchiellaro (2023) interviewed LGBTQ+ corporate employees and found that some LGBTQ+ employees have leveraged and capitalized on their 'diversity' to the benefit of their careers and success. Burchiellaro acknowledged that 'it is important to recognize that inclusion is not simply being levied from above – it is also an object of desire for LGBTQ+ people themselves. After all, who would not want to be(come) more "productive"' (2023: 10). While we should pay attention and be critical of capitalist co-option and marketization of LGBTQ+ identities, activism and platforms, such as Pride, it is equally important to acknowledge not only the restricted agency actors have, but also the active and complex levels of complicity and reward for LGBTQ+ communities that are offered by capitalism.

The gentrification of LGBTQ± activism and the rise of 'career queers'

The advance of capitalism into terrains that was once the preserve of the women, Black and LGBTQ+ protest movements has led to pressures of gentrification on these movements. Ward (2008: 13) believes that if LGBTQ+ organizations become dependent on having corporate partners and/or funding, these organizations 'have become *culturally* and *ideologically* dependent on corporations'. As previously discussed, Ward documents how Los Angeles Pride was 'gentrified' and its working-class and Latinx roots erased. Ward also points to the 'sanitization' of Pride when 'homonormative' concerns about being 'family friendly' is prioritized over 'the right to public sexuality and an environment free of the glorification of innocence, reproduction and the nuclear family' (2008: 17). The celebration of 'homonormative' same-sex marriage and the presentation of this legal change as the ultimate achievement of LGTBQ+ progress have been criticized for serving the needs of the highly lucrative wedding industry, attendant consumer practices such as obtaining property and also surrogacy rights in territories where this requires significant monetary costs (Butler, 2010; Conway, 2022; Duggan, 2004; Scott, 2013).

As will be expanded upon in Chapter 4, SM Rodriguez (2018) explored the negative impacts on Ugandan grassroot LGBTQ+ activists caused by the elite, international group of 'gentrified' LGBTQ+ advocates who work for international agencies and LGBTQ+ umbrella organizations. Rodriguez names these gentrified global elites 'career queers': professionals who 'have created successful careers out of queer activism' (Rodriguez, 2018: 83). Career queers 'are more likely to approach activism as a form of business; they are less likely to situate the activism in the perspective of a community, even if they argue that their activism is in and of itself for the community' (Rodriguez, 2018: 84). International umbrella organizations employing educated professionals are symptomatic of the 'trickle down philanthropic structure' of the international 'non-profit industrial complex' (Rodriguez, 2018: 84). The rise of LGBTQ+ non-profit organizations, from umbrella groups like InterPride, which now has Consultative

Status at the UN, EuroPride and the International Lesbian and Gay Association (ILGA), to transnational lobbying organizations such as the Kaleidoscope Trust and Outright International, 'redirects activist energies into career-based modes of organizing instead of mass-based organizing capable of actually transforming society' (Rodriguez, 2018: 84). This changes the social movement and activist landscape, leading to funding processes and expectations that 'encourages social movements to model themselves after capitalist structures, effectively halting any major critique of those structures' (Rodriguez, 2018: 83). The rise of career queers has led to the phenomenon of 'high profile celebrity activists' (Rodriguez, 2018: 14), some of whom are also Pride organizers. Rodriguez quotes one grassroots LGBTQ+ activist in Uganda who comments that the new era of the movement relies on celebrities who believe 'being famous is better than being courageous' (2018: 14). Pride events, particularly World Pride and its Human Rights Conference, provide an important networking and fundraising forum for 'career queers', many of whom change jobs between Pride organizing, LGBTQ+/Human Rights advocacy, transnational governmental organizations, such as the UN, and corporate LGBTQ+ advocacy umbrella groups. Large-scale Pride and Pride umbrella organizations, such as InterPride and EuroPride, and the transnational LGBTQ+ advocacy umbrella organization ILGA are pre-eminent examples of this gentrified new elite of 'career queers'.

As with my discussion about LGBTQ+ corporate employees, I am not, necessarily, arguing that individual 'career queers' be held responsible for the extractive politics and marginalization of grassroots communities and issues, for they also have limited agency. Exercising individual agency and freely expressing our opinions at work are not always possible, but I have been struck with the apparent disregard by some career queers about grassroots activists, in terms of considering them or including them in elite LGBTQ+ events, even when presented the easy opportunity to do so. As I will discuss in Chapter 6, my repeated efforts to get grassroots activists from South Africa included in the World Pride Human Rights Conference in Copenhagen were unsuccessful. The Conference included almost the same group of Global North LGBTQ+ advocates and corporate EDI professionals as had dominated the previous conference in New York. While there may have been constraints on agency and possibly just poor planning by the organizers, I have heard numerous anecdotes about LGBTQ+ grassroots activists from Africa and Asia being excluded from high-profile international LGBTQ+ rights forums, and feeling that they are not 'seen' by LGBTQ+ advocacy elites if and when they are included. It is important that we are always honest about what Pride and LGBTQ+ advocacy events are and do, who they include and exclude, and what potential they really have to transform or conceal social injustice.

Many Pride events, including London, New York and Sydney, are registered as corporate entities and can have salaried staff and professional governance structures. However, as Roy notes, 'neoliberalism looks very different in different parts of the world' (2022: 5). The pressures of capitalism make it difficult to draw 'dividing lines between different and even oppositional political projects' (Roy, 2022: 5). In most international contexts, grassroots queer activists struggle to obtain reliable sources of funding and income. In the Global South, even queer activists with anti-capitalist politics can find themselves approaching potential corporate donors in contexts where there are few, or no other sources of reliable funding. Furthermore, although homocapitalism privileges whiteness, just as it privileges patriarchy, this does not mean that people of colour cannot participate and reinforce the exploitation of other marginalized groups. Rao explains that 'homocapitalism does not simply fraction populations along lines of race and caste but also aligns with and intensifies ideological tensions within racialized and oppressed caste groups over the putative merits of capitalism as a vehicle for social mobility' (Rao, 2024: 90). The expansion of corporate diversity and inclusion policies across the world created opportunities for advancement and status for previously marginalized groups. In contexts, including New York, Johannesburg and Mumbai, Pride as a visible and transnational platform has also afforded the opportunity for queers to gain status, reward and simultaneously disregard and disavow the struggles that less privileged LGBTQ+ communities face.

The positive, celebratory and happy emotional tenor that institutional expressions of diversity and inclusion engender leaves little place for the anger and indignation that have traditionally been part of feminist, Black and queer social protest movements. Institutional diversity talk creates a 'feel good politics' (Ahmed, 2012: 69) that allows the organization to retain 'good idea of themselves' (Ahmed, 2012: 71) and also to communicate images to the wider public that 'establish and maintain goodwill' (Ahmed, 2012: 143). Ahmed claims that university diversity policies and the statements of senior managers and public relations staff about the valuing and protecting diversity often 'perform a lie insofar as they represent the university as if it has principles that it does not have' (Ahmed, 2006). Thus, these statements and policies are 'non performative speech acts' in that they do not do what they say, and if they do anything, they can in fact act against the very people they claim to protect and celebrate. Ahmed provides evidence of ethnic minority students at an elite UK university who had complained of racist treatment by the university, being dismissed by the institution that argued the university did not tolerate racism; it had a policy on antiracism and therefore the students' complaints could not be true and was not acted upon (2006). Thus, diversity talk maintains the institutions whiteness, mitigates against confrontation and complaint and 'the smile of diversity stops the "rotten core" from surfacing' (Ahmed, 2012: 72). Ahmed identifies institutional expressions of support for LGBTQ+ employees and consumers as an ideal means for concealing racism, sexism and class exclusion. This is because institutions can choose to celebrate Black, educated, 'successful' and 'happy' LGBTQ+ individuals and hide the struggles of 'unsuccessful' Black and working-class communities, including LGBTQ+ people in these communities (2012: 151–2; see also Conway, 2022; 2024; Ward, 2008). The happy, celebratory, smiling face of 'diversity talk' can fit seamlessly with Pride's positive, celebratory emotional tenor, making it the ideal platform for an uncritical 'feel good politics' and for institutions to, literally, parade their ostensible commitment to diversity and inclusion.

Pride and the political economy of the rainbow

The rainbow has become synonymous with Pride, LGBTQ+ identity and the celebration of LGBTQ+ communities. The controversies around business and products using the rainbow to symbolize Pride and LGBTQ+ rights lie within the history of the origin of the rainbow flag and the belief of Gilbert Baker, the artist who made the first rainbow flag, that the more institutions that used the rainbow flag and image to ally with the LGBTQ+ community, the better. The rainbow flag was first displayed for this purpose at San Francisco Freedom Day Parade in 1978 (Rossi, 2020). The LGBTQ+ rights activist and politician Harvey Milk had asked Gilbert Baker and a small group of LGBTQ+ activists and artists, to design a symbol for the parade. Crucially, Baker did not apply for copyright of the rainbow flag because he wanted it to be used by any person or group to symbolize Pride, LGBTQ+ identity and rights (Rossi, 2020). While this was presumably motivated by a desire to enable all LGBTQ+ activists and causes to utilize the rainbow in their campaigning, and this has certainly been the case, it has also enabled commercial enterprises to use the rainbow as an LGBTQ+ symbol in any way they see fit. For example, Baker collaborated with several companies on 'official' Pride Flag merchandise, including the Finnish vodka distiller, Absolut. Absolut began targeted LGBT advertising in 1981 and produced the first 'Absolut Colors' Pride bottle in the 2000s (Absolut, n.d.). Absolut explained that the 2019 edition of the bottle was 'the latest demonstration of Absolut's long-standing support to the LGBT community' (Absolut, n.d.). Encouraging the free use of the rainbow flag ensured it became centrally and powerfully associated with Pride, LGBTQ+ communities and causes. It also meant that any group or institution can use the rainbow to symbolize support for Pride and LGBTQ+ communities without committing to any other material, political or legal stance. The ease with which the rainbow can be used and adapted and its vibrant and easy recognizability make it at once a powerful, positive and successful symbol for LGBTQ+ identity and activism, but also potentially superficial, over-used and meaningless. It is this rebranding of corporate logos using rainbow colours that critics argue is disingenuous 'Pink' or 'Rainbow-washing' (Schulman, 2012b), or a 'non performative speech act' (Ahmed, 2006). The value of commercial companies using the rainbow as a sign of solidarity and a symbol of progress is questioned by queer critics who consider capitalism as incompatible with the achievement of social justice and LGBTQ+ liberation.

Pride parades are seldom homogeneous, or exclusive, platforms for the celebration of corporate diversity policies and 'homocapitalism', they are also sites of controversy, protest and open contestation of corporate involvement and the commercialization. For example, at Brighton Pride in 2019, British Airways sponsored a large aeroplane shaped float occupied by uniformed BA staff waving rainbow flags. In the same parade, the Queers Support the Migrants group marched with placards depicting BA logos with 'No Pride in Deportation' written on them. This opposed British Airways collaboration with the UK government's deportation of LGBT asylum seekers who had had their applications rejected. British Airways, along with other airlines, withdrew from the government's deportation programme, indicating that these protests had been successful. Conceptualizing Pride as part of a 'regime of truth' is not synonymous with claiming that Pride has been fully captured by capitalist governmentality; rather, Pride can be a site for ideological contestation, or a 'politics of truth', whereby political and social confrontations become struggles about what is accepted as the truth (Foucault, 2001). As Foucault (1998: 95) famously remarked, 'where there is power, there is resistance'; power is not only disciplinary

Figure 6 Saks 5th Avenue, Stonewall Anniversary/Pride Month fashion range.

and repressive, it can also liberate. In this way, 'resistance is both an element of the functioning of power and a source of its perpetual disorder' (Dreyfus and Rabinow, 1982: 147). Contesting a particular regime of truth is therefore possible. Foucault (1980: 133) argues that the political imperative of our times is to try to change the 'political, economic, institutional regime for the production of truth' in order to constitute a 'new politics of truth'. As will be discussed later in this book, queer protests at and against Pride for being too commercialized are examples of these contestations, as are Pride events that eschew corporate involvement and critique capitalism.

Queer activists protested at the sponsorship of Reading Pride by BAE Systems, a major weapons manufacturer and exporter to homophobic states, such as Saudi Arabia (Glass, 2020). Rossdale (2019) argues that although criticizing the sponsorship of Pride by BAE Systems is legitimate, it can imply that businesses are moral actors, something that reinscribes the moral authority of Western capitalism. As Burchiellaro

(2023: 32) argues, 'the very existence of corporations ... exerts an "unfriendly" influence on the world, perhaps especially when their business is that of making weapons'. As discussed at the beginning of the chapter, queer activists have protested the commercialization, race and class politics of Johannesburg Pride. There have been protests about these issues at Prides elsewhere in South Africa, Hong Kong and India (Conway, 2022, 2023, 2024). There have also been alternative, queer, or Reclaim Pride marches, most notably the Reclaim Pride march attended by 45,000 people a few streets away from the 'official' World Pride parade held in New York in 2019. Pride, therefore, can be the site of political and queer contestation of capitalism and the Reclaim Pride movement seeks to reject capitalism altogether and articulate a vision of radically queer future.

Conclusion

This chapter has conceptualized Pride as part of a 'politics of truth' that articulates the lives, needs and culture of LGBTQ+ individuals. As such, the extent to which Pride reveals, or conceals, the intersectional realities of LGBTQ+ lives and needs has profound political, ideological and social implications. Much of the existing literature on Pride makes bold and universal claims, claims that should be questioned and analysis expanded to Pride events outside of the Global North and West. Pride's role in providing a platform for LGBTQ+ people to collectively 'come out' and create visibility to change social, cultural and political norms is not a universal good across the world, nor do participants have free agency to shape and define the nature of Pride, its displays and messages. Official regulations and organizers' rules and expectations can play a significant role in constraining and shaping the kinds of bodies, messages and communities in the parade. While adopting contentious politics approaches to conceptualizing and analysing Pride can be useful, they can lead to reductive and problematic universal claims that belie epistemological whiteness and gentrified analytical frameworks that ignore the ideological impacts of Pride and the perspectives and needs to marginalized LGBTQ+ people in local and international terms. Adopting a queer approach to understanding Pride locates queerness at the margins and in subculture. From this emerges a radical and transgressive politics that articulate a different social reality, way of organizing and being in the world. ACT UP is a key example of how queer activism emerged from a subculture and marginalized communities and its radical politics made precarious lives, and deaths, visible and matter.

The pressures of economic, spatial and social pressures of gentrification are essentially part of the expansion and re-orientation of late-capitalism. These changes in the market seek to incorporate, profit from and de-radicalise once marginal and politically threatening communities. The ability of subcultures to form and create in major urban centres depended on affordable living and levels of state welfare support, the retreat of the state and the transformation of these urbanscapes into expensive, gentrified areas has displaced, contracted and radically changed the populations and cultures that once existed in those spaces. Queer, at its essence, is to make strange, to contest, to reject conformity and to imagine new and radically different ways of being. Gentrification co-opts, but also homogenizes and conforms. These cultural processes have radically politically conservative effects. Businesses now position themselves as advocates for the LGBTQ+ community and a new generation of 'career queers' have formed an international elite that adopts the language of activism without any necessary connection or understanding of grassroots queer activist history or needs. Pride has become a pre-eminent location for businesses to advertise and parade their ostensible queer credentials. The tensions between the capitalist co-option of Pride and Pride as a platform for radical queer activism began almost as soon as Pride emerged in the early 1970s. The next chapter will explore whether Pride can be a utopic and queer 'microcosm' of an alter-society in much the same way as queer subculture, or whether it just serves as a 'mirror' of heteronormative white conformity and co-option by capitalism.

Chapter 3

PRIDE AS A 'MIRROR', NOT A 'MICROCOSM', OF SOCIETY: CONFLICTS OVER RACE, CLASS AND GENDER

> We call for a Pride that is a microcosm of the society we wish to live in, and not a mirror of the divided one that we currently live in. We wish Pride to be a space that all can access, where all can be free, and where every voice is important.
>
> – Johannesburg People's Pride Manifesto 2013

> They [the organizers of Mumbai Pride] are not interested in caste or Hijra [trans, intersex or eunuch] … In India we cannot isolate queerness, caste plays an important role in the queer community … People stop talking to me on Grindr once they find out I'm Adivasi [indigenous] … What does Mumbai Pride's slogan 'Pride for all' mean in the minds of the organizers? Just saying the theme is 'Pride for all' doesn't mean it happens!
>
> – Tata Institute of Social Sciences (TISS), Mumbai students' Queer Collective (interview with the author, 2019)

In 2018, the LGBTQ+ advocacy charity Stonewall UK pulled out of London Pride on the grounds that the event was not doing enough to include Black and ethnic minority communities (Khomami, 2018). In 2021, the organizing committee of London Pride resigned after a Black member of the committee stood-down and publicly accused London Pride of institutional racism (Mohdin, 2021). That Pride serves as a 'mirror' to pre-existing social, political and economic divisions, rather than an inclusive, transformational and utopic 'microcosm' of a society that should exist, has become a commonplace criticism of Prides across the world. Lewis and colleagues' study of queer people of colour's experiences in Sydney argues that in white-majority societies, Pride mirrors 'social structures and power relations which privilege individuals from that group. The normative whiteness that shapes these societies influences the dominance of whiteness in queer spaces and Pride events which take place in them' (2023: 520). The interviews with queer people of colour in Australia found evidence of deeply embedded racism with multiple accounts of racist experiences in clubs, while dating and a broader 'inherent racism' in the presentation of the LGBTQ+ people in popular culture (Lewis et al., 2023). In North America and Europe, Black Lives Matter and other anti-racist protestors have protested and disrupted parades arguing that Pride parades are racist (Boston and Duyvendak, 2015; Walcott, 2017). Alternative Pride events have been organized to include Black and ethnic minority communities, including London's Black Pride, which was first held in 2005 (*UK Black Pride*, no date). This chapter will explore the socio-economic, political and spatial tensions that manifest at Pride events. This addresses one of the key questions that inspired this book: whether, why and to what extent queer criticisms of Pride's racism, sexism and classism are reproduced in contexts outside of the West/Global North.

Chapter 2 discussed Ward's (2008) study of Los Angeles Pride, where working-class people of colour were edged out of Pride's organization and replaced by middle-class white organizers, who then profoundly changed the nature and rationale of the event to reflect their own interests and worldviews, at the expense of the grassroots communities that had previously been included. As will be discussed at greater length in Chapter 4, the commercialization of Pride, with the involvement of brands, advertising and corporate floats in the parade, has also been criticized for reinforcing the exclusionary whiteness of Pride (Lewis et al., 2023: 531). My research found that Pride in South Africa, Hong Kong, India and Shanghai all point to how the organization, location and representations at mainstream Pride events reflect and exacerbate underlying socio-political divisions and are a focus for queer contestation and protest. Pride is all too often a 'mirror' of social, political and economic divisions, rather than a queer 'microcosm' of the world we should inhabit.

Pride on the margins of South Africa

South Africa has extreme levels of economic and racial inequality (Chancel et al., 2021: 39–40). The legacies of the legal, institutional and societal racism of apartheid, and the brutal violence of the State of Emergency the 1980s and 1990s, continue to resonate throughout the country's politics, economics and society. The spatial dynamics of the past continue to define life in South Africa's cities today, with many formerly white-only areas remaining enclaves for the country's wealthy white minority and a new Black middle class. Numerous academic studies have argued that although South Africa is an international role model for LGBTQ+ legal rights, Pride in Johannesburg and Cape Town is the focus, and cause, of bitter race, class and gender divisions (Conway, 2014, 2022; Gevisser and Cameron, 1994; Hoad, 1999; Mathebeni, 2018; Milani, 2015; Moreau, 2017; Scott, 2013). Zethu Matebeni (2018) and others tried to engage with Cape Town Pride in the 2010s in an effort to democratize and make the event more inclusive but without significant success. The desire of the Johannesburg People's Pride for Pride events not to be a 'mirror' of the 'divided' nature of South African society has yet to be realized.

South Africa's significant socio-economic divisions have led to 'rival Prides' in Johannesburg and Cape Town that take place in the historically privileged [white] and historically disadvantaged [Black] areas. These separate Prides have different levels of resource, visibility and aims. In Johannesburg and Cape Town, conflicting accounts about Pride can often appear to be a war of words between activists, and between the different Pride events held across the city. However, these disagreements and criticisms are not merely interpersonal. They stem from contentious histories of protest that themselves draw from underlying social divides. Johannesburg Pride now takes place in Sandton City, a luxury shopping mall in Africa's wealthiest suburb, Cape Town Pride takes place in Greenpoint, a gentrified tourist hot spot next to De Waterkant, Cape Town's picturesque 'gay village'. In Cape Town, Khumbulani Pride takes place in the predominantly Black townships, distant from the gentrified Greenpoint and in areas with some of the highest rates of violence and social deprivation in South Africa. As will be discussed below, Soweto Pride began in 2004, but its politics became particularly significant following Black queer activist protests at Joburg Pride in 2012. Alongside protests about Pride's location, activists also protested Joburg Pride ignoring the issues of homophobic violence, particularly against Black lesbians, and socio-economic inequality for the Black majority.

LGBTQ+ activism in South Africa is deeply enmeshed with the country's history of racism and the Liberation Struggle against apartheid and reflects the country's activist history and its tense and ongoing racial, gendered and economic divisions (Conway, 2014; Gevisser and Cameron, 1994). Johannesburg Pride emerged out of the broader history of international LGBTQ+ activism and from the

Liberation Struggle against apartheid. The first Pride march in South Africa (and the African continent) was held in Johannesburg in 1990. The first Johannesburg Pride resembled many other apartheid-era protests, weaving through the streets of central Johannesburg and led by prominent liberation struggle figures including Simon Nkoli, Beverly Palesa Ditsie and Edwin Cameron (De Waal and Manion, 2006; Gevisser and Cameron, 1994). In the 1980s, within the African National Congress (ANC), Simon Nkoli and others had successfully campaigned for the liberation movement to commit to delivering LGBT rights in a future non-racial South Africa (Conway, 2014; Gevisser and Cameron, 1994). As a result, South Africa's transitional and final democratic constitution in 1996 was the first in the world to enshrine rights for sexual minorities. The Constitutional Court, with Edwin Cameron as one of its justices, became the venue for a succession of LGBTQ+ rights victories, including the right to same-sex marriage, surrogacy and adoption. However, these legal protections belie ongoing social, educational and employment-based discrimination and physical violence against LGBTQ+ people.

Despite South Africa's progressive legal framework for LGBTQ+ rights, the disparity between legal rights and everyday experience can be stark, particularly for Black South Africans (Judge, 2017; Scott, 2013). South African civil society and academia are well served by gender and LGBTQ+ rights organizations and specialists. The 2024 Government of National Unity, the prominent LGBTQ+ rights advocate and lesbian Mmapaseh 'Steve' Letsike was appointed as Deputy Minister for Women, Youth and Persons with Disabilities. Despite legal rights and high-level representation, violence against Black lesbians, from 'corrective rapes' to murder, has steadily increased from the 2000s onwards and has been accompanied by a general lack of official action or broader societal concern (Fletcher, 2016; Judge, 2017; Moreau, 2017). LGBTQ+ asylum seekers in South Africa are often subject to xenophobic prejudice and violence as well as a lack of sympathy or due process from immigration officials (Beetar, 2016; Camminga, 2019). Despite clear hate crimes laws, there is no clear statutory means of recording and monitoring these crimes and victims of hate crimes are not guaranteed a sympathetic reception at police stations and clinics. Constitutional rights have not been mirrored by social attitudes towards LGBTQ+ communities. Public opinion surveys reveal that only a slight majority of South Africans believe LGBTQ+ citizens should have equal rights and protections (Conway, 2014; Morris, 2017) and a majority of LGBTQ+ respondents fear discrimination based on their sexuality, with 44 per cent experiencing such discrimination (De Barros, 2016). During the Covid-19 lockdowns in 2019 and 2020, homophobic and gender-based violence in South Africa significantly increased (Coopoo, 2023; Harrisberg, 2021). Scott (2013) has argued that because of high levels of homophobic and gender-based violence, same-sex marriage rights in South Africa are a 'murderous inclusion' because they enable local and international groups to celebrate the country as a beacon of LGBTQ+ progress, when in reality LGBTQ+ lives are precarious and widespread prejudice remains. South Africa's high-levels of gender-based and homophobic violence, socio-economic inequality and prejudice, makes the issues and communities Pride highlights and includes, or obscures and marginalise, of particular political and social significance.

South African societal attitudes towards LGBTQ+ communities and rights were vividly illustrated when I exhibited a photography exhibition on Soweto and Ekurhuleni Prides at the Rand Club in 2023 in downtown Johannesburg. At a roundtable discussion to launch the exhibition with government, civil society, academia and the diplomatic community, one of the members of the audience remarked how there was a lack of societal awareness of the LGBTQ+ clauses in the constitution and why they were there. The following weekend there was an 'Open House' weekend across Johannesburg and hundreds of people came to see the historic Rand Club. Most were probably not expecting to see an exhibition on Pride and I was struck by the number of people who were indeed unaware that the country had LGBTQ+ rights in the constitution and were totally surprised that Pride took place in the region. The older white men who walked into the room looked at the photographs of Pride rather uncomfortably and quickly after took a close interest in the view out of the windows onto the taxi rank below, before leaving the room. The broader social context in which LGBTQ+ communities exist in South Africa was summed up by the response of a Black woman who walked round the exhibition. Chatting to me she remarked that the activists were 'brave' and she 'had no idea' there were Prides in Soweto and Ekurhuleni. After sharing with me that she was a corporate social responsibility consultant, I asked if she could help the organizers of Soweto and Ekurhuleni Pride connect with potential sponsors, she paused and replied, 'I'm all for people being themselves, but I wouldn't want my son or daughter to be gay' and there was no offer of help.

Pride and the queer politics of place and space

The spatial dynamics of apartheid and the continued racial and classed significance of urban space in South Africa mean that the location of Pride parades and afterparties is highly significant. The changing location of Pride in Johannesburg and Cape Town has been a continual source of tension. In Johannesburg, the years following the end of apartheid the Pride march moved from the centre of the city, which was perceived to have become too dangerous to hold a march in, to the formerly whites-only and affluent northern suburb of Rosebank. This provoked criticisms about the representativeness, accessibility and inclusivity of Pride. Mpumi Mathabela, an LGBTQ+ and gender rights activist, felt that the location of Pride in a middle-class suburb removed the political and visibility purposes of Pride: 'violence on our bodies happens in our backyards [in the townships], it doesn't happen in Rosebank … we didn't feel that Rosebank for us worked as a space'. Mathabela continued that following the change of location from the centre of the city,

> now there's a class issue because also now people from townships must get themselves to Rosebank, right. So, if you know how South Africa is designed, if you know the history, you know that Black communities were moved right away from the industrial area, which was Johannesburg, right, and placed over there on the [southern] end. So getting ourselves to this [northern] side of town is quite a mission on its own. So people start getting attacked on their way there, insults, hate crimes, verbal hate crime, some get beaten on their way back, because now it's late. So there was a lot of that. And we kept saying this is an issue.

Tensions became particularly acute when Pride organizers started to charge an entrance fee to the Pride enclosure at the park surrounding Zoo Lake following the parade in 2004 onwards. Many Black attendees sat outside the fence of the enclosure with picnics because they were prohibited from taking their pre-prepared food and drink into the enclosure and could not afford the entrance fee, while wealthier and mostly white attendees partied inside. Mpumi Mathabela recalled that the decision to start charging to enter the enclosure led to a 'peeling off layers of people. So we start excluding this group of people who cannot afford it. So black middle class can come in, but a certain class is left out.' Pride as a 'safe space' for LGBTQ+ communities was contradicted by the fact that transport to the parade across the city was itself dangerous and expensive, unless you already lived in the affluent northern suburbs.

Tensions over the spaces and places Pride in Johannesburg was held and the communities it included and excluded erupted in open protest in 2012, when members of the One in Nine campaign disrupted the parade route. Protesting about the location of Pride, its de-politicization, commercialization and its focus on partying, rather than serious social issues, such as gender-based violence, activists wore t-shirts with 'STOP the war on women's bodies', 'Dying for Justice' and 'No Cause for Celebration' and held a silent protest in front of the Pride parade route (Scott, 2017; Shelver, 2012). The protest was also about broadening Pride's conception of LGBTQ+ community in intersectional terms. Mpumi Mathabela was one of the protestors and explained:

> We felt that Joburg Pride was not really speaking to the issues of black lesbian women in the townships ... We had t-shirts with different identities of those they thought left out we had trans, we had lesbian, we had gay, we had feminist, we had sex worker, we had foreigner, because these are all our identities as queer people. We're not just queer. We're all of these other things.

When the Black women and gender non-binary protestors attempted to stage a 'die in' in front of the parade route, the then Pride organizer began shouting out of the window of her gold Mercedes. As Methabela recalled, the intention of the protest was to say:

> Can we acknowledge that people are dying before we do this extravagance ... and the security and everyone else decided 'mmm... nah. This is our Pride'. And you can see from the video [later posted on social media] 'This is my Pride!'. She [the Pride organizer] clearly said, 'this is my Pride!' and she said 'This is my route! Get off my route! This is my route. If they don't move run over them!' And they did exactly that. So one guy on a bike went over someone's foot. The other one head butted an unarmed woman standing there with a banner.

These shocking scenes were accompanied by racial abuse and violent threats from the mostly white Pride parade participants, who began to step over the bodies of the protestors lying on the road. Some of the protestors were assaulted, and a security guard set his dog loose to attack them. Jade Madingwane, now an organizer of Soweto Pride, recalled that 'I was one of the people that was hit by a white man at Pride, because we were just like, we were having a parade in an area where there are high walls. If you are having a parade in an area where no-one is going to see you, what is the point of even having that parade?'. Videos of the confrontation were posted on YouTube and circulated via social media, causing widespread furore in media, activist and academic communities in South Africa (Shelver, 2012). As Martin notes, the protest at Joburg Pride 'intensified conversations over the meaning of Pride: who could claim the space as their own; how queerness and transness intersects with race, gender and class; and exposed how power operates at this annual moment' (2017, 5). Following the protests, the organizing committee of Joburg Pride resigned, and a new committee was formed to hold a renamed Johannesburg Pride in 2013. Johannesburg Pride was moved further north to Melrose Arch, a luxury mall and hotel complex and then in 2021 to Sandton City. Here, a small parade route takes second place to a live music stage, outside bars, stalls and an evening party.

Following the protests in 2012, the Johannesburg People's Pride collective was formed, its manifesto accused Joburg Pride of taking place in 'spaces that re-enforce discrimination, violence and exclusion' and that the 'fun aspect' of Pride had been

> racialized and marked by class,... the relegation, then, of the majority of people into an outside area which they can afford to be in, which is inadequately resourced and literally turns them into the periphery of the 'centre', which remains predominantly white and wealthy,... how all of the above has led to many people either not attending the JHB Pride parade as an act of defiance, or feeling like second-class queers when they do – Pride organizers have failed to engage this constituency in any meaningful way.
>
> (Johannesburg People's Pride, 2013)

The collective organized a Johannesburg People's Pride parade that retraced the route of the original route of 1990 Johannesburg Pride through the streets of the city centre and stopped at various points to commemorate LGBTQ+ struggle heroes, including Simon Nkoli, who had died from AIDS in 1998. Johannesburg People's Pride was organized for three years before the activists organizing it moved onto concentrating on Soweto Pride, the Forum for the Empowerment of Women, One in Nine Campaign and other projects. As previously mentioned, the reformed Johannesburg Pride committee decided to hold Pride in Melrose Arch, which, as Mpumi Mathabela explained, 'is worse than Rosebank' because it is further north from the city centre and whereas at Rosebank, the parade had been along a public highway and in a park (albeit in an enclosure), Melrose Arch is a private shopping mall and hotel complex. Zandile Matsoeneng, who had been one of the protestors in 2012, explained that 'I wanted to experience the "white Pride", as we normally call it, or the "white Pride parade"' and while she conceded that at Melrose Arch 'it is a safe space', but that 'what you're wearing there also matters because now you're going to meet all the celebrities. They always go there because Melrose Arch is a top-notch place. So, it's about who and who can afford it, and what about the people that cannot afford it?'. Mpumi Mathabela acknowledged that the organizers of Johannesburg Pride 'they wanted a safe space, they were complaining about safety and the glitzy parts of Johannesburg are safe', but she wondered about the significance of holding Pride and a luxury shopping mall where

> No one cares. People go and they do their own shopping. They don't care if you're gay or flaunting around. They don't care, they're just there to do their shopping or eat in an expensive restaurant and then leave. Is it making any difference because maybe they are already converted?

Jade Madingwane concurred that the location of Melrose Arch is 'classist because if I'm not able to get to Johannesburg Pride, because I'm in Soweto, I have to take double transport to get to Melrose, and when I get there I have to spend an exorbitant amount of money for drinks, etc'. In 2016, Beverly Palesia Ditsie, one of the organizers of the first Pride in Johannesburg, told the media she no longer supported the event because it had become an elite celebration of 'whiteness and freedom while LGBTQ+ people living in townships continue to be persecuted' (Ndabeni, 2018). The changing location of Pride in Johannesburg is significant for the class, race and ideological impacts of Pride. Moving Pride further north in the city on the grounds of 'safety' reinforces the class and race-based safety concerns of white South Africans and overlooks the needs and lives of the Black majority.

It was perhaps unsurprising, given the continual criticism of Johannesburg Pride, that when I met with the organizer of Johannesburg Pride, Kaye Ally, she seemed defensive. In 2016, Ally had told the media that critics of Pride were 'mischief makers' and that 'there is a different kind of Pride associated with being in a world-class complex such as Melrose Arch … it lets Pride have the same quality as [those in] New York, San Francisco [and] London' (Van Niekerk, 2017). Ally continued:

> Having it in a mainstream environment such as Melrose Arch [makes] it convenient for everyone. Taxis are parked right outside the entrance. And the other community members can park in the basement parking and know their cars are still there when they get back.

In 2018, Ally repeated this justification of the choice of Melrose Arch, explaining to me that it was the 'perfect place' for Pride and that one of her 'proudest moments' was when a friend had mistaken photographs of Johannesburg Pride on social media for New York Pride. Ally explained that for Pride to be at a shopping mall meant:

> You just park your car in the basement, you came up the escalator, you checked out the Pride scene, there's an entire Pride village catered to you, you had a few drinks, you waited for your friends, you could go anywhere for a meal and you could come back at any time.

Ally is of Muslim Indian heritage and in 2016 had told the press that 'I love the narrative that goes out there that it's a white Pride board that doesn't cater for the non-white community. Because the last time I checked I was very much a person of colour.' Yet Ally's embrace and justification of Johannesburg Pride to be held in a shopping mall in the historically privileged area of the city reveal not only the deep ideological divide between the different Pride events and LGBTQ+ communities in the region, but also how capitalism can co-opt people of colour, human rights discourses and activist platforms, to maintain capitalism's racial and class hegemony. Jade Madingwane also identified the contestations over spaces and places in which Pride is held to be essentially about contrasting politics and ideologies:

> If you don't have a collective voice or people saying, 'Actually, let's have a Pride in Bree Street', the busiest street in Joburg CBD, 'let's have a Pride there, so that these people can see that we exist'. As much as it's dangerous there, if the Joburg Pride organizers do not have shared politics with other people around a collective voice on what Pride should look like, then I don't necessarily think there will be a Pride in the CBD.

In the 2018 Pride parade, some of the marchers openly critiqued the politics of Johannesburg Pride, one person carried a banner with the slogan 'There's no pride in marching where it's safe', another, dressed in a hat with a Melrose Arch security badge, wearing a tutu made of pink dollars and a sash proclaiming 'sell out', carried a sign with the caption 'Move the Porsche bitch, Pride is here!'. Wanting Pride to be held in an area that resembled the locations of mainstream Prides in New York, London and Sydney and to be convenient and 'safe' for middle-class attendees, inevitably excludes LGBTQ+ communities who cannot travel to, feel safe or welcome in such spaces.

While the organizers of Johannesburg Pride have dismissed criticisms about Pride's location, they have sought to expand the activities that take

Figure 7 'Move the Porsche Bitch, Pride is here!', Johannesburg Pride parade 2018.

place to address the charge that Johannesburg Pride does not address the social and political issues. In 2018, Johannesburg Pride organized an event titled 'Beyond the Closet: The Lifestyle Conference'. However, 'Beyond the Closet' and 'Lifestyle' were specifically chosen as names for the conference to emphasize the claim that LGBTQ+ visibility, equality and human rights had been achieved in South Africa. When I asked Kaye Ally if the conference would discuss human rights, she replied that it would not because 'that's why it's a lifestyle conference! It's no human rights no, no. It's a lifestyle conference because we've gone beyond the human rights now'. Ally continued:

> There are members of the LGBT community [in South Africa] who are quite comfortable, blacks, whites, Indian, coloured… expat. Quite regular. Comfortable. Normal! Professional. Two-income households, fancy houses, fancy holidays. Adopting children, getting married, going out to dinners. Very, very normal lifestyles! So… there's no one catering for that. When we looked at the Lifestyle Conference, we did that with the express purpose of saying, where are the gaps?

This explanation of why the Lifestyle Conference was necessary indicates Johannesburg Pride is premised on a very particular understanding and representation of LGBTQ+ lifestyles. A representation that is at odds with the reality of the majority of LGBTQ+ experiences in contemporary South Africa. Having positioned the conference as 'beyond human rights', Ally explained that the purpose was to share information: 'people don't know what is the requirement for a civil union. People don't know how taxing it is for an adoption process, or if you want your own child via a surrogacy, how expensive is it.' The rights to surrogacy and protection for LGBTQ+ workers draw from human rights enshrined in the constitution. Yet the advice offered at the conference raised troubling questions about what constitutes rights and what constitutes privileges, or indeed whether these were only rights for the privileged, considerably out of the reach of most South Africans.

Held in a corporate event space close to Melrose Arch, the room was adorned with crystal chandeliers and prominently displayed LGBTQ+-focused advertising from the conference's corporate sponsors, including EY's rainbow Pride banners and Accenture's 'Diversity Makes Us Stronger' slogan. The session on workplace harassment and discrimination law gave examples of best practice and how the law can protect LGBTQ+ employees, but was aimed at and most useful for those in professional jobs, or in organizations with clear policies and HR procedures. Such advice would be of little use to the 30 per cent of South Africans who work in the informal sector, the over one million domestic workers, or the 32 per cent of South Africans who are unemployed (Yu and Nackerdien, 2019). Similarly, the lawyer who specialized in surrogacy explained at the conference that the average cost of this process was ZAR300,000. This is out of reach of most South Africans, because the average salary is ZAR254,000 (BusinessTech, 2019). This information was useful for those who had income high enough to afford the 'right' of surrogacy in South Africa. This evidenced Ally's intention to provide information for those with privileged 'lifestyles'. Broader issues such as violence, negotiating encounters with the police and health services as an LGBTQ+ person, applying for asylum as an LGBTQ+ migrant, trans rights, or everyday discrimination and prejudice were not mentioned at the conference. Ally's claim that 'we've gone beyond the human rights' rests on the limited understanding that where formal legal rights have been achieved there is no need for social justice activism but in South Africa access to these rights is highly limited by class and race. However, as the earlier quote from Ally makes clear, the lifestyles in mind were 'normal', 'professional people', with 'fancy' lifestyles.

Pride and the politics of race in Cape Town

In 2016, Cape Town Pride's slogan 'Gay, Proud, Colour Blind' angered activists who thought the claim that Cape Town Pride was 'Colour Blind' was an effort to obscure and 'whitewash' the ongoing salience of race and racial inequalities at Pride, in the city and in wider South Africa (Igual, 2015). Although race, class and place are also at the heart of queer criticisms about Cape Town Pride, there are significant demographic, spatial and political differences, which are mirrored in tensions surrounding Pride in the city. Until recently, the so-called Coloured community comprised the majority of the Western Cape's population and in Cape Town, the white and Coloured community outnumber Black South Africans (City of Cape Town, 2023). Largely because of this, the white-led opposition party, the Democratic Alliance (DA) (which from 2024 became part of the Federal Government of National Unity), governs the city and province. Unlike Johannesburg, the CBD of Cape Town has not seen dramatic change following apartheid and has experienced significant gentrification, with loft apartments, boutiques and luxury hotels lining the city's streets. Cape Town is a major international tourist, and in particular is marketed as an LGBTQ+ destination (Williams, 2008). Reinforcing this LGBTQ+-friendly image, the city hosted the 2024 ILGA World Conference and will host World Pride in 2028. At the foot of Table Mountain and close to the seafront, the De Waterkant and Greenpoint districts are widely known as Cape Town's 'gay village' with LGBTQ+ clubs, bars, guest houses and shops. Like other LGBTQ+-friendly districts in the Global North, there is now a rainbow-painted pedestrian crossing connecting De Waterkant and Greenpoint and an 'inclusive love' mural depicting a same-sex couple kissing on a wall nearby.

Despite the ostentatious display of LGBTQ+ friendliness in the city centre and waterfront, Cape Town and the surrounds continue to have the highest levels of violence in South Africa, with poverty and crime endemic in the outlying townships and squatter camps on the outskirts of the city (Turok, Scheba and Visagie, 2020). The picturesque streets and gentrified glamour of De Waterkant and Greenpoint belie anecdotal accounts of Black and Coloured LGBTQ+ people feeling either uncomfortable, or excluded, from these predominantly white spaces, even if they can afford to travel and spend money in the bars and clubs of the gay village. As will be discussed below, the close connection between Cape Town Pride and the governing Democratic Alliance creates further tensions. Cape Town Pride begins in front of the De Waterkant gay village and has a small parade before ending at a paid for entry afterparty in Greenpoint stadium and as with Johannesburg Pride, the space and place it exists in, the people included and excluded and the issues it chooses to highlight, or ignore, have become major points of tension and contestation.

'People travel for hours and hours and hours to come to Cape Town Pride', said Matthew Clayton, then a manager at the LGBTQ+ NGO, the Triangle Project, 'especially people from the small towns, because this is the only place where they can actually be openly gay in public. And it's very important for them.' The Triangle Project is a grassroots LGBTQ+ organizing providing a range of support services, advocacy and also organizes Khumbulani Pride. Over the last few years, however, the Triangle Project has boycotted Cape Town Pride. Thozama Njobe, also with the Triangle Project, told the media in 2022:

> Cape Town Pride is white, it's male, and it caters for the economic elite. It caters for no one else. And if it did, it wouldn't be organized the way it is. It wouldn't be an event of feather boas and floats …

What does that mean for black trans people who are in the township, who don't have access to affirming healthcare?

(Guerandi, 2022)

Sindiswe Thafini, who organized Khumbulani Pride, told me, 'We really didn't want division between us and Cape Town Pride, but there is division and the division has the race card in it'. Sindiswe continued:

> It's good to have Pride, but with the scourges of rape and murder happening in South Africa, especially in the Western Cape, what is Pride doing? Is there a platform to talk about this issue with the broader society? And Pride marching in town, the same street every time, what does it really mean for us poor people back in our communities and facing discrimination and homophobia every day of our lives in our homes and in the streets, and in our workplaces?

Khumbulani is Xhosa for 'to remember' and the Triangle Project had chosen the name Khumbulani Pride to remember victims of homophobic and gender-based violence. Khumbulani Pride was held in different communities across Cape Town, often where there had been recent homophobic attacks, but as Sindiswe Thafemi explained, unlike Cape Town Pride, Khumbulani Pride had struggled to obtain government or commercial funding because, she believed, of its 'Blackness' and because it was held in places in the city which were considered dangerous and where white people avoided going.

For some, holding separate Pride events in different places for different communities was a pragmatic, possibly inevitable and workable solution in divided societies. Matthew Clayton, however, argued that the holding of different Pride events for different communities in the city was unfortunate because 'explicitly and implicitly, Cape Town Pride has got this idea that it doesn't need to be political because now there's Khumbulani Pride. It's almost as if this has been outsourced. It's almost like that is their outreach activity'. In 2018, when I spoke to the then organizer of Cape Town Pride, Matthew van As, he claimed to have helped establish a Pride event in the townships and was a 'mentor' to the organizers. Both Mathew Clayton and Sindiswe Thafeni disputed this, saying Van As was not involved in Khumbulani Pride and had actually tried to set up a rival to Khumbulani Pride in the townships. 'He's a mentor to no one,' commented Sindiswe Thafeni and had tried to 'pit Blacks against Blacks', which she felt was an apartheid-era strategy, 'which was perhaps the worst thing of all!'. The tensions between Cape

Town Pride and grassroots LGBTQ+ communities and other Pride events are the same as the racial, class and spatial tensions, and although, unlike in Johannesburg, they had not spilled into open protest, there were bitter interpersonal and ideological differences between LGBTQ+ activists and different Pride events.

Pride and party politics

In 2018, I attended a Democratic Alliance (DA) LGBTQ+ event held in Cape Town's council assembly chamber. The DA has consistently been present at Pride events across South Africa wearing rainbow-branded party t-shirts and waving flags and the party has a number of high-profile LGBTQ+ MPs, councillors and now national Cabinet ministers. I had struggled to get a response from the then organizer of Cape Town Pride, Matthew van As, and while I had spoken to David Lee, a Taiwanese member of the organizing committee living in Cape Town, I wanted to speak with Van As, given the multiple accusations of racism and exclusion that I had heard. I correctly predicted that Van As would be at the DA event, given the strong connections between the DA and the organizing committee of Cape Town Pride. Like David Lee, Matthew van As told me that the organizers of Cape Town Pride are volunteers and that anyone was welcome to join the committee and contribute to the organization of Pride. Van As pointed to the expense of organizing Pride and that the existing committee were often the only people willing to do the work. Dion George, a gay DA MP (and now a Cabinet minister in the government of national unity), and Roberto Miguel Quintas, a gay member of Cape Town's municipal council executive, spoke and answered questions at the event. During the meeting, members of the audience pointed to the fact that despite South Africa's clear protections against hate crime, statistics on homophobic hate crime were, at that time, not collected by the South African Police Services or Home Affairs, something the provincial and city authorities could do little about. From the floor, a speaker started to criticize Cape Town Pride saying:

> What are we celebrating? Lesbians and gays in South Africa are bullied all the time! Why are we doing it! The tickets are too expensive 50 Rand – not everyone can afford it. Why is it in Green Point? Why can't it be in Khayelitsha [a black majority township and squatter camp with high levels of violence]? Pride should not just be at Green Point!

Mathew van As responded from the floor that 'people can get in for free. People say the same thing every year, but they are apathetic and don't volunteer. Greenpoint is in Cape Town and is part of the city.' Roberto Miguel Quintas added that free buses were being provided for people to attend Pride from outlying areas. As discussed above, Cape Town Pride has continued to be criticized following 2018 and in 2023, Matthew van As and a number of other members of the organizing committee stood down and Wentzel Ryan, a member of the Coloured community, took over as main organizer.

In the days leading up to the 2024 Pride parade, the often tense racial and class politics of the city became visible, municipal authorities cleared a squatter camp that was located close to the Pride route in Greenpoint, a fire had started and burned most of the tents and possessions of the squatters (Thebus, 2024). The DA was one of the largest contingencies at the Pride parade, wearing blue t-shirts with the party's logo adapted to include a rainbow. The Pride march began and walked past the DA's 2024 provincial election 'battle bus' with a large picture of DA Provincial premier, Alan Winde on the side. As the march reached the rainbow pedestrian crossing in Greenpoint, the DA contingency carrying a large banner 'Standing together for LGBTQIA rights in Africa' on it, paused and press photographers gathered. Dion George MP started pointing at the rainbow crossing in front of him and repeatedly shouted, 'The DA did this for you! The DA did this for you! The DA did this for the LGBT community in Cape Town!'. While Cape Town Pride receives financial support from the city of Cape Town, which is led by the DA and therefore it is unsurprising that the DA would be present, I was struck how close the visible association between the party and the Pride parade and how this frames the nature of the event. 'It was like a DA rally,' remarked a friend of mine who had also attended Cape Town Pride. The DA and ANC had arrived early at Soweto Pride when I attended in 2018, but the organizers of the Pride march had asked them not to march wearing any party-political t-shirts or banners during the parade. Cape Town's local politics relate to broader sociopolitical tensions about race, and the DA branding of Cape Town Pride is one very visible aspect of the controversies surrounding the event.

I had heard from contacts that the new Coloured organizers of Cape Town Pride had made efforts to reach out to a broad range of local communities and had tried to expand the activities in the lead up to the parade. In the week leading up to the parade several events were arranged, including drinks and drag parties and attended by mostly white men, but also smaller 'book talks' held in Zer021, an LGBTQ+ nightclub in District 6, known for being more welcoming for Black and Coloured

Figure 8 Dion George MP, Roberto Quintas, Cape Town Executive Member, and the Democratic Alliance at Greenpoint Rainbow Crossing, Cape Town Pride 2024.

communities. Here, issues focusing on race, religion and homophobia in family backgrounds and communities were openly discussed. There was a community Pride discussion event in the Cape Flats, a predominantly working-class Coloured area with high crime rates. However, the main Pride event remained in Greenpoint, with a comparatively expensive ticketed afterparty in Greenpoint stadium. At the stadium, there was a VIP bar at which invited guests had free drinks. In the stadium itself, there was a stage, but no speeches were given. On the pitch, in between drinks tents and food stalls, there were representatives from LGBTQ+ civil society and services, such as the Ivan Toms STI clinic and the Western Cape's newly established Hate Crime reporting centres. South African companies also had stalls attempting to attract qualified graduates to apply for jobs. 'Didn't you find it boring?,' a Coloured man asked me a few days later as he cut my hair, 'there was nothing really to do at that stadium and I didn't think it had anything to do with Pride', he said. 'Those Pride organizers don't know what they are doing,' he continued and said that for him, as an older Coloured gay man, he felt 'judged, very excluded and isolated' by the younger and predominantly white gay scene in Cape Town. Pride had done nothing to address that, he said. Cape Town Pride has sought to engage with a broader community and wider set of issues, but its location in Greenpoint, close association with the DA, ticketed and expensive afterparty and focus on listless drinking, rather than considering what the region's diverse population might want or need, meant it remains an exclusive space.

'HomoHindunationalism' at Mumbai Pride

Like South Africa, India has internationally high levels of socio-economic inequality (Chancel et al., 2021: 19–20). The Humsafar Trust, an organization that provides LGBTQ+ health services and advocacy for LGBTQ+ rights, organizes Mumbai Pride, the largest Pride event in India. The leadership of the Humsafar Trust has been criticized by queer activists for being upper-caste, predominantly cis-gendered male and for openly supporting the ruling Hindu-Nationalist BJP Party and the right-wing populist Prime Minister Narendra Modi. The founder and chair of the Humsafar Trust, Ashok Row Kavi, has been described as a 'homoHindunationalist' who is 'openly casteist' and Islamophobic (Upadhyay, 2020: 427). Before the parade, I spoke with Ankit Bhuptani, a member of the Humsafar Trust, who was tasked with organizing Mumbai Pride. Bhuptani complained about the 'politicization' of Pride by queer activists and blamed

> Lesbian groups making slogans against the ruling party [the BJP], that is something we don't appreciate in Mumbai Pride! ... Don't mix everything at once! Queer people, especially on the left, are so keen to talk about these issues ... They're using Pride as a vehicle.

The Pride parade began and ended at a stage set up in August Kranti Maidan, a market place next to a large park. The stage and marketplace were surrounded by the orange and blue banners of the ruling BJP party adorned with face of Prime Minister Modi. While this scene was related to the upcoming regional elections, but as at Cape Town Pride, it was symbolic of close association between the Pride organizers and the political party in power. The march was attended by thousands of people and weaved through the streets of Mumbai. The theme of Mumbai Pride was 'Pride for all!' and many attendees were celebrating the repeal of Section 377, the colonial-era law that banned homosexuality, by the Supreme Court months earlier. Towards the end of the Pride march was a group of students who carried banners protesting for Trans rights in India [and against a proposed and restrictive Transgender Bill in the Indian parliament], for Dalit [lower caste] and Hijra [trans, intersex or eunuch] communities, against the BJP party government, against the privatization of public services and against gender-based violence. The group carried protest signs with 'Smash Brahminical Patriarchy', 'fuck Rainbow-washing', 'Azaadi [liberation] from private schools and hospitals', 'Queer Undocumented and Unafraid. We Exist!', 'Police Violence in a Queer Issue', and with clear references to Indian politics 'Stop the Trans Bill', 'down with Islamophobia', 'Queer Dalit, Queer Muslim', and 'Vote 2019!'. As we arrived back at the August Kranti Maidan, I saw Ankit Bhuptani who said, 'Did you see them! Did you see those protestors! They were trying to disrupt the Pride parade! Those are the ones I told you about!'. The protestors were students from the Tata Institute of Social Sciences (TISS) who had formed a Queer Collective. While speaking to them after the march they told me that they had had a conflictual and tense relationship with the organizers of Mumbai Pride and were there to introduce a queer politics and protest to the Pride march, which, they felt, would be apolitical and conformist otherwise.

Figure 9 TISS Queer Collective at Mumbai Pride 2019.

Following the parade, I met with members of the Queer Collective on the campus of the TISS and we talked about their experiences with and attitudes towards Mumbai Pride. As the quote at the beginning of this chapter makes clear, the members of the TISS Queer Collective had debated the theme 'Pride for all' with the Humsafar Trust and had argued that the Humsafar Trust was not an inclusive space for all of India's LGBTQ+ communities, not least because Mumbai Pride meetings were conducted only in English. One of the collective told me that 'there are very few Hijra who are involved in the decision making process, last year I said during one of the Humsafar meetings, "look around you at the meeting! There are only cis-gendered men involved." So where is the community at Pride?' The Queer Collective believed Ankit's Bhuptani's criticism of the politicization of Pride was borne out of the upper-class/upper-caste privilege of Mumbai Pride's organizers: 'The moment you say apolitical, that is your privilege that is talking … I do not have this privilege of being apolitical. It is a political statement to say "I am apolitical"', said a member of the collective. Another member of the collective continued that 'the whole Pride narrative in India only focuses on the upper caste narrative, the cis-gendered, middle-class narrative of coming out, accepting yourself and there's no diversity in how queerness is experienced'. For the members of the Queer Collective, the marginalization and erasure of Dalit (lower caste) people and their struggles from Mumbai Pride was the result of the (a)political aims of the Pride organizers. The following year, fifty queer activists were arrested, and it was rumoured that the detainees' details had been given to the police by the organizers of Mumbai Pride (The Wire, 2020). In 2022, open divisions between queer activists and the organizers of Mumbai Pride contributed to Mumbai Pride being cancelled that year.

The TISS Queer Collective had begun as a reading group at TISS and had read and debated, among others, Judith Butler's writings. This had informed TISS's queer perspectives and arguments about Mumbai Pride. As one of the collective explained, 'Butler argues that the queer movement needs to be democratized and that's what definitely needs to happen in India.' As in South Africa, the predominant focus on the achievement and celebration of LGBTQ+ legal rights overlooked the reality for LGBTQ+ communities on the ground in India. In 2019, TISS were critical of Mumbai Pride's celebration of the repeal of Section 377:

> The entire focus [of Pride] is on 377 and there are multiple other issues. I've heard some people say now we are done with 377, there's no need for Pride, let's just celebrate the 377 judgement. But what are

you talking about! Just look at the kind of laws that are being passed by the BJP. There are multiple other issues. This is just a baby step the Supreme Court has taken and they should have done it years ago!

The Collective were very aware of Ankit Bhuptani's criticism that the Queer Collective wanted to make Pride inappropriately political. Bhuptani had told them in a planning meeting: 'This is a queer Pride we should stick to queer issues we should not talk about other issues, you wouldn't carry a Pride flag in a Dalit march!' The collective member's response was:

> There are Dalit students who have supported queer issues, there are Dalit queer people and how can we bracket these issues. I am a Dalit queer person. How can I go to Pride just as a queer person? They're argument is completely flawed. It is coming from a very upper caste space.

During the planning meetings the Collective had said they wanted to display protest banners and had been asked by the organizers what kind of banners and that political protest banners 'should have a disclaimer message that it was not part of Mumbai Pride. I was genuinely shocked. It signified so much!.' In the weeks following Mumbai Pride, the Modi government launched cross-border air force bombing raids on neighbouring Pakistan and I observed Bhuptani and other members of Mumbai's LGBTQ+ upper echelons celebrating India's air strikes on social media. As in Johannesburg and Cape Town, Mumbai Pride's organizers have a narrow conception of politics and one that excludes intersectional, queer and social justice frames. Yet as in those other contexts, in Mumbai the narrow and conservative politics of Pride is openly contested and protested by queer activists.

As discussed in previous chapters, the class privilege of Pride organizers relates to a broader critique of LGBTQ+ advocacy, the 'NGO-ization' (Choudry and Kapoor, 2012) of LGBT activism and the privileges it can bestow on a global elite of LGBT advocates, or 'career queers' (Rodriguez, 2022: 83). The evolution of Pride organizing and LGBTQ+ advocacy as a profitable and high-profile career option (for some) has, in the view of many queer activists, led to the marginalization of radical politics and the mainstreaming of 'homonormative' complicity, much in the same terms as discussed above. 'It's quite scary these people are making careers out of queer identity. They work in NGOs ... they hold power,' said a member of the

TISS Queer Collective. One of the Collective recalled an encounter with a well-known gay business executive at Mumbai Pride: 'he stopped me and said "Can you say something to me for my podcast?" I said "No!" He said "Can't you just say, "It get's better!" It's only three words". I said "No!". It is everything they are about. Just this positive message that appeals to the Global North'. The Collective believed that the 'simplistic' and 'positive' framing of Mumbai Pride around celebration of the recent decriminalization of homosexuality in India, rather than protest about social and political issues was why the organizers of Mumbai Pride had been successful in gaining diplomatic and corporate funding and broader international recognition and why queer activists were unfunded and marginalized.

Conclusion

The Johannesburg People's Pride manifesto called for a Pride that was a utopic microcosm, not a mirror of socio-economic and political divisions. As this chapter has argued, Pride in South Africa and India continues to hold a mirror to broader divisions and tensions in local society. The controversies and contestation of Johannesburg and Cape Town Pride are one of a number discursive struggles that reveal the 'hidden transcripts' (Conway, 2016; Statman and Ansell, 2000) of racial tension and South Africa's unresolved nation-building project. In Cape Town, Sindiswe Thafuni remarked sadly that 'racism in this country is still so strong and it's embedded in every department of life'. For Mpumi Mathebela, the fraught politics of Johannesburg Pride reveals how racial tension is woven into the fabric of South Africa's history 'a history we have never really paid attention to … all we did was sweep the dust under the carpet there and played nice (laughs), but when you do that the dust kind of sort of comes out once in awhile. And I think it's reflective of our country'. I interviewed Mpumi using my iPhone, which was resting on the desk between us, and she continued:

> It's so exhausting! I think it's a clear reflection of who we are in South Africa as a country right now, and all of the issues I think we have sort of bottled but haven't really dealt with. So if I am fighting with them and we are fighting over why is your phone sitting on my desk, and that boils, that grows, and then I remember you stole my land, and then you remember I did something, and then it becomes a thing, right, and it becomes a white versus a black thing, and poof!

The iPhone is just a catalyst into a bigger problem. And so I think that whole, that incident [the protest at Joburg Pride in 2012] was about space. So 'you're occupying my route, it's my route, it's my space, it's mine, it's my thing', it's not our thing, it's my thing.

Mpumi's allusion to racial and settler privilege, land rights, ownership and privilege also underpins the political, social and economic significance of the places and spaces Pride is held, the communities it considers, includes and celebrates and the communities and causes it ignores and excludes. As the next chapter will argue, this politics is inherently entwined with capitalism. Pride's relationship and co-option with commercial institutions and capitalist values are at the heart of queer contestations of Pride.

Chapter 4

CORPORATE PRIDE, COMMERCIALIZATION AND THE GLOBAL PRIDE CIRCUIT

And we started seeing all the commercialization. I mean, the space had been commercialized right. So, you started by seeing a banner from PowerPlay saying 'Joburg Gay Pride brought to you by PowerPlay' and you go hmmm, oh wait, there's a problem here!

– Mpumi Mathabela, queer activist at the One in Nine Campaign, Johannesburg (interview with the author, 2018)

They look in the mirror and think it's a window, believing that corporate support for and inflation of their story is in fact a neutral and accurate picture of the world.

– Sarah Schulman (2012b: 28)

In 2023, the organizers of Soweto Pride and Ekurhuleni Pride in South Africa participated in London Pride. Standing on the stage in Trafalgar Square, they told the thousands watching, 'We see the rainbows on London's streets, and we feel welcome!.' The activists from Soweto and Ekurhuleni told me that they had been thrilled by rainbow branding in shop windows, the 'Pride Month' adverts in Underground stations and the rainbow flags flying in the sky along Regent Street, a contrast to the rainbow free streets and shops of Johannesburg. As I discussed in Chapter 3, Pride in South Africa has a complex relationship with privilege. The protests at Joburg Pride in 2012 were in part against Pride's commercialization and Johannesburg Pride's location in a luxury shopping mall remains a key point of tension. Funding and logistical support remain perennial problems for the organizers of Soweto Pride and Ekurhuleni Pride, and as the committee of Soweto Pride explained, despite their critique of capitalism and the exacting racial and gendered logics it perpetuates in South Africa, they are willing to consider corporate funding 'if their intentions are right'. The criticisms of Pride's commercialization and the 'Pink' or 'Rainbow-washing' by companies during 'Pride Month' have become commonplace. So too have the dilemmas of how to navigate the challenging funding, political and legal environments for many LGBTQ+ activists. Many LGBTQ+ activists and organizers in the Global South have either no recourse, or cannot rely, on state support for their work. Considering how to respond to the opportunities, pressures and threats of the commercialization of Pride and more broadly, LGBTQ+ politics and identities, are at the heart of some of the most critical questions for LGBTQ+, feminist and more broadly, social justice activism.

World Pride in 2019 took place on the fiftieth anniversary of the Stonewall Riots and encapsulated many of the dynamics and debates about the commercialization of Pride. Manhattan's buildings were ablaze with rainbows and department stores had designed Pride fashion ranges with accompanying video footage of individuals described as LGBT activists talking about their lives and activism. T-Mobile, a major sponsor of World Pride, had t-shirts, merchandize and huge banner advertising on Times Square with 'Mobilize for Equality' alongside the T-Mobile logo. As explained in the introduction, the first event I attended at World Pride was a ticketed Pride Luminaries Brunch, held at a rooftop bar in downtown Manhattan. At the entrance there was a notice informing attendees that by entering they agreed for photographs and videos of themselves to be used for marketing purposes by New York Pride and their sponsors. A Pride volunteer wearing a T-Mobile 'Mobilize for Equality' t-shirt was distributing free Pride 'goodie bags' with rainbow, corporate sponsor-branded merchandize, but only if you agreed to post a selfie picture with a rainbow clad, T-Mobile 'Love Your True Self' frame and rainbow sunglasses on attendees social media account. I thought that posting such a thing on my social media account would leave my friends and followers puzzled, as well as contradict my discomfort with rainbow corporate branding, but this was my first event at World Pride and I was determined to get the 'goodie bag'. I realized I could post the picture 'privately' on Facebook and that this would look as if I had publicly posted the advert to the bag distributor. I was duly given the Pride bag. Other sponsors were present with branded rainbow freebies, including British Airways and American Airlines, the tourist board of New Orleans and free drinks were provided by Barefoot Wines and Skky Vodka, whose staff wore 'Proudly American' t-shirts.

The Pride 'Luminaries' were handed awards and tried to make speeches above the din of the increasingly inebriated guests. Beverly Tillery, then the head of the New York City Anti-Violence project, became emotional as she spoke about the murders of trans prisoners in New York over the past few months. 'Please listen', she said to the guests at the brunch, who were mostly distracted at the bar chatting, 'I would say to all of you while you're having your drinks and celebrating today to think about what you can do more. You have privilege, you have money, you can use your voice to shine a light on those dark spots where we don't want to look'. As I listened, I thought about the irony that Tillery was frustratedly addressing an issue to an indifferent audience about violence against trans people of colour, almost the same experience and exactly the same issue that Sylvia Rivera had raised at New York Pride in 1973. I spoke with Beverley Tillery afterwards and said how sorry I was that most people were not listening to her. She replied that she was not surprised and that the organizers of New York Pride were not much better, because they had initially been unwilling to highlight the issue of violence against trans prisoners in New York state, and they had only eventually agreed to 'issue just 3 tweets' about violence against trans prisoners.

'Oh, that makes me sick', said Sister Hucklefaery Ken, a queer activist involved in planning the Reclaim Pride March, when I told them about the Pride Luminaries Brunch and T-Mobiles 'Mobilize for Equality' slogan, 'what really strikes me as hollow about that is they're not supporting activists. They're not supporting activist groups. They're turning it into a branding.' As well as the alternative Reclaim Pride March, the annual Drag March and Dyke March in New York also expressly rejected the commercialization of New York and World Pride. An organizer of the Dyke March told me: 'I come from Russia, where my big issue was at the time Citibank wasn't allowing homosexual couples or homosexual people to have bank accounts and here they were in New York with their big Pride float.' On the evening of the fiftieth anniversary of the Stonewall Riots, the Drag March arrived in front of the Stonewall Inn and met with the 'official' World Pride stage also outside the Stonewall Inn. The World Pride official, speaking from the stage objected to singing and chanting by the participants of the Drag March, accusing them of 'not listening' or 'showing respect' to her. Many of the Drag Marchers shouted back that she was not listening or respecting them and it was they who were honouring the true legacy of Pride. The next day an organizer of the march told me it summed up the contrasting worlds and beliefs the Drag Marchers and the organizers of World Pride occupied. These starkly contrasting visions and enactments of Pride, with their opposing capitalist and anti-capitalist politics, summed up the divisions and debates about the purposes and politics of Pride.

The rainbow branding of transnational and many national corporations in the Global North for Pride Month, rather like Christmas advertising over in December or sales marketing in January, has become commonplace. Yet the backlash, or pushback, against LGBTQ+ rights across the world has tested corporate willingness to be visibly associated with LGBTQ+ causes and communities. For example, and as discussed in the introduction, major retailers in the United States and the United Kingdom have either dropped or scaled back Pride branded merchandize and events following homophobic and transphobic online and physical threats. This has led some LGBTQ+ activists and academics to debate if the critique of corporate involvement in Pride needs to be revisited. Some have wondered if we will miss rainbow branding if it is gone, and whether visible corporate support for Pride, and by association LGBTQ+ communities and rights, is important now that these rights are now being questioned and rolled back, even in Europe and North America. These are important questions to ask, but as I will argue in this chapter, corporate 'support' for Pride and LGBTQ+ communities and rights has always been contingent and inconsistent across time and place.

The lineage and development of corporate social responsibility policies and EDI policies, which LGBTQ+ staff groups, involvement in Pride and rainbow branding is part of, emerged from US corporate efforts to neutralize and sidestep activist challenges to exploitative and unjust business operations in apartheid-era South Africa. The contemporary discourses of 'diversity politics' (Ahmed, 2012) and 'homocapitalism' (Rao, 2015, 2020) are an extension of the displacement of social justice activism with a neoliberal 'regime of truth' (Foucault, 2001) that presents social problems as either solved or effectively managed and on a positive direction in the hands of corporate actors. This chapter argues that the involvement of business in Pride, with the heavy emphasis on consumer advertising, participating of corporate employees and the attendant positive emotional tenor of such involvement, inevitable privileges certain kinds of LGBTQ+ communities, messages and causes over others. For example, commercial institutions are unlikely to consider questions of poverty, disability or precarity in their advertising at Pride and should their employees engage in political protest while at Pride, they will probably be in breach of contract. The commercialization of Pride and the involvement of corporations as sponsors, advertisers and attendees at Pride have profound implications for the understanding of LGBTQ+ identities, activism and the extent and need for political, legal and social change.

The chapter will also reflect on my, possibly naïve, attempts to be a 'critical friend' to LGBTQ+ advocacy groups and the mixed record of success in these efforts to make access to these events more equitable and socially just. In reflecting on these efforts, the chapter develops Rodriguez's (2022) decolonial critique of 'career queers': LGBTQ+ advocates working at state and international agencies, NGOs and advocacy groups, mostly from and in the Global North, but focused on the Global South. As Pride events have increased in number and scale and as institutions from multinational corporates to diplomatic agencies have become increasingly involved in Pride, considerable status and power have been afforded to a small group of Pride organizers and LGBTQ+ advocates. 'Career queers' are a development emerging out of the institutionalization of 'diversity politics'. Diversity politics reframes LGBTQ+, and other forms of, activism as a professional career in the service of the institution, rather than a basis for struggle and protest for broader socio-political change. This chapter will explore the dynamics and politics of this process and pose the question of whether 'career queers' help connect, or displace local grassroots activists and issues, defining what issues, discourses and communities are made visible and invisible. The chapter explores examples from Johannesburg, Mumbai, Shanghai and Hong Kong, where corporate actors create worldviews and constructions of progress and LGBTQ+ identities that obscure the lived realities of LGBTQ+ lives in those contexts and reinforce global hierarchies of privilege.

The emergence and dynamics of corporate Pride

The involvement of business in Pride follows significant social, legal and political change towards tolerance and legal rights for LGBTQ+ communities in many parts of the world, but also key shifts in neoliberal capitalism in relation to diverse communities. Hooper (2001), writing about *The Economist* magazine's construction of Anglo-American corporate visions of the world, documents how business advertising in the late-1980s and 1990s changed from being dominated by images of white male captains of industry to include South and East Asians and women as corporate executives. This was due to the rise of the 'Asian Tiger' economies and also the advance of employment law identifying women and people of colour for special protection. This led to a new emphasis on the importance of diversity and inclusion employment policies and a belief that the embrace of diversity was a positive good for business in terms of attracting and retaining talented employees and accessing new markets.

The involvement of Western business as advocates for LGBTQ+ communities and models of LGBTQ+ inclusion follows the business community's adoption of elements of the feminist movement's demands for women's equality in the workplace, and to a lesser extent the anti-racist movement's demands for equality. However, the inclusion of a more diverse racial group and women as model employees and markets in the 1980s and 1990s was not combined with claims by corporations to be activists on their behalf, or to be at the vanguard of efforts of positive societal and legal change for these communities. Contemporary business celebration of LGBTQ+ communities and employees is very invested in such claims to advocacy and activist change. Corporate D&I executives, Todd Hewlett and Sylvia Ann Sears (2024), write,

> with governments and international blocs in retreat, where can LGBTQ+ employees turn to for support? The not-so-obvious answer is global companies. Looking back on what has driven dramatic gains in the life prospects of LGBTQ+ people over the last twenty years, legislative action and culture shifts have been important, but at centre stage have been multinational companies.

As discussed in Chapter 2, this homocapitalist (Rao, 2015, 2020, 2024) argument rests on a confidence that businesses, as institutions, are effective agents of social, political and legal change; that LGBTQ+ individuals can be liberated by being 'out' in their workplaces and that personal productivity and career success will be maximized by being able to express their 'authentic' selves, or as corporate D&I/EDI advocates frequently argue, to 'bring their whole (or true) selves to work'. Furthermore, LGBTQ+ individuals can exercise their newfound freedom as consumers in a marketplace of unlimited choices, where products and experiences are increasingly tailored for them. This not only privileges certain kinds of LGBTQ+ subjects over others, namely privileged LGBTQ+ people with the education and income to enjoy freedom in these terms, but it presents homophobia as 'merely cultural' with business 'outside' the problem of homophobia (Rao, 2020). The presentation of business as activists for LGBTQ+ liberation has profound implications for understandings of how socio-political and legal change happens and what freedom means. It also enables the seamless commercialization of Pride and the belief that this is logical and desirable.

The divisions created by and contestation of the commercialization of Pride have become commonplace across the Global North, yet each year new Prides emerge across the Global South and East. This raises the question of whether the same tensions and debates are experienced in these socio-political and legal spaces, or whether activists and organizers consider the corporate involvement in Pride as being not only a pragmatic compromise, but even an important strategy in enabling visibility for LGBTQ+ communities in politically and socially hostile spaces. Rao (2024: 81) writes that the emergence of advocates of the 'business case' for LGBTQ+ inclusion across the Global South and East is integral to the efforts to 'make the business case hegemonic by demonstrating the universality of its benefits'. A key element of the universal applicability of the 'business case' is that neoliberalism both transcends and renders categories of race, class, gender and sexuality as anachronistic and irrelevant to an individuals' success in life (Conway, 2022: 160; Rao, 2024: 82). As Rao (2024) argues, 'homocapitalism' creates divides and illuminates class and other social-fissures within racial groups, as well as reifying a global hierarchy that privileges whiteness, with some people of colour arguing that capitalism offers the best opportunity for social advancement and the reduction of homophobia. Pride in South Africa, India, China and elsewhere is also subject to tensions and contestation over commercialization but has also seen the emergence of prominent local LGBTQ+ advocates who believe that business is the pre-eminent, and sometimes the only, means to achieve progress and rights for LGBTQ+ communities.

Race washing and corporate social responsibility

The decision of institutions, from state institutions from the police, military and embassies to commercial entities including banks, technology firms, shops and airlines to sponsor floats and take part in Pride parades, as well as the rebranding of their logos in rainbow colours for 'Pride Month' fits within a broader move of these institutions to celebrate their commitment to 'diversity', 'inclusion' and often to offer visible proof that they are paragons of equitable employment policies, that they value LGBTQ+ employees and that rainbow branding demonstrates real societal progress has and is being made for LGBTQ+ communities. As discussed in Chapter 2, Ahmed is highly critical of this institutional turn to 'diversity speak' (Ahmed, 2006, 2012). Writing about elite British universities advance into 'diversity politics', with institutional websites displaying the smiling faces of 'diverse' students and staff and considerable effort spent on writing documents and processes for race, gender and LGBT equality. Ahmed argues that this 'smiling face' of diversity is actually a means of 'avoiding actually doing anything' about advancing equality, or tackling the racism, sexism or homophobia staff and students of these institutions may and do face (2012: 71).

It is common for Pride organizers who accept corporate sponsorship and involvement to justify this involvement not just by stressing the economic necessity of such support. In Johannesburg, Kaye Ally explained, Pride 'is registered with the express purpose of engaging with sponsors to plan and execute a Pride parade and market'. Ally continued: 'I'm a realist ….You want a comfortable Pride? There are bills that need to be paid and big business does have the means to assist.' The organizer of Cape Town Pride until 2023, Mathew van As, concurred:

> Prides are expensive, even here in South Africa, you're looking at a minimum of 500,000 Rand for a one-day event … you need to be able to pay for those costs … I'm okay with corporates being involved. I mean, if they're willing to show the support to the LGBTI community and they have strong LGBTI connections and brands within their organizations, I'm saying why not?

Pride organizers also commonly argue that to accept such sponsorship they need to be convinced of the genuine commitment of these corporations to policies that value and protect their LGBTQ+ employees and customers. This, of course, mirrors the companies themselves, who often argue that their commitment to LGBTQ+ communities is genuine and long standing. Kaye Ally, the organizer of Johannesburg Pride, argued that 'I don't enter into a sponsorship agreement with them [corporations] just as a branding exercise. So as a brand, you have diversity policies, and you have inclusion mechanisms in place.' The evolution of companies adopting employment and other codes of conduct that encompass moral, social and political positions is relatively recent. As Burchiellaro (2023) argues, an 'EDI industrial complex' has developed involving career trajectories, consultants, conferences, lobbying groups and award ceremonies. Pride organizing and EDI advising for corporations have also become interchangeable. Kaye Ally is a former employee of the US-based technology company IBM and explained:

> IBM has one of the oldest diversity policies in the world I think its 40 or 50 years old if not older. So from that perspective I think it's a good

thing that corporates want to be involved. I think it's important that the community sees the involvement a) particularly identifies with those logos but b) also hears that they have those diversity policies.

As Ally spoke to me about IBM, I remembered having interviewed a white British former employee of IBM in South Africa for a previous research project on the British in South Africa. He had told me of his experience of working at what he believed was the racially tolerant environment of IBM in the 1970s and how this disproved the claim that apartheid in South Africa was as bad as international activists and media outlets had argued (Conway and Leonard, 2014). This claim, premised on interactions mediated by racially defined management hierarchies, belied the fact that IBM's technology underpinned the apartheid government's security apparatus and enabled its ability to monitor and maintain racial segregation. The pragmatic defence for corporate funding of Pride is often tied to the claim that corporate support is genuine based on their EDI policies. Yet these policies can be a mere 'exercise in documentation' (Ahmed, 2012) with little actual meaningful commitment to change and even worse, they can exist to conceal exploitative and discriminatory business practices.

'We are standing together, shoulder to shoulder, all working for the common good', proclaimed IBM's founding Chairman and CEO Thomas Watson Sr in the 1950s. This quote was repeated at the beginning of IBM's publication titled 'Supporting the journey gender transition in the global workplace: A best practices study based on IBM's comprehensive approach', co-authored with the Human Rights Campaign Foundation and distributed at the World Pride Human Rights Conference in 2019. As discussed above, analysing IBM's history reveals that the company has not always, if ever, been working for the common good, or standing shoulder to shoulder with oppressed people. In addition to IBM's operations in South Africa in the 1970s and 1980s, there is a further South African link between the development of 'corporate social responsibility', business practice policies and being engaged in the very unjust practices that such policies claim to repudiate. IBM, Kodak (who provided the means to print 'Pass Books' that underpinned racial segregation) and other US corporations had lobbied the Nixon administration to develop a voluntary code of conduct in South Africa, to ward off formal sanctions that would prevent companies from doing business in what was the most lucrative market in the world (Larson, 2020). The Sullivan Principles were developed as a code of conduct for US businesses in South Africa and the first a voluntary code related to human rights and race for business. The Sullivan Principles were difficult to monitor and contained many contradictions. Larson (2020) judges the Principles to have been a 'failure' in their aim to ameliorate or oppose the injustices of apartheid, but they gave companies 'an alternative path for demonstrating opposition to apartheid' and 'dissuaded them from joining with activists to actually challenge the regime'. The Principles also split the international apartheid movement, some of whom argued that it would be better to engage with business to promote positive change in South Africa, whereas others argued that business underpinned apartheid and there should be boycotts and economic sanctions.

Larson argues that despite the Sullivan Code's failure, it continues to be held up as a model of corporate social responsibility in Western business studies literature and teaching at Business Schools. Larson concludes the Sullivan Code 'augured the future of corporate responses to globalization concerns, and their structure was designed to mollify criticism without solving the attendant issues' (Larson, 2020). While it may seem a stretch to compare the evolution of corporate social responsibility in apartheid-era South Africa to contemporary corporate involvement in Pride, the example evidences Ahmed's claim that corporate diversity and inclusion commitments require little action

Figure 10 IBM 'Legendary Pride', 2019.

4. Corporate Pride and Commercialization

and hides the ongoing and systematic racism of these same institutions (2006, 2012). This also mirrors Rao's (2020) claim that companies who proclaim their LGBTQ+ tolerance and opposition to homophobia as a cultural problem that they play no role in. The evolution of corporate social responsibility and corporate commitments to EDI should be approached with caution and with an understanding of the structural effects of contemporary neoliberal capitalism.

At the 2019 World Pride Parade in New York, IBM employees carried placards depicting 'Key IBM Diversity Moments'. These placards included '1997 IBM discusses LGBT Rights at the Vatican', '2012 IBM endorses first official rainbow flag' and '2017 IBM launches legendary 8 bar rainbow logo'. It looked as if the history of IBM's EDI policies related to LGBTQ+ communities was indistinguishable from the actual struggle for LGBTQ+ rights in the world. To underscore IBM's presentation of itself as an activist group or social movement for social justice, a large advert in the New York World Pride magazine proclaimed;

> For more than a century, IBM has been committed to creating an equal and open workplace where IBMers feel comfortable bringing their full selves to work. In 1984, IBM became one of the first companies to include sexual orientation as part of our commitment to non-discrimination ... we've expanded same-sex partner benefits in over 50 countries around the world and have tirelessly championed policies that accommodate all of our employees-most recently by urging the US Congress to pass the Equality Act. Standing up for diversity and inclusion in the workplace is a part of who we are.

At the World Pride Human Rights Conference, which took place in the week leading up to the Parade, IBM had sponsored a panel titled 'Corporate Advocacy: The Role of Corporations in Affirming LGBT+ Equality around the Globe'. At the panel, a corporate executive announced that 'we're the ones at the state courthouses supporting LGBT and abortion rights cases'. In the question-and-answer session she briefly acknowledged that in homophobic parts of the world the company may keep its counsel on such issues 'if it endangers our staff' and since 'the bottom line is profit, things can get a bit tricky'. The presentation of corporations as being both at the vanguard and the embodiment of LGBTQ+ acceptance and equality is part of the ongoing development of corporate social responsibility policies, which are themselves part of broader shifts in global capitalism as it responds to changes in the market and potential challenges from social and political movements. The presentation of corporations as activists on behalf of marginalized communities from women, people of colour and LGBTQ+ and even that the self-described history of corporate advocacy on behalf of these communities is something to be documented and commemorated as achievements for social justice, should be interpreted in the broader context and history of corporate social diversity. This history demonstrates that corporate social responsibility emerged in direct response to activist challenges and the threat of sanctions against operating in the profitable territory of the 1970s and 1980s South Africa and to sidestep accusations of complicity in apartheid. In similar terms, loud corporate proclamations of commitment to LGBTQ+ communities often belie inconsistent application of these commitments across the territories corporations operate and the rapid and quiet ditching of these commitments is commonplace should profit be jeopardized.

Global corporate Pride in Asia

While the commercialization of Pride can be critiqued from a queer anti-capitalist and social justice perspective, investigating the actual political and material levels of support for Pride and LGBTQ+ activism also reveals troubling evidence. A Baring Foundation and Give Out report (Baring Foundation and Give Out, 2023) found that 'we could only identify a small number of corporates which championed LGBTQI organizations through their larger corporate philanthropy budgets'. Despite the UK being home to major transnational corporations, many of whom are at the forefront of 'global homocapitalism' and prominent at Pride parades across the world, only 6p out of every £100 spent on corporate social responsibility projects was focused on LGBTQ+ issues and most of this came from the relatively small amounts of funding dedicated to staff LGBTQ+ groups. These staff groups were most likely to spend the money on internal events, and on rainbow-branded clothing and merchandize for employees attending Pride.

In Chapter 2, I discussed how Gilbert Baker had opted not to trademark the rainbow flag and was happy for any group or institution to use it as a symbol of Pride and LGBTQ+ rights. This has enabled the rainbow branding of corporate logos for 'Pride Month' and for some companies to proclaim that they have the 'official' Pride merchandize, as Absolut Vodka does for its rainbow-coloured 'official Pride Absolut Vodka'. The example of Absolut's 'official' rainbow Pride bottle of vodka is indicative of corporate involvement and support for Pride.

Absolut will not disclose financial details about its 'Absolut Rainbow' marketing campaign and advises staff that if they are asked whether the company adopts 'any specific political positions regarding LGBT equality ... [for example] do you believe in full equal rights including same-sex adoption?', the reply should be 'Absolut does not comment on political matters – we are not a lobbying group, nor a plaintiff. We are supporting the right to freedom of expression regardless of who you love.' When I asked a Hong Kong-based marketing executive at Pernod Ricard, Absolut's parent company, whether he saw any contradictions in this stance, he replied that to take a stand in different territories was inappropriate internal interference in the politics of that country. It is difficult to see how a company can meaningfully claim to be at the vanguard of social, political and legal change for LGBTQ+ communities and simultaneously refuse to speak up for LGBTQ+ people's legal and political rights in the territories' the company operates in.

In societies where there are legal restrictions on public gatherings and marches, or in conservative societies with high levels of homophobia, the support and participation of business can be viewed as vital for Pride organizing and for increasing the visibility of and community building for LGBTQ+ people. As pushback and backlash against LGBT rights are increasing in both the Global North and South (Ayoub and Stoeckl, 2024), there is evidence that the pragmatic engagement with business and the commercialization of Pride are not an effective defence against homophobia. This has been the case for LGBTQ+ organizing in China. Shanghai Pride had multiple corporate and diplomatic sponsors and used the spaces of Western chain hotels, transnational corporate offices, foreign consulates and some local businesses for conferences, exhibitions, film screenings and parties. Such was the concern about potential sanctions against meetings and events discussing LGBTQ+ lives and rights, that one year the Chinese branch of Parents and Friends of Lesbians and Gays (PFLAG) held their annual convention on a cruise ship, commencing the conference only once the ship had left port. When I attended Shanghai Pride in 2018, PFLAG held a large conference at a Western-owned hotel in the city, with delegates attending from across China.

Charlene Yiu, the main organizer of Shanghai Pride, believed the international business played an important role in both enabling Pride to take place in a legally hostile terrain, but also in delivering Prides' mission to raise visibility and influence social and legal change. 'They are the big push because they are business right?', commented Charlene, 'if they support [LGBT] employees ... employees are the consumers, right? ... So it's a win-win ... and then governments will see that, "Okay, yeah, LGBT people have big support ... you are not bad, it's not causing any chaos" and then slowly hopefully there will be change'. One of the events for Shanghai Pride was an Out & Equal China Corporate Summit on the campus of General Electric and compered by Wei, a member of the Shanghai Pride committee. Wei believed that the commercialization of Pride in China was the only way that there would be progress for LGBTQ+ communities:

> The big face here is money. Everything is valued and can be valued ... If we talk about human rights or we talk like 'politicals', the Chinese people wouldn't care. What they care is money. So, let's talk about money. Let's use money to talk ... So we are using this kind of soft approach to get attention and awareness from other communities.

Wei also believed that adopting a language of human rights or using protest to try and achieve human rights was not only naïve but counterproductive and provoke a harsh response from the authorities. The organizers of Shanghai Pride had been very successful in running multiple events, catering to different people from those who wanted social parties, LGBTQ+ film screenings, 'rainbow' fun runs and bike rides in place of a parade, and discussion events on issues from being disabled and LGBTQ+, to HIV+ and gender issues within LGBTQ+ communities and they, like some of their counterparts in other conservative societies in the region, argued that the language and partnership with business was the only and the most effective means to hold these events and lead to positive change.

A banner displaying their multiple corporate and diplomatic partners always accompanied Shanghai Pride's events, but it became clear that this support had its limits. A member of Shanghai Pride's organizing committee had recently transferred from the US headquarters of a transnational corporation. His employer is heavily involved in Pride in the United States, Europe and Australasia and even organizes a large Pride of its own at its Florida headquarters and theme park. Naturally, he had assumed that they would welcome the opportunity to be involved in Shanghai Pride. When he approached his managers for support and told them he was co-organizing the Out & Equal Conference, they responded that no rainbow-branded merchandize from the corporation could be on display at Shanghai Pride and that if he participated in its events, he should take annual leave and do so as a private individual, not a representative of the company and this is what he did. While

Figure 11 Out & Equal Asia Conference, Shanghai Pride 2018.

Chinese regulations stipulate than any international business can only operate in the country if 51 per cent of the local company is owned by the Chinese state, and this may be a reason for this cautious approach, other Western companies did decide to be involved in Shanghai Pride. Corporate decisions are inevitably based on minimizing business risk and maximizing profitability. It is unsurprising, therefore, that there would be reluctance and sometimes refusal to become involved in Pride and LGBTQ+ advocacy in conservative contexts.

In 2018, Shanghai Pride celebrated their tenth anniversary. The organizing committee had skilfully negotiated the sensitive legal and political context despite continual challenges. Each year some events had been cancelled because of official interference, but the committee believed their cautious 'business case' strategy had been broadly successful. I asked Charlene Yiu, 'In terms of thinking about the future, do you worry that political circumstances could make LGBT life difficult here?' Charlene replied, 'I think it will be okay. Because at the end of the day, the economy thrives on peace. Peace and harmony really. So, it will be okay, we're good.' Yet, over the following two years, police harassment of the Pride organizers significantly increased. A Malaysian member of the organizing committee, who was a long-term resident of Shanghai, had his work visa renewal application denied, for no apparent reason, and other members of the committee were repeatedly called in for police questioning. The situation reached the point where the committee decided it was no longer safe to organize Pride and the event was put on an indefinite hiatus in 2021. Charlene Yiu and her partner also left China, in part, because of the police harassment they had faced (see Bernot and Davies, 2024; Bernot et al., 2024). Ward (2003) poses the question of what will happen to the corporate celebration of LGBTQ+ communities if it is no longer considered to be profitable to do so. The experience of the US employee in Shanghai, who discovered his 'gay friendly' employer wanted nothing to do with Shanghai Pride provides an answer to that question. Rao's (2024: 99) claim that 'yesterday's folk devils may have become today's gay patriots, but they may yet be spat out of a system that cannot metabolize them' finds evidence in the regrettable demise of Shanghai Pride. The case study of Shanghai Pride reveals the contingency of corporate support and limits of the 'business case' for LGBTQ+ rights.

Along the coast from Shanghai, Hong Kong hosts a wide range of LGBTQ+ advocacy, activist and corporate events which have suffered less legal and political interference. These include Hong Kong Pride, Hong Kong Migrants Pride, Pink Dot and Pink Season. While homosexuality in Hong Kong was legalized by the British administration in 1991, there are few positive legal protections or rights for LGBTQ+ people (Kong, 2011, 2019, 2023). The lived experience of LGBTQ+ people in Hong Kong is fragmented along lines of wealth, race, nationality and gender and the different LGBTQ+ events cater to different racial, class and national groups within the LGBTQ+ community and articulate different visions of progress and social justice. Hong Kong Pride was started in 2008 and is organized by local Cantonese activists. It draws from the territory's history of political protest, has a close relationship with the pro-democracy movement and makes open demands for legal protections and equality. Betty Grisoni, one of the organizers of Pink Dot, was keen to emphasize the 'soft approach' they adopted, one that did not 'demand change', but was family and corporate friendly. Phillip

4. Corporate Pride and Commercialization

Howell-Williams, the UK-born organizer of Pink Season, explained that his series of events were 'not directly political' and focused on sport, parties and some discussion of legal rights in corporate contexts. Hong Kong Migrants Pride started in 2015 and emerged out of a broad coalition of MDW support groups and from local LGBTQ+ activists, particularly those involved in Hong Kong Pride (Lai, 2018). A range of corporate LGBTQ+ umbrella and lobbying groups also exist including Interbank, the Hong Kong Gay and Lesbian Attorney's Network and Community Business. These corporate advocacy groups were supported by several transnational businesses to bring forward the 'QT Case' that successfully won the legal right for internationally registered same-sex marriages to be recognized, albeit only for immigrants on professional work visas in Hong Kong (Suen, 2019).

The intersectional differences and divisions between LGBTQ+ communities could be vividly illustrated by Pride and other LGBTQ+ events in the territory. In 2019, I attended the Out Leadership Asia Summit and reception held high up in HSBC's corporate headquarters and a few days later Hong Kong Migrants Pride, which take place in the exact same location in the city, with Migrant's Pride weaving beside and beneath HSBC's headquarters. The two events reflected different communities and very different understandings of politics and society, albeit around shared discursive framings and symbolisms of Pride. HSBC is a powerful economic, social and political actor in Hong Kong. Its headquarters occupy a commanding position and as the information panels placed at the foot of the building make clear, the history of the bank is interwoven with the colonial history and development of the territory. Primarily operating between London and Hong Kong, HSBC regularly serves as a mouthpiece for the collective interests of Hong Kong and the broader global corporate sector. As Jack Guest, a UK-born HSBC employee and co-founder of the Hong Kong HSBC Pride group, explained:

> HSBC in Hong Kong is in an absolutely unique position. Our influence in this city is absolutely unchallenged, we are almost a monopoly in the banking sector, just the sheer scale of the organization and its deep roots into Hong Kong are very evident and so we have all eyes on us at all times.

In recent years, HSBC has engaged with LGBTQ+ issues. In 2013, HSBC employees established an LGBTQ+ employee group, HSBC Pride. Since 2014, the Out Leadership Asia Summit has been hosted at HSBC's headquarters in Hong Kong, with the skyscraper lit in rainbow colours for the week. In 2018, HSBC Pride was a prominent contingent at the Hong Kong Pride march, with over a hundred staff wearing HSBC-branded rainbow t-shirts and marching with large HSBC Pride banners. Jack Guest explained, although HSBC had 'a very visible presence at Pride', but 'I don't see us becoming a sponsor' of Pride, whereas HSBC does sponsor Pink Dot. This was because, he explained, Pride was perceived as being 'too political', 'too aggressive' and too closely associated with the pro-democracy movement in the territory, unlike Pink Dot.

In 2018, the Out Leadership Asia Summit's closing event involved senior executives from a number of different financial, legal and media organizations in Hong Kong and across Asia, as well as prominent actors in Hong Kong and the region's LGBTQ+ advocacy community. The event began with 'uplifting' videos highlighting Out Leadership's LGBTQ+ advocacy work in the corporate sector and showcasing the role of HSBC and other corporations in making LGBTQ+ employees feel accepted, valued and able to be 'out' at work. At the event, senior HSBC executives, all of whom identified as being heterosexual, emphasized the corporation's commitment to diversity simply by the fact that the bank operated across numerous territories. Kevin Martin, an HSBC executive, said: 'The bank was founded more than 150 years ago to finance trade between Europe and Asia and we have always brought different people and cultures together. Diversity is at the heart of our business model.' Another executive agreed that 'HSBC's roots are forged in diversity. Without diversity we could not understand and service the needs of our 48 million customers around the globe'. As with IBM's proclaimed long lineage and commitment to diversity, HSBC's commitment to diversity obscured the historical and contemporary power relations inherent to the group's powerful role in shaping colonial and postcolonial capitalism.

At the closing event of the Summit, the mostly white speakers from Hong Kong's financial, legal and media sectors' emphasized their corporations' global role in advancing diversity and inclusion. Roundtable-style discussions between prominent LGBTQ+ corporate employees in Hong Kong portrayed a dynamic, positive and hopeful future for LGBTQ+ employees in the territory: as one speaker remarked, 'I think we've turned the corner' for LGBT rights in the territory (field notes). Speakers at the event were selected to portray the important influence corporations have in advancing LGBTQ+ rights. Jennifer Lu, a prominent Taiwanese LGBTQ+ rights activist, was interviewed on stage, saying that 'corporate support is extremely important' and thanked the corporate sector for their support in the forthcoming Taiwanese referendum on same-sex marriage. I subsequently discovered that HSBC, like most other transnational corporations, had made no financial contribution or public statement about the referendum in Taiwan. Perhaps the most incongruous and revealing scene at the Summit was that of gay US Olympic athlete Gus Kenworthy, who had been flown in for the occasion, and spoke about leadership, courage, strength and being an LGBT 'role model'. Kenworthy's presence emphasized the impression that this was an event mostly populated by and aimed at Western and global elites, framed in terms that assumed an empowered present and progressive future for LGBTQ+ subjects, and one that was enabled by transnational corporations and embodied by their professional employees.

The Summit's final reception was a glamorous affair, with rainbow-themed canapés to match the skyscraper's lighting scheme. At the reception, I asked a Hong Kong-based human rights advocate where he had gone after he had spoken on the stage earlier in the afternoon. 'I couldn't stand to listen to their hypocrisy,' he replied and then spoke at length at how HSBC had refused to publicly call for pro-LGBTQ+ legislation in Hong Kong or to formally support legal cases, such as the QT case. At the event, various claims about the extent of LGBTQ+ progress and the ability of transnational corporations to deliver and protect such progress were articulated, but in private conversations and based on evidence of previous corporate action, and inaction, it was clear that there was more complex and contradictory reality behind the carefully curated narrative of institutional support for LGBTQ+ inclusion at the Summit.

'It's always business that makes change happen', a UK-born Hong Kong corporate executive remarked to me during the Summit's drinks reception. She was echoing a remark made by an HSBC executive from the stage who had said that 'nothing will change in Hong Kong unless we lead that change'. She had been discussing with me the broader pro-democracy protests and the prospects for legal advances in LGBTQ+ rights in Hong Kong. As her comment implied, she was sceptical of the potential for pro-democracy, or LGBTQ+ activists, to effect change, but confident that transnational corporations in the territory would do so. This understanding of political, legal and social reality as being predicated on, and refracted through, corporate power is also at the heart of how LGBTQ+ identities and rights are understood as valid only when they become part of what has been termed, by both advocates and critics, what the 'business case for diversity and inclusion' claims. Thus, it becomes a self-evident truth that it makes 'business sense' to advocate for and celebrate LGBTQ+ individuals as employees and customers.

At the Summit, Kevin Martin, HSBC Asia's Group General Manager, explained that 'we must develop a safe and supportive environment where everyone can bring their whole selves [to work] to whatever they do and achieve their goals'. This has also been a consistent theme of HSBC's articulation of its involvement in LGBTQ+ issues. Diana Cesar, CEO of HSBC Hong Kong, explained that HSBCs lighting the building in rainbow colours each year demonstrated 'our commitment to achieving a truly open and diverse working environment'. This claim is premised on the commodification of LGBTQ+ subjects as productive employees who increase profit for business. Even the residency rights won for same-sex partners of corporate employees in the QT case were justified by one legal executive at the Summit not as a triumph for LGBT rights, but a logical step that increased Hong Kong's economic competitiveness: '[the QT case] was important to Hong Kong's ability to attract and maintain talent'. However, despite the outward display of rainbow colours by HSBC, this 'business case' was inward facing and defined as creating a better working environment for corporate employees. For HSBC, LGBTQ+ identities, rights and individuals confer value only through productive professional work and understand the achievement of authentic LGBTQ+ subjectivity in and by work.

The importance of the business case to the framing of LGBTQ+ rights and commitment to LGBTQ+ equality was apparent in the readiness to de-prioritize and adapt positions if they conflict with commercial interest. In 2016, Jack Guest and others in HSBC Pride organized the painting of the HSBC's symbolic bronze lion statues in rainbow colours. Jack explained this generated a 'phenomenal [positive] response' on social media. In 2018, the painting of the lions was hailed as a proof of the bank's commitment to 'leading' progressive LGBT rights change: 'We've lit the building. We've put rainbow lions outside,' remarked an HSBC executive. However, a petition protesting against the rainbow lions was initiated by the Christian activist, Roger Wong, who also criticized HSBC at its annual shareholder meeting for equalizing same-sex employee benefits without consulting shareholders (AFP, 2016). Media coverage of these protests made some 'very senior clients' approach senior managers and express their concern about HSBC becoming involved in LGBTQ+ issues. As Jack Guest explained, while HSBC's official response was to deploy a 'boilerplate' line about valuing diversity and inclusion, he admitted that it had made senior managers 'a little bit uncomfortable' and that had led to a 'dampening of our overt messaging' and that HSBC had not done anything as 'big and bold' as painting the lions: 'I can't touch the lions again!' he exclaimed. HSBC's (and wider corporate) commitment to LGBTQ+ rights was proclaimed by corporate elites first by the painting of the lions in rainbow colours and pointing to this as evidence of leadership and change, yet this concealed the reality of caution and compromise in response to homophobic opposition.

As discussed above, HSBC and other corporations have been reluctant to sponsor Hong Kong Pride because it is perceived to be 'too political', but groups of employees have participated in the Pride march. Hong Kong Pride emerged in the late-1990s and is organized by Cantonese activists who had a close relationship with the pro-democracy movement in the territory. Like the attitude of the organizing committee of Shanghai Pride, Wylie Yeo, the main organizer of Hong Kong Pride, explained:

> I think this is important for Hong Kong, as a commercial city, that Hong Kong people like to stress the commercial side of everything, so if they think that are some big names joining in then they may consider it not to be something too extraordinary to support. So, it creates a kind of trend or, 'Oh, those big brands are supporting Pride then it may not be too bad for me to support'.

Yeo also revealed that there had been tensions with commercial sponsors. A corporate sponsor had objected to their logo being featured alongside a sex toy and condom company that had also sponsored Hong Kong Pride. The conflation of business and activism and the presentation of businesses *as* activists in challenging contexts came into sharp focus in Hong Kong. In 2019, Mac Cosmetics employees and a group of models hired by Mac marched in the Hong Kong Pride Parade carrying placards. These Mac-branded placards had 'Love is Love' and "Free to be You' 'Mac Stands with Inclusion' posted on them. This 'protest for hire' encapsulated the neoliberal conflation of business and activism. At the end of the march in front of Hong Kong City Hall, I took a picture of the placards piled next to the refuse bins. The image symbolized the ersatz protest that Mac had sponsored and summed up my concerns about the transient and superficial nature of corporate involvement in Pride.

For Hong Kong Pride, the close association with the pro-democracy camp had caused difficulties. One year a sponsor had insisted that no pro-democracy figure should be allowed to speak from the stage

Figure 12 Mac Stands with Inclusion by the refuse bin, Hong Kong Pride 2018.

at the end of the Pride march. The organizers had ignored this and allowed pro-democracy activists to speak and the sponsorship from that institution was not forthcoming the following year. Many corporations in Hong Kong choose to fund Pink Dot and Pink Season, because they are non-confrontational and less political. Vincy Chan, a queer activist involved in Hong Kong Pride, acknowledged that there is a pragmatic rationale for involving corporations in LGBT advocacy in Hong Kong, but

> I do think it is very problematic that that is the only strategy we're using to try and push this [LGBT rights] conversation forward … If we continue to let corporations drive that conversation and drive any sort of activity around the movement, it will just continue to be that, like people who are rich, and white, and cis, and gay, and able-bodied, to be the head of that movement. That isn't something that I want to see in the long run.

While the organizers and activists involved in Hong Kong Pride could see the pragmatic value of having corporate sponsors, in what is one of the world's major financial and legal centres, the involvement of such support came with strings that sought to restrict the discussion of political and legal issues that mattered to the activists and place conservative pressures on the celebration of sex and sexuality. Tensions and divisions around race, class, nationality and gender were also exposed and exacerbated by corporate involvement, or lack of, in Pride.

In Mumbai, the rapid growth in India's economy has been accompanied by a growth in corporate LGBTQ+ advocacy groups such as Pride Circle and the Godrej India Cultural Lab. In Chapter 3, I discussed the divisions between the Hindu-nationalist organizing committee of Mumbai Pride and local queer activists. As well as these political divisions, the commercialization of Pride and LGBTQ+ advocacy was also a source of tension. Mumbai Pride can be considered an expression of 'HomoHindunationalism' (Upadhyay, 2020) and also what I would term HomoHinducapitalism. Ankit Bhuptani, the organizer of Mumbai Pride, told me that 'any support is welcome and corporate support is more than welcome. T-shirts are great- to get the branding and get the pink money! And at the end of the day, what's wrong with it? Any corporate engagement more than welcome'. In the Pride march, the students from the TISS Queer Collection clearly disagreed and carried protest banners opposing the commercialization of Pride and the privatization of state services in India.

During Mumbai's Queer Azaadi 'Pride Month' several LGBTQ+ events were held at the glossy corporate headquarters of Godrej, a major soap and chemical manufacturer in India. Parmesh Shahini, a Godrej executive and head of Godrej's India Culture Lab, has been termed a 'self-described "inclusion advocate" and principle cheerleader for homocapitalism in India' (Rao, 2024: 81) having published *Queeristan: LGBTQ+ Inclusion in the Indian Workplace* and being feted by global elites as a Yale World Fellow, Future Young Leader of the World Bank and a TED talk speaker. The designer-clad Shahani was dismissive of criticisms of the commercialization of Pride and derisory of my questions about the tensions between transnational corporations and local grassroots activism. Comparing the global spread of Pride to McDonalds he concluded, 'that's capitalism! It happens everywhere!'. The students from the TISS Queer Collective later told me that 'it is difficult to get tickets to Godrej's events, because they are given out to elite people ... I went there for one of the meetings and personally, I was intimidated ... The venue itself is intimidating to marginalized people and many marginalized queer people will not get to go to Godrej .... The crowd is an elite crowd'. As discussed in Chapter 3, a number of queer protestors were arrested at Mumbai Pride in 2020 and it was rumoured the organizers of Pride had given their names to the police. There are significant rewards for Global South LGBTQ+ figures who participate in homocapitalism and who can establish high-profile lucrative careers and travel the world attending corporate D&I conventions, LGBTQ+ conferences and Pride events. Mumbai Pride also reveals the authoritarian instincts of those complicit in homocapitalism and their desire to prevent and discipline those who wish to protest and/or talk about broader social justice issues at Pride.

Corporate 'skills', the gentrification of Pride organizing and 'career queers'

In Johannesburg, Kaye Ally argued that there is not just a need for corporate sponsors to be involved for the money, but that professional employees of corporations are better at organizing than political activists, 'I've got a 22 years IT background,' Ally explained:

> I've spent lot of time in project management and sales. So I have very good understanding of putting something together end to end, with purpose, and finding solutions to things ….NGOs and activists want a Pride with no corporate involvement and they don't care if there's nothing as simple as toilets or drinks, or a place for people to actually rest, or a place for people to enjoy themselves. And that makes us no better than a mine-workers strike, or truck-drivers strike.

Having attended activist and NGO organized Pride events in South Africa, Taiwan, Hong Kong, the United Kingdom and the United States, I believe this is an unfair characterization of the activists' and NGOs abilities. The valorization of a professional class of LGBTQ+ organizers in place of community activists is part of the gentrification of LGBTQ+ activism that Shulman (2012b) identifies. As discussed in Chapter 2, Ward (2008) analysed how the original working-class and Latinx organizers of Los Angeles Pride were replaced with university-educated white professionals and argues that this professionalization and gentrification replaced a radical politics that served the needs of the local community with a conservative politics than was distant from the local population. The commercialization of Johannesburg Pride has led to the same displacement of community activists and the issues they represent. Mpumi Mathabela commented on how this commercialization of Pride was reflected in who made up the organizing committee and the skills that were deemed necessary, the kind of priorities and factors that believed to make a 'successful' Pride event. Mathabela recalled that one of the committee members of Johannesburg Pride had told her:

> I know nothing about the politics of the LGBTI community. I'm queer, yes, but I am just a marketer. I was brought onto the committee to market Pride. And so I did that, I marketed Pride. And for me to market it, I need advertising, I need to advertise it. I need people to actually buy into the idea and so for me it was the numbers. So when we get people on board who are giving us money, if this year 9000 people attend, next year must be 10,000, and the following year it must be even bigger, and that's what this space is, because I was brought on to do that.

This lends evidence to support Schulman's claim that the LGBTQ+ community has 'doomed' itself by framing Pride as large-scale events that need levels of security and facilities that require corporate funding when these are all factors that are 'choices' made by Pride organizers (Schulman, 2012a: 119).

The valorization of professional skills and the attendant belief that activists are unqualified and/or too chaotic to organize a 'successful' Pride event reveal the ideological motivations of Pride organizers and who they imagine Pride to exist for. The professionalization of Pride organizing mirrors the broader critique of LGBTQ advocacy, the 'NGO-ization' (Choudry and Kapoor, 2012) of LGBTQ+ activism and the rise of a new global elite of 'career queers' (Rodriguez, 2022: 83). This has created divisions between LGBTQ+ activists and elites in both the Global North and South and that puts grassroots activists at an even greater disadvantage when they try to access funds for campaigning.

Transnational, and often Global North-based, LGBTQ+ organizations and 'Umbrella Groups', such as InterPride, EuroPride, ILGA and its regional caucuses, Outright, The Kaleidoscope Trust and nationally based groups such as Stonewall UK and The Other Foundation in South Africa have become hubs for 'career queers', easily identifiable targets for philanthropic and governmental donations and have developed the professionalized infrastructure to meet the, often lengthy and complex, application and evaluation requirements of funders. These organizations are not necessarily entirely siloed from grassroots organizations. For example, The Other Foundation has a rapid reaction small grants programme and has funded the Forum for the Empowerment of Women. The Kaleidoscope Trust administers a UK government-funded scheme to build the capacity of thirty-one LGBTQ+ NGOs in seven Commonwealth territories (Jackson and Jackson, 2023). 'Career queers' can also have a genuine desire to assist grassroots activism and some may come from a grassroots activist background themselves. However, the growth of umbrella groups has created a privileged and relatively closed global ecology of networking opportunities focused on costly international conferences, such as the ILGA World Conference and InterPride's World Pride Human Rights Conference. Relevant government and diplomatic officials, corporate LGBTQ+ advocacy groups and the activists who can afford the visa, travel and registration fees also, and sometimes only, attend these events. Rao (2020) writes about how the Kaleidoscope Trust emerged in the context of the UK's 'expression of regret' about the colonial roots of homophobia across Africa, Asia and the Caribbean. The British government and parliamentarians did not extend this 'expression of regret' to the legacies of slavery and the colonial roots of racism in those territories. Rao argues the Kaleidoscope Trust is indicative of the ongoing global racial hierarchy where the UK admonishes postcolonial territories for their homophobic 'backwardness' and continues to position itself as a 'civilizing' force in the world. Rao also discusses accusations that Kaleidoscope acted as a 'gatekeeper' for a chosen few LGBTQ+ activists. During my research, I encountered the same small group of LGBTQ+ advocacy professionals time and again at various Pride and LGBTQ+ advocacy events across the world. International forums, such as the World Pride Human Rights Conference and the ILGA World Conference have registration fees of US$350+ and I have heard numerous anecdotes, as well as personal experience, of organizers being unhelpful with visa applications and not responding to grassroots activists from the Global South's request to speak at these forums. Several grassroots activists have commented to me that even if they do get to be in the same spaces as international umbrella organizations, they seldom feel 'seen' and taken seriously by those groups.

The global location and privileged circle of 'career queers' can lead to a complete absence of grassroots queer activists and 'alternative' Prides. For example, a recent Outright Report on Pride events worldwide, overlooked the many Pride events in South Africa, and only highlighted Johannesburg Pride (Outright International, 2021). Following the 2019 World Pride Human Rights Conference in New York, I tried to connect the organizer of the following World Pride Human Rights Conference due to be held in Copenhagen in 2021 with the grassroots activists I had spoken to in South Africa, India and Hong Kong. I had a number of zoom conversations with the World Pride official and yet, despite all the activists I had connected him with (and myself) having filled in online application forms to participate, none received a reply or were invited. The Human Rights Conference in Copenhagen had many of the same speakers that had been at New York and still emphasized corporate participation. While this may have been an oversight due to disorganization, I wondered if the grassroots activists from Soweto, Ekurhuleni, Mumbai and Hong Kong jarred with the 'homocapitalist' tenor of the Human Rights Conference and it was simply too inconvenient to expend energy and expense on helping activists from the Global South navigate the complex and costly visa regimes in order to travel to Copenhagen. As previously mentioned, while the Other Foundation in Johannesburg does make grassroots donations on a case-by-case basis, some activists in South Africa cynically commented on how an influx of international funding had led to the Other Foundation moving to new and presumably expensive corporate headquarters in the upmarket Rosebank suburb. In 2024, the Other Foundation released a glossy report titled 'Size Matters' attempting to quantify the size and emphasize the value of LGBTQ+ people to the South African economy, localizing the international' homocapitalist' discourse of the 'productive' value of LGBTQ+ people to economic growth and further distancing policy discourses from grassroots struggles in the country.

The Pride organizing committee in Ekurhuleni, South Africa and Hong Kong are unpaid volunteers and although Soweto Pride was organized by the salaried staff at an NGO, the Forum for the Empowerment of Women (FEW), FEW has struggled for funding and in some months, had barely been able to fund their payroll. For Jade Madingwane, the root of this struggle was the fact that FEW was run by Black lesbians, and she explained 'we call funders, we call to people but they have no confidence solely on the fact that it [Soweto Pride] is organized by Black women'. While attending a reception to celebrate LGBTQ+ inclusion at a major bank in Hong Kong, a diversity and inclusion professional, who led the bank's LGBT staff group, told me that he had been 'embarrassed' when watching the organizers of Hong Kong Pride struggling to use PowerPoint software during a pitch for funding and by their 'limited' English-language ability. It was no surprise to him that they struggled to find sponsors and he believed they needed 'training in professional skills'. Class privilege, race, homonormative 'positive' messaging all serve to exclude grassroots Pride organizers from becoming part of a visible, rewarded and well-travelled global elite of LGBTQ+ 'career queers'. Relatedly, an LGBTQ+ philanthropist told an audience at the 2022 Global LGBT Rights Funding Summit in London how he likes to fund organizations based on what is presented on their website and the contents of their monthly email newsletters. I reflected how despite the success of Soweto Pride and Ekurhuleni Pride to organize large and meaningful events each year, neither organization has a website, an email list or even a dedicated bank account, with money currently channelled via the GALA Queer Archive of South Africa. Both Prides use social media, word of mouth and WhatsApp to effectively communicate their plans, but by not conforming to the norms of Global North corporate advocacy, with a website, an email list and a recognizable institutional structure, they will continue to struggle for consistent funding.

The struggle for salaries and funding for events leads grassroots LGBTQ+ activists to face what Moreau and Currier have termed a 'queer dilemma' (Moreau and Currier, 2018). In a context of homophobic, indifferent or unreliable governments, there are scarce resources for LGBT civil society and any potential source of funding is difficult to refuse. 'Alternative' Pride organizers in South Africa and Hong Kong are caught in this 'queer dilemma' and were willing to consider corporate sponsorship on a case-by-case basis. Yet, efforts to get such sponsorship were often unsuccessful because these Pride events were perceived as too 'political', or not sufficiently beneficial for the potential sponsors. Jade Mandingwane explained that Soweto Pride was willing to consider sponsorship if 'their intentions are right and genuine', but that corporate sponsors would not be allowed to participate in the Pride march because, as was discussed in Chapter 3, the purpose of the march was political protest and mourning victims of homophobic violence. The year I attended Soweto Pride a local, Black-owned estate agent had sponsored a stall at the afterparty. However, wider efforts to obtain sponsorship, even from companies that support Johannesburg Pride, have been unsuccessful. At the request of the organizers of Soweto Pride, I tried to broker sponsorship with a major transnational bank that has sponsored multiple Prides. The bank declined because although they operate in South Africa, they explained that their customers were mostly elite investors and wealthy expatriates, and they do not have the customer base in the country to 'justify' sponsoring an event 'like Soweto Pride'. As discussed earlier in the chapter, the organizers of Hong Kong Pride were also keenly aware of corporations who very visibly displayed their rainbow colours at the Pride march and other events in Hong Kong, only to refuse to officially support or sponsor Hong Kong Pride because it was considered 'too political' and thus a potential business risk.

Pride organizers can choose to accept corporate sponsorship and then ignore the instructions or wishes of the sponsor. Kates and Belk (2001) argue that this approach to subverting, or repurposing, corporate sponsorship and advertising during Pride was evident in their research on Pride attendees in Toronto. My anecdote about obtaining a free Pride goodies bag at the New York Pride Luminaries Brunch also demonstrates how I subverted corporate sponsors' intentions to use the merchandize for advertising on social media. The organizers of Hong Kong Pride explained how they had subverted corporate sponsors' conditions in the aftermath of the large-scale 'Umbrella Movement' pro-democracy protests in 2014:

> One of our sponsors asked us to sign an agreement to be non-political. And we signed it, but we also did our event. And that year ... we invited those student leaders [from the Umbrella Movement] to be on our stage. And we discussed how we would answer if they [the sponsors] asked us why we were inviting them and we said we would answer that, in our interpretation, this is not political to invite them, but we would not explain it further. Finally, they didn't ask. So, I think it was just a gesture and they understand that we will do it our way.

As discussed above, Hong Kong Pride has struggled to attract significant and ongoing corporate sponsorship because of the perception it is 'too political'. This raises questions of whether the short-term tactic of subverting the wishes of sponsors to be 'non-political' led to reluctance to support and sponsor in the longer term. Corporate support for Pride places pressures on the nature and content of Pride and in politically tense contexts, seeks to restrict the ability of Pride to engage with broader political debates and human rights concerns. While there can be pragmatic workarounds for these issues, they are often not sustainable and corporations will back away if their wishes are not met.

Conclusion

After presenting a paper on the 'business of human rights' with Olimpia Burchiellaro at the 2024 International Studies Association (ISA), where we had criticized corporate involvement in human rights advocacy and presented many of the critiques discussed above, I was approached by a woman who introduced herself as the employee of a corporate and individual philanthropy organization. Somewhat perturbed, she asked, 'What do you expect corporations to do? What is a good model of corporate involvement in LGBT advocacy?' I have been posed this question numerous times by Pride organizers and LGBTQ+ corporate employees, many of whom feel frustrated, defensive and sometimes just puzzled, by queer academic critiques of their work. As previously discussed, I fully concur with Rao (2015) that corporate employee's agency is limited, as are Pride organizers and queer activists, and it is not my intention to criticize individual efforts to support or be involved in Pride, an event that can be very meaningful and enjoyable for LGBTQ+ people. Nor do I *necessarily* criticize Pride organizers' desire to obtain funding and support for the parade or associated events, with the proviso that Pride organizers need to have clear principles of engagement grounded in a social justice purpose. Pride should fully reflect, encompass and be inclusive of all the facets, intersections and precarities of the LGBTQ+ communities it is supposed to represent. My interlocutor at the ISA had added, 'Starbucks spent a lot of money on diversity training and it didn't achieve anything' and then implied the company would have been better off giving the money to Pride. I replied that I was unaware of the Starbucks case, but that the 'failure' of their diversity training was likely due to the low pay and poor employment conditions that Starbucks and similar companies are notorious for and that this was the point I was trying to make. Capitalism will not and cannot deliver liberation, equity and value every individual for their own inherent worth.

The incorporation of Pride by consumer capitalism has been aided by the decisions of early Pride organizers themselves, to eschew protest for alcohol fuelled street parties, and to enable the rainbow to be adopted by any institution or company. More than this, however, it is the growth and development of capitalism to first include women and people of colour as model employees and consumers, and then 'homocapitalism' that frames and addresses LGBTQ+ people in the same neoliberal terms. As this chapter has argued, the inclusion of LGBTQ+ identities and rights as part of a celebratory 'diversity talk' has gone further than the 'diversity talk' that ostensibly celebrated gender and race. This is because Pride has been an easily accessible platform for corporate and other institutions to parade in colourful, celebratory and happy ways, in terms that are not easily possible for the anti-racist movement, which tends to be characterized by anger and protest about ongoing injustice and inequality. This is further aided by the fact that a predominantly, albeit not exclusively, white, often male and educated sections of the LGBTQ+ community have been major beneficiaries from the turn to diversity and celebration of LGBTQ+ employees. These same groups have then themselves articulated this celebratory politics at the expense of LGBTQ+ people of colour, working class and other minoritized communities.

Ward writes: '[W]hat happens when diversity is no longer profitable?' (2008). Corporations have perennially retreated from spending on diversity and involvement in Pride in the face of an assertive backlash and pushback against LGBTQ+ rights and communities across the world. Corporations have always been reticent in their support for LGBTQ+ communities when there has been a need for political or legal rights to be articulated, and ultimately the pursuit of profit is the main rationale for all commercial organizations. I argue that the response to corporate involvement in Pride should not be one of gratitude, but to point to the logics of capitalism that make all individuals and communities dispensable should we no longer be perceived to be a profitable investment. The development of corporate social responsibility policies emerged in response to fears of activist attacks on business complicity and enablement of the racist system of apartheid in the highly profitable territory of the 1970s and 1980s South Africa. It is therefore unsurprising that contemporary diversity and inclusion policies and pronouncements should be framed in similar terms, to disavow ongoing racism, sexism and homophobia and to silence critics. As will be discussed in Chapter 6, there are examples of 'alternative' Prides that seek to celebrate LGBTQ+ identities but also to critique capitalism and its injustices, such as the Reclaim Pride movement and grassroots Prides in South Africa, Hong Kong and elsewhere. There are also examples where grassroots have accepted limited corporate funding and involvement on specific terms, or even subverted this funding for their own political ends. The evolution of Pride from protest to consumer capitalism is a major and ongoing matter of concern and should continue to be the focus for queer critique and protest.

Chapter 5

PRIDE, THE STATE AND RAINBOW DIPLOMACY

> Yes, it is a pinkwash, because we don't agree to open political liberties to the people, 'let's open this area here for all the gays, lesbians and trans people to show that we're a democratic country to the West'.
>
> – Isbel Diaz Torres, Cuban LGBTQ+ activist
> Havana (interview with the author, 2019)

'Sweden Loves Equality' was emblazed on the t-shirts worn by the marshals at Cape Town Pride in 2024. The embassy was a key financial partner of the event and had also held an LGBTQ+ film evening about queer representation in Swedish cinema and a drinks reception a few days before. In the Pride parade, there was a group of US diplomats carrying large US flags and wearing t-shirts with 'US Consulate General Cape Town supporting Pride'. While chatting to the US diplomats in the drinks tent at Greenpoint stadium, I noticed that the flags on their t-shirts had only 6 stars rather than the correct 50. Jamie, a junior diplomat at the consulate, laughed and said 'that's the thing, I issue passports, how am I supposed to know how to do t-shirt design?'. Talking more generally about diplomatic involvement in Pride, Jamie said 'It always falls on the LGBT staff to do the labour for LGBT rights. They just delegate it to us regardless of what our job role is and they can say they have demonstrated commitment to LGBT rights, whether they are committed to them or not'. Since 2012, the US State Department has mandated the reporting on LGBTQ+ rights in all the territories it is represented in and encourages diplomatic staff to be present at Pride events, but Jamie recalled the 'awkward coming out' conversation she had with a senior diplomat, who was unaware she was a lesbian and had assumed her spouse was a man, when they were discussing how to engage with Cape Town Pride. This senior diplomat had spoken from the stage of Cape Town Pride the year before, but he had said he 'felt uncomfortable' and would rather 'that an LGBT diplomat speak', 'but

Figure 13 'Sweden Loves Equality', Cape Town Pride marshall 2024.

he's exactly the sort of person that should be speaking at this event' said Jamie.

Western diplomats were a visible presence at almost all the Pride events I attended across the world, with rainbow national branding and slogans indicating their country's commitment to LGBTQ+ equality and rights. Yet the increase in international governments, NGOs and transnational organizations prioritizing LGBTQ+ rights has not been matched by material funding or always by meaningful action. In 2021, I was invited to participate, via Zoom, at an LGBTQ+ rights event held at the Swedish embassy in Kampala, Uganda. Two Swedish academics were organizing the event and spoke first, using a PowerPoint that presented graphs showing the increase in Western funding for international LGBTQ+ rights. I had seen this PowerPoint in advance and knowing that LGBTQ+ rights funding is a fraction of, already limited, broader human rights and development budgets, I wondered how this information would be received by Ugandan activists. It quickly became clear they were not happy and disputed these figures. 'We don't see any of this money', said an activist who had been involved in Pride Uganda, 'when Western funders talk about our lack of capacity as a reason we can't access funding, how can we build capacity without money, and without money to eat or live?' Other activists talked about how they struggled to get employment in the NGO sector, while they saw Western LGBTQ+ advocacy professionals building successful careers and talking at international forums on their behalf. The organizer of Pride Uganda also criticized Western governments that classified HIV/AIDS funding in Africa as LGBTQ+ advocacy, when unlike in Europe and North America, HIV is predominantly spread via heterosexual sex in Africa. The Ugandan activists' responses were the result of lack of consideration for the local context by the Swedish academics who prepared the opening remarks, but it also revealed the fact that the very visible presence of Western embassies at international Pride events is not matched by material support, and the material support given can cause division between LGBTQ+ activists and discriminate against queer activists who do not have the capacity to meet the funders' criteria.

Western governments have proven to be capricious and unreliable LGBTQ+ rights advocates. The UK government adopted a markedly pro-LGBTQ+ rights foreign policy position under the premierships of David Cameron and Theresa May, the latter announcing record funding for a project to tackle homophobia in Africa. Yet this funding was quietly cancelled by May's successor, Boris Johnson, and a UK-hosted international conference on LGBTQ+ rights dramatically collapsed after being sabotaged by the Johnson government weeks before it was due to be held (Waites, 2024). Germany, Sweden and the United States have also seen dramatic changes in foreign policy relating to LGBTQ+ and gender rights, and inconsistent framings of feminist and LGBTQ+ commitments when they do exist. Asylum policies and procedures are also disproportionately harsh and challenging for LGBTQ+ individuals seeking asylum in Western states (Lopes Heimer, 2020; Murray, 2014). Despite the actions and swift changes in human rights policy by national governments, individual diplomats continue to demonstrate meaningful commitment to LGBTQ+ rights advocacy, can ignore the removal of national commitments to LGBTQ+ rights and can make dramatic differences to grassroots LGBTQ+ activists and enable Pride events. However, these individual commitments are haphazard and subject to change with changes in staff alongside just the sheer lack of time and conflicting priorities in diplomats' working lives.

Rainbow diplomacy

International advocacy of LGBTQ+ rights by politicians and foreign ministries and diplomatic involvement in and support for Pride events has become a significant factor in global politics. The complexities and contradictions of Pride symbolizing freedom, progressiveness and modernity have been used by multiple states. The advocacy of LGBTQ+ rights by Western states and their admonition of homophobic states in the Global South have been criticized by queer academics as being 'homocolonialist' (Rahman, 2014) and, as with the criticism of international corporations pro-LGBT stances, viewed as hypocritical and part of a 'civilising mission' (Rao, 2014). The inclusion and mainstreaming of sexual orientation and gender identity (SOGI) rights have become a defining, albeit a contingent and sometimes sidelined, feature of the foreign policies of several European, North American and Oceanic states (Langlois, 2022). Sweden and the Netherlands have included LGBTQ+ rights among their foreign policy priorities since the mid-2000s. The United States adopted a commitment to LGBTQ+ rights as an international priority in 2011, with President Obama pledging to 'put American diplomacy at the service of the global promotion of gay rights' (Encarnación, 2016). The UK's passing of same-sex marriage act in 2013 was accompanied by Prime Minister David Cameron's pledge to 'export gay marriage around the world' with a new emphasis on LGBTQ+ diplomacy and a particular focus on the Commonwealth (Rao, 2020). The prioritization of LGBTQ+ rights can sit alongside the emergence of 'feminist foreign policies', as is the case with Canada's 2017 'feminist international assistance policy' (Parisi, 2020). In the Global South, Brazil was the first country through its Department of Foreign Affairs to propose a normative test on LGBTQ+ rights and took pro-active international leadership on LGBTQ+ rights promotion (Nogueira, 2017). The Equal Rights Coalition was founded in 2016 by forty-three states to help inform and coordinate pro-LGBTQ+ diplomatic work. Despite these foreign policy commitments, contradictions and policy reversals have been commonplace. Reversals of policy and funding commitments to LGBTQ+ rights advocacy have happened in recent years following changes of government in the United States, the United Kingdom, the Netherlands and Brazil. Commitments to LGBTQ+ rights can belie a lack of actual funding and even rhetorical support can be reversed following changes of government or policy.

Since 2012, US embassies have been required to engage with outreach and engagement, with Pride recommended as a focus. In 2017, the US State Department issued guidance saying embassies could recognize LGBTQ+ Pride month and this continued even under the first Trump Presidency (Burack, 2018). Canada, Sweden, the Netherlands and the EU are a visible presence at many Pride events internationally. In 2018, the British LGBTQ+ organization Stonewall produced a guide for UK diplomats recommending showing solidarity by flying a rainbow flag or lighting the embassy in rainbow colours, offering in-kind support and attending Pride. UK diplomats can draw from development funding focused on gender and human rights, the British Council's resources and the 'Britain is Great' branding to use 'Love is Great' and rainbow-branded UK flags (Khambay and Dorey, 2018). Participation in Pride parades by diplomats, accompanied by rainbow versions of their national flags and LGBTQ+ rights slogans, is a visual representation of support, but it can also be done without any financial or other diplomatic commitments to advance LGBTQ+ rights in the host society.

Western states' pro-LGBTQ+ diplomacy has been critiqued by queer scholars who point out the hypocrisy of many states' international stances. Criticisms have focused on the imperfect legal and social conditions for LGBTQ+ communities in Global North states and the 'homocolonialist' (Rahman, 2014) implications of framing new standards of 'civilization' and 'modernity' by which to judge their former colonies and other societies in the Global South (Delatolla, 2020). For example, Encarnacion argues that the United States 'should not be the face of the effort to sell gay rights to the developing world' because of its own poor record on LGBTQ+ rights and the evidence of significant 'backlashes' which include a rise in homo- and transphobic legislation in the aftermath of US LGBTQ+ rights diplomacy (Encarnación, 2016: 21–2). Assuming that Global North states are vectors of LGBTQ+ tolerance and rights advancement can overlook hostility to LGBTQ+ rights within Global North states (Browne and Nash, 2014). Transnational conservative networks, such as the World Congress of Families and Evangelical Christian churches, are also based in the Global North, and advocate homophobia transnationally in the Global South and East and often target Pride events (Ayoub and Stoeckl, 2024). The practice of assessing LGBTQ+ progress based on the legal right to same-sex marriage has also been criticized for its reductionism and homonormativity (Delatolla, 2020). For queer critics, judging LGBTQ+ rights performance on the basis of Western norms of LGBTQ+ identity and legal codes of monogamous marriage typifies the colonial assumptions of Western states.

As discussed in Chapters 2 and 3, queer critics of the Global North's LGBTQ+ rights have singled out Pride as an example of 'homocolonialism', 'homonationalism' and as a vehicle to pay lip service to Western norms of LGBTQ+ legal rights. As such, these critics argue states use Pride and LGBTQ+ rights discourses to 'rainbow wash' their foreign and domestic policies. Franke (2012) and Schulman (2012a) detail Israeli state sponsorship of and visible presence at North American Pride parades, alongside the heavy marketing of Tel Aviv as an international LGBTQ+ tourist destination. This was to 'rebrand Israel', particularly for the 18–30-year-old demographic in Europe and North America, and to distract from Israeli domestic and regional policies. Slootmaeckers (2017) documents how Serbia organized a 'ghost Pride' to portray the state as suitable for EU membership. Similarly, Franke (2012) discusses how Romania obscured the country's poor record on women's and Roma community rights when demonstrating its progressive 'Europeanness' by organizing a Pride parade. Canada's presence at Pride parades across the world, with rainbow Canadian flags, belies the fact that Canada spends less on development aid than UN-recommended goals, and barely more than the UK's modest budget on LGBTQ+ rights advocacy (Othen-Reeves, 2020). Canada's 2017 commitment to a 'feminist international assistance policy' was not met by an increase in funding and was contradicted by an increase in defence spending, with arms sales agreed to anti-LGBTQ+ states such as Saudi Arabia (Brown and Swiss, 2017). Delatolla (2020) witnessed the Canadian embassy actively encouraging skilled immigration at Tokyo Pride in 2018 by their active promotion of Canada as an 'open and welcoming space for the LGBTQ+ community', yet argues that this obscures Canada's hostile policies and practices towards LGBTQ+ asylum seekers. Queer critics thus consider diplomatic involvement in Pride not as an example of the positive advancement of LGBTQ+ rights and protection of communities, but rather the homocolonial and homonationalist rainbow washing of Global North states' poor record on LGBTQ+ and broader human rights.

A debate has emerged in response to these queer critiques of LGBTQ+ diplomacy. Burack (2018) argues that queer criticisms of diplomatic efforts to support and advance LGBTQ+ rights discount the genuine intentions that diplomats and policymakers have to advance LGBTQ+ rights internationally. Rainer (2021: 31–2) acknowledges

Figure 14 Canada at Taiwan Pride 2018.

that 'while American ambassadors march in foreign LGBTI Pride parades, the LGBTI equality movement faces powerful opposition at home', but argues that US diplomats listen to local grassroots activists on whether to speak out on LGBTQ+ rights or not, and can provide valuable funding and support when needed (Rainer, 2021: 83). As with LGBTQ+ corporate employees, Rao (2015) acknowledges the structural constraints and limited agency that institutional LGBTQ+ advocates face, and that it is important to acknowledge and explore the constraints and agency such advocates can have. Given diplomats' restricted agency, the complex interplay between personal beliefs, foreign policy priorities and limited budgets should be analysed in relation to the ideological, financial and symbolic outcomes created by rainbow diplomacy.

The individual agency, interests and identities of diplomats can lead to significant foreign policy change. Individual prioritization of LGBTQ+ rights and civil society engagement are a key factor when diplomatic missions become involved in or demonstrate commitment to LGBTQ+ rights. These individual interventions can make significant impact in a local and international context. Neumann writes that the mainstay of diplomacy is reporting back to the home foreign ministry and that 'different people, with different social traits, will report different things, so one key issue concerns in what measure such differences result in different outcomes' (Neumann, 2012: 131–2). Individual diplomats have had significant impacts on national foreign policy. For example, Brazil's international leadership on SOGI issues emerged somewhat unexpectedly, following the individual initiatives of mid-ranking LGBTQ+ Brazilian diplomats at the UN who had drafted an LGBTQ+ rights proposal that quickly gained international and high-level Brazilian support (Nogueira, 2017).

That moral, ethical and human rights commitments would be premised on individual conviction and belief is perhaps not surprising, but it can create inherently precarious foreign policy commitments, particularly towards LGBTQ+ rights. The Stonewall report on LGBTQ+ advocacy by the UK Foreign Commonwealth and Development Office (FCDO) quoted a diplomat who said 'one of the challenges with all diplomatic missions is consistency. There is very little institutional memory that transfers with change in leadership, so we have to start from scratch' (Khambay and Dorey, 2018: 19). This inconsistency was aided by frequent diplomatic rotations. When diplomats committed to LGBTQ+ rights move post, the embassy's focus on LGBTQ+ rights can be lost, with financial and other implications for local civil society. The FCDO staff that spoke to Stonewall also said they needed more support and capacity to work on LGBTQ+ rights and that such work could feel like an additional 'task' on top of already heavy workloads. Without clear and consistent leadership from the national foreign ministry with the resources to support LGBTQ+ rights work, commitments to and involvement in rainbow diplomacy can quickly fall away.

The Global North as unreliable LGBTQ+ allies

When Western diplomats engage in Pride, and support LGBTQ+ activism, they are balancing different and sometimes contradictory goals and interests. Previous research has shown that despite rhetorical commitments to LGBTQ+ human rights by states like Canada, UK and the Nordic countries, other strategic, military or economic priorities often override LGBTQ+ concerns, and relatively little money is spent on LGBTQ+ issues. According to the Global Philanthropy Project, funds directed to LGBTQ+ projects and organizations were equivalent to 4 cents out of every $100 of total worldwide official development assistance (ODA) in 2021–2. The two largest per capita donors to

LGBTQ+ purposes, the Netherlands and Sweden, spent only 0.47 per cent and 0.17 per cent, respectively, of their development budgets on LGBTQ+ advocacy and support in 2021–2 (Global Philathropy Project, 2024). Commitments to funding international LGBTQ+ advocacy and support may be cancelled following changes in government ministers, or political opposition to such funding. National and foreign policy claims to support LGBTQ+ rights must be assessed against the actual material commitments underpinning these claims for support.

Foreign policy commitments to LGBTQ+ rights can rapidly change and be cancelled. The UK announced a major LGBTQ+ funding initiative to tackle homophobia in Africa in 2018 and this funding was abruptly cancelled in 2020 (Othen-Reeves, 2020). In 2024, the German government's plans to devote funding to international human rights advocacy, including LGBTQ+ rights, were stopped following a judgement by the German constitutional court cancelling the budget (Arnold, 2023).

In 2019, the Cuban government, which provided the oblique reason of 'regional tensions', abruptly cancelled the Cuban equivalent of Pride, the Conga for the International Day against Homophobia, Transphobia and Biphobia. Other activities about LGBTQ+ rights continued as usual, including the official Conga afterparty and an LGBTQ+ film festival held by the organizer of the Conga, Senator Dr Mariela Castro Espín, Director of the Centre for Sexual Education (CENESEX) and the Swedish and Norwegian embassies. It was clear from social media that a number of Cuban LGBTQ+ activists were angry with the Cuban government for cancelling the Conga and decided to organize an 'unofficial' Conga march. I attended the march on Saturday and a few hundred Cuban activists sang and waved large rainbow flags as they marched through the streets of Havana. All was well until we reached the Malecon which stretched along the bay. The activists had intended to walk along the Malecon and 'gatecrash' Mariela Castro Espin's official afterparty. At this point, a large group of older men in baseball caps appeared almost from nowhere and the marchers at the front were picked up on all fours and bundled into police cars. Two coachloads of police arrived and as they poured out scuffles and fights started. It transpired that more activists had been arrested before the march began and had spent the previous night in police custody. Castro-Espín later branded the marchers as 'counter-revolutionaries' and accused them of being sponsored by Cuba's enemies in Miami. Given that the Norwegian and Swedish embassies were official partners of CENESEX and advocate human rights as part of their foreign policies, I was interested to find out what position diplomats involved in the LGBTQ+ film festival thought and did, if anything, about the situation. A diplomat at the Swedish embassy in Cuba explained that no position was taken on the situation:

> It is definitely a tough one for an Embassy; we can't really take a stand on one of those issues […] of course we have to, in order to work here and in order to do all the different things that we do in Cuba, we do need to have good relationships. Good relationship with the Cuban regime and good doesn't necessarily mean that we agree. It does mean that we need to be able to work and that does mean, also, cooperating with the [Cuban] Culture Ministry. We've been doing this Film Festival together with them. There are several advantages to that. They are the ones with access to all of the cinemas […] I'm very sure that good diplomacy can find ways to not only support one side and to manoeuvre a difficult situation like that. It takes some skills. It is challenging.

The diplomat went on to further explain that the duty of the embassy was to 'report' on issues to Stockholm, rather than take an active stance and get involved in them on the ground. This was also the position the Norwegian embassy. LGBTQ+ activists are aware of such competing priorities and that these may overshadow LGBTQ+ support. Over the following months the activists who had arrested continued to be harassed and the ones I spoke to now live in exile. While the events surrounding the 'unofficial' Conga, which was one of the first illegal protests in post-revolutionary Cuba, were complex and challenging for diplomatic partners, the LGBTQ+ activists arrested should have received more support from the Swedish and Norwegian embassies, even if it was behind the scenes advocacy on their behalf, given those national government's purported commitments to human rights.

In 2019, the UK Parliament's Global LGBT Rights All-Party Parliamentary Group held a special session on LGBTQ+ rights in the Commonwealth followed by a discussion at the FCDO. At the events, much was made about the 'leadership' the UK had ostensibly taken on tackling homophobia in Commonwealth countries. Yet on the walk between parliament and the FCDO, one of the activists who was based in a Commonwealth country where homosexuality was illegal, explained that efforts to hold any event on LGBTQ+ rights at the UK High Commission in the country had been met with resistance and refusal from the diplomatic staff. The cancellation of the UK's LGBTQ+ international funding commitments in 2021, and the subsequent cancellation of an international LGBTQ+ rights conference due to be hosted by the UK government in 2022, caused consternation in LGBTQ+ activist communities, and several activists have told me that they had lost confidence in the UK as a dependable ally.

LGBTQ+ rights foreign policy commitments sit alongside and are often superseded by trade and economic diplomatic goals. In the previous chapter, I discussed how transnational corporations based in the Global North frame LGBTQ+ rights as a 'homocapitalist' good for economic good for staff productivity and accessing new markets. As partial and flawed as this rationale is, Global North states do not frame LGBTQ+ rights in terms of the economic value and trade opportunities they deliver. They are framed in Human Rights terms and are frequently relegated and dispensed with should they clash with trade priorities. I suspect this reveals the essential shallowness of 'homocapitalism' and whereas business can pick and choose which territories to rainbow brand products and become involved in Pride and where to remain invisible and silent, states realize that foreign and trade policies are less agile than individual businesses and the 'homocapitalist' articulation of foreign trade policies could jeopardize and prevent their ability to freely trade. It is also possibly why active engagement with LGBTQ+ advocacy and participation at Pride is often delegated to junior diplomats, or LGBTQ+ diplomats regardless of their job role or other commitments, rather than more senior diplomats who do the 'serious' work of negotiating trade and security policies. Speaking with a mid-ranking gay UK diplomat in India, who wanted to emphasize the UK High Commissioner's support for being involved in Mumbai Pride, I asked if the High Commissioner had ever made a direct representation to the Indian government for LGBTQ+ rights when homosexuality had been illegal and he replied that the issue had not been raised. Ultimately, the UK's priority was for good trade and security relations. Relatedly, a Taiwanese LGBTQ+ activist expressed a sense that Western allies could not be trusted to maintain their support if LGBTQ+ rights conflicted with other priorities:

> Unfortunately, we live in a capitalist world. Everything is about money, so I think the foreign affairs offices are still thinking about trade and economy a lot more than human rights, which is stupid of them.

Thus, tracking actual financial commitments to these policies and exploring how consistently (or not) LGBTQ+ advocacy is applied across diplomatic missions reveals that when pitted against other priorities, such as trade or security, LGBTQ+ rights can be easily sidelined. Furthermore, changes in government, or societal or political hostility to funding on LGBTQ+ rights can lead to the deprioritization of LGBTQ+ diplomacy.

Pride and managing (in)visibility

As discussed in Chapter 2, Pride epitomizes the struggle for LGBTQ+ visibility. Visibility and collectively 'coming out' are not always desirable or legally possible, and can place LGBTQ+ individuals and communities at the risk of hostile reactions from the state or other actors. LGBTQ+ activists often negotiate the benefits and dangers of visibility through multiple strategies, which may include 'strategic invisibility', as is the case in many African, Middle Eastern and Asian contexts (Currier, 2011; Olouch and Tabengwa, 2017). International diplomats engaging in Pride negotiate complex dynamics of visibility and a lack of sensitivity or awareness can be counterproductive.

Diplomatic engagement in Pride can be very public, and visible diplomatic support for LGBTQ+ rights is controversial. At almost every Pride parade I attended I saw diplomats marching with large banners and often rainbow-themed national flags. This was particularly the case for Canada, the United Kingdom and the United States. However, Western states involvement in international Pride events have been criticized by queer critics. Encarnacion argues that the United States' advocacy of LGBTQ+ rights internationally were counterproductive, because they endangered activists in Uganda and Kenya, justified the belief that LGBTQ+ identities are Western and 'un-African' and gave rise to homophobic legislation across a number of African states (Encarnación, 2016). This claim is contested by other authors, such as Rainer (2021) and Burack (2018), who argue that open diplomatic support for LGBTQ+ rights can provide a vital lifeline for grassroots LGBTQ+ activists.

At Taiwan Pride, a significant contingency from the European Union's office was present with EU rainbow flags, and the EU representative stood on the Pride float of a local NGO. The EU office published an article in a Taiwanese newspaper before Pride, about its human rights work, encouraging people to come to Pride. According to an EU diplomat, the EU's visible participation in Pride was appreciated by local LGBTQ+ activists:

> People who are involved in this issue, they're very happy that we do things like this to help […] They are happy that there is an international community presence there.

According to diplomats, visible manifestations in support of LGBTQ+ rights enacted by embassies were primarily intended to empower and inspire LGBTQ+ people locally, by showing that they have international backing. A Swedish diplomat in Cuba elaborated:

> I do believe that what we've done is we've shown that Sweden and Norway, we are committed to these issues [...] We have managed to be a voice, especially on social media, for LGBTQI rights. I do think people have seen that on Facebook, for example, and hopefully people have felt that they're not alone in this. The LGBTQ community is local, but it's also a global one and we are fighting some of the same struggles and we can learn from each other and we can help each other in these battles. Hopefully we've inspired a bit and we've lightened a few hearts and shown that it might be very difficult now but keep fighting.

Visible support for LGBTQ+ rights by Western diplomats can also have unintended, negative consequences. It may reinforce and confirm narratives of LGBTQ+ identities as a foreign, Western phenomenon. Diplomatic pro-LGBTQ+ visibility may be perceived as illegitimate outside interference in domestic politics, something diplomats were aware of. For example, an EU diplomat in Taiwan spoke about being surprised when the EU ambassador publicly encouraged people to vote in favour of two pro-LGBTQ+ bills in a 2018 referendum, as there had previously been internal hesitation about whether the EU could take a public position on how Taiwanese people should vote. The EU's representative changed her mind after speaking with local LGBTQ+ activists. The same diplomat argued that visible Western pressure on LGBTQ+ issues can impact local legislators who want to be seen positively by the international community, but can also cement impressions that LGBTQ+ rights are imposed by Western states in 'homocolonial' terms:

> On our Facebook page, there's always comments that are very, very negative. Every time we post something on human rights, especially on the death penalty and on LGBTI, there will be comments saying it does not apply here. This is Western, this is European and don't tell us what to do.

The visibility of rainbow diplomacy can create risks. Shanghai Pride often used the spaces and support of Western consulates and cultural organizations, such as the British Council and Goethe Institute, for funding, discussion events, film screenings and exhibitions. For a long time, this had provided a safe space free from official interference. However, in 2018 a Twitter/X account linked to the Chinese authorities had warned people to not attend LGBTQ+ events 'at foreign embassies', and the police had arrived at an event hosted by an international consulate.

Rainbow branding national identity

Pride has become a potent political symbol in national identity construction, geopolitical claims and public diplomacy. Hosting Pride can be a way to manifest a 'modern' progressive, European or Western identity, to both domestic and international audiences, as shown in research on Israel and candidate EU accession states. Indeed, when I began researching Pride in 2018, I noticed how Tel Aviv Pride started to be consistently advertised on my Facebook and Instagram feeds. I came to realize that this evidenced Sarah Schulman's (2012a) research on the Israeli government's funding and promotion of Tel Aviv Pride and its marketing to European and North American audience in an effort to change perceptions of Israel and convince foreign audiences that the state was a beacon of liberal tolerance in the Middle East (see also, Press-Barnathan and Lutz, 2020).

As discussed above, Senator Dr Mariela Castro Espín organizes the Conga, the equivalent of Pride in Havana. Castro Espín is the niece of Fidel Castro and daughter of Raul Castro and the feminist activist Wilma Espín, and pictures of her in a pink vintage Cadillac at the front of the parade surrounded by rainbow flags have been regularly disseminated across the web and in international media (Kirk, 2017). Each year, Castro Espín's CENESEX centre invites and awards an international LGBTQ+ activist. In 2019, although there was no Conga parade, the veteran US LGBTQ+ and AIDS activist Cleve Jones was given the award at a gala event the evening before the Conga was due to have taken place. Giving one of the original rainbow flags made by Gilbert Baker to Castro Espín, Jones called for an end to the US economic sanctions and travel restrictions against Cuba. Isbel Diaz Torres is an LGBTQ+ anarchist environmental activist and was one of the people arrested the evening before the Conga. I spoke to him after he had been released and asked him if he thought the Conga was a 'pinkwash' of Cuba's national identity. He replied, 'It's a pinkwash, yes, that's what it is, but not only that … I don't want to sound so hyper-critical about it but I have to be critical in a way, because I'm not saying it's only like a pink wash but it's part of the deal.' Torres acknowledged that having Castro Espín as an LGBTQ+ advocate 'opens a lot of doors' and 'no one else would have been listened to by the government'. Castro Espín's doctoral thesis was on trans rights and she has been instrumental in positively changing the law for trans people in Cuba. Torres acknowledged that Castro Espín was committed to LGBTQ+ rights, but that ultimately, she was 'a Castro', 'part of the regime' and is a 'straight ally', not LGBTQ+. Torres continued:

> But the government is a different thing. They say we are heterosexual, we are sexist, we're macho, we don't like that [LGBTQ+ rights], but we want to get inserted in the logic of the world. We want to be accepted in Europe and other countries, the US etc. So then we need to show a different part of Cuban society. Since we don't agree to open political liberties to the people, let's open this area here for the gay, lesbians and trans people, just to show that we are a democratic country. It works like that too. Of course, the Conga is very important. We've got the space where you can match with other countries. You can show, okay, we're exactly the same as you.

Torres had established a queer anarchist community centre with a small events space and library and was a notable commentator on LGBTQ+ rights in the country and beyond. Along with others involved in the 'unofficial' Conga, he was branded 'counter-revolutionary' and faced further harassment from the police. He and his partner left Cuba and now live in Florida. The Cuban Conga for the International Day against Homophobia, Transphobia and Biphobia is not entirely superficial and meaningless, but nor does it embrace the LGBTQ+ community and issues in its entirety. When a group of LGBTQ+ activists held their own Pride march, they were arrested. While Castro Espín may be personally committed to LGBTQ+ rights and can evidence having changed certain aspects of Cuban law, the presentation of the Conga regionally and internationally feeds into broader geopolitical Cuban aims, particularly in relation to its hostile neighbour, the United States. Like other states, such as Israel, the Conga helps present Cuba as more progressive, liberal and free than it actually is.

'Queer Friendly Taipei', says a poster promoting the 2006 Taiwan Pride. The Taiwanese Ministry of Foreign Affairs encourages its international missions to publicize Taiwan Pride not only as evidence of the island's progressiveness, but to buttress more profound claims for the acknowledgement of Taiwan's international sovereignty and stress its difference from mainland China. Taiwan lacks recognized statehood at the UN and has few formal diplomatic ties. In 2019, Taiwan legalized same-sex marriage rights and it has a groundbreaking Gender Equity Education Act. Taiwan Pride has grown to be the largest in Asia with 140,000 people marching through Taipei's streets. Despite the Taiwanese government periodically using LGBTQ+ rights as a means to attract the attention of international institutions and governments, Nai-Chia and Fell argue that the country 'does not have a sophisticated … LGBT rights foreign policy agenda … it should be understood as the product of both government and nongovernmental forces' (Nai-Chia and Fell, 2021). A former Taiwanese diplomat explained how the Ministry of Foreign Affairs would promote Taiwan Pride through their international missions' channels and that Taiwanese diplomats would tell their counterparts in Europe and North America, 'see, we're an open society, a free society. People can do whatever they want, we are different from China … because we value freedom and we value human rights'. This strategy has the support and significant participation of many in Taiwanese LGBTQ+ civil society. Yi, a human rights activist with Amnesty explained:

> I personally think that human rights are a great way to distinguish that Taiwan is not part of China: 'We're very different. We are a lot more like you guys [the West] and so you guys should help us so we don't get bullied by China all the time'.

In the aftermath of the Taiwanese Constitutional Court instructing the government to pass same-sex marriage in 2017, the Taiwanese government sponsored a significant contingent of LGBTQ+ activists, including Jennifer Lu, a leading campaigner for LGBTQ+ marriage rights, to attend World Pride held in New York in 2019. Carrying a large banner proclaiming 'Taiwan: The First in Asia!' in the parade, the government had also sponsored an exhibition held in Manhattan called 'The Wedding Banquet' that told the story of LGBTQ+ rights in Taiwan alongside holding a number of public events to discuss LGBTQ+ rights progress in the country. Merchandize including t-shirts, posters and towels depicted a map of Asia with a large arrow pointing to the island of Taiwan coloured in rainbow with the slogan 'Taiwan: The First in Asia!' Jennifer Lu has been sponsored by the Taiwanese government to speak at multiple international forums on LGBTQ+ rights and the

5. Pride, the State and Rainbow Diplomacy

Figure 15 Taiwan, First in Asia.

Taiwanese LGBTQ+ contingency at World Pride made clear and bold visual and human rights discourse claims for Taiwan's recognition as an independent state in Asia and one that was part of the Global North community, and not part of China.

There are contradictions and criticisms of Taiwan's presentation of itself as a vanguard of LGBTQ+ and wider human rights. A former Taiwanese diplomat explained that when Taiwanese ambassadors used human rights to distinguish Taiwan from China, she had felt: 'they're not thinking about what it means' and gave the example that Taiwan continues to use the death penalty with no plans to abolish it. She also worried that the Ministry of Foreign Affairs' highlighting of Taiwan's LGBTQ+ rights record may make other human rights problems invisible: 'they [the international community] will think that there's nothing to worry about here, while there's still a lot to be worried about'. For example, Taiwan has punitive laws criminalizing HIV+ people who have sex (Taiwan [PRC], no date). The Constitutional Court had ordered same-sex marriage in 2017, but the government of President Tsai had been slow to enact the legislation and the main conservative opposition party, alongside a campaign sponsored by US

Evangelical Churches, had petitioned for an advisory referendum on same-sex marriage and the Gender Equality Education Act. At Taiwan Pride in 2018, many activists were angry with Tsai's government and believed high-profile activists had been too willing to collaborate with Taiwan's disingenuous rainbow diplomacy. The subsequent referendum rejected same-sex marriage and the Gender Equality Education Act. Although this did not prevent the passing of same-sex marriage into law the following year, it demonstrated a lack of societal support for LGBTQ+ and gender rights. Kao (2024) disputes the queer critique of homocapitalism, homonationalism and homonormativity in relation to Taiwan's same-sex marriage laws. Kao argues that these criticisms do not take account of the perspectives of local LGBTQ+ rights activists, or the socio-economic conditions of Taiwan, which, unlike the United States, include universal healthcare and greater equality. Kao also argues that Taiwanese LGBTQ+ rights advocates are 'far removed' from the privileged elites of Western EDI and LGBTQ+ policy elites (Kao, 2024). As will be discussed in the next chapter, Taiwan Pride is much more inclusive, attendant to grassroots issues and intersectional causes than most Western Pride events. Taiwan Pride is the largest in the region and is organized by volunteers. While it is true that Taiwan's gender and LGBTQ+ rights extend beyond same-sex marriage and there is an excellent public health service, I did speak with local Taiwanese activists who expressed concerns about the existence of death penalty, gaps in LGBTQ+ protections and also complained about the high cost of living, particularly for young people. Jennifer Lu, Taiwan's pre-eminent advocate for same-sex marriage rights, has spoken on numerous corporate and international LGBTQ+ advocacy platforms and is now a senior manager at Outright in New York. Lu is very much part of the LGBTQ+ global elite. Taiwan's presentation as a beacon of LGBTQ+ rights thus belies both contradictions in human rights law in the country and a lack of domestic political will and broader popular support for LGBTQ+ rights.

There was awareness by some diplomats about critiques of Western 'homocolonialism' (Rahman, 2014) and a desire to refute the narratives of the West as imposing its own model of LGBTQ+ rights. A Swedish diplomat in Cuba, having arranged screenings of Swedish LGBTQ+ films, said:

> That was actually very important to me to avoid that as much as possible. I really do believe that we are often seen, the Nordic countries are often seen as the blueprint and that goes for Europe and

the West in general […]. I refuse to believe that and I refuse to see us as that blueprint. I think that we have so much to learn from others and how other countries have chosen, the paths they've chosen or been forced upon to go down […] To me it is very important to step out of that perfect picture of Sweden and Norway.

Similarly, in the days before Cape Town Pride in 2024, the Swedish embassy held a well-attended film screening about queer representation in Swedish film. The deputy ambassador repeatedly stressed that Sweden was not a model of LGBTQ+ equality and that he wanted dialogue and to learn from South African LGBTQ+ communities. Such critical self-reflection and learning are also reflected in recent policy changes by Western states, such as Canada's 'do no harm' principle, and an awareness that the West's open support for local LGBTQ+ activists can sometimes put them at risk, as happened to two Bangladeshi LGBTQ+ activists who were supported by the United States and were killed in 2016 (Siddiqi, 2019). Whereas many diplomats were clearly aware of risks and expressed both modesty and self-reflection, I heard other Western diplomats explaining that 'we have a good story to tell about LGBT rights'. To some extent, much LGBTQ+ diplomacy is still implicitly guided by a 'leveraged pedagogy' (Kulpa, 2014) where LGBTQ+ rights promotion remains a mostly one-directional process of transferring Western experiences and supporting activists in accordance with Western standards and expectations of LGBTQ+ liberation. While 'learning from each other' is an argument made by some diplomats, the focus of LGBTQ+ diplomacy is largely on the promotion of LGBTQ+ rights 'elsewhere', rather developing genuine cross dialogues, learning or applying experiences from other contexts in the diplomats' home state. Efforts of individual diplomats to make Rainbow Diplomacy a more egalitarian and mutual process were constrained by structural factors such as lack of leadership, funding and consistency over time.

Supporting grassroots activism and advocacy

There was a strong emphasis on the importance for international actors to follow the lead of local activists among the diplomats and foreign policy officials I spoke to. Diplomats' support and cooperation with local activist groups are therefore important foci for analysis. While this was a shared discourse among Western diplomats, it was particularly explicit in the case of Swedish LGBTQ+ diplomacy. As argued by Svennson, Edenborg and Strand (2024), the principle of 'local ownership' is considered central to Sweden's promotion of LGBTQ+ rights in foreign and development policy. The idea was emphasized by a diplomat at the Swedish embassy in Cuba, speaking about the embassy's support of a local LGBTQ+ organization:

> Through a workshop with them [local activists] and through close collaboration with them, they've taken the reigns and they've really been the ones leading this project [...] To me it's been very important to make sure that there was a Cuban ownership and there was a local ownership.

Similarly, a diplomat at the EU embassy in Taiwan spoke about the EU's funding of LGBTQ+ events, organized by local activists.

> We have this budget for human rights issues and we would always use them to have events with the NGOs, with the local NGOs. We cannot do it by ourselves, we have to contract it to another party and do it together with them [...] We're, in a way, helping the NGOs to amplify their voices.

The emphasis on local activists having agency and leading change reflects a more general discursive trend in international LGBTQ+ promotion. For some years, NGOs, scholars and even states have stressed the need to move from top-down models where donors decide the priorities, and instead support activists on their own terms. As expressed in a recent report by the, now defunct, US Agency for International Development: 'follow the lead of local LGBTQI+ activists and groups and act with humility and in allyship' (USAID, 2023). Following criticism that Western states are pushing their LGBTQ+ agendas onto Global South contexts in neocolonial ways, recent expert and civil society reports have recommended how foreign policy and development frameworks can be made more inclusive and how LGBTQ+ activists can be supported (Rainer et al., 2021).

The ambition to empower local activists presents its own challenges. First, grassroots groups, without sophisticated governance and reporting structures, can be disqualified from obtaining diplomatic funding, and diplomats can be prevented from committing to open-ended funding, making meaningful and long-term support difficult.

5. Pride, the State and Rainbow Diplomacy 135

Decisions about which groups should be supported for funding and visibility rely on the time and expertise to develop knowledge of the local activist and NGO landscape. Even in contexts where LGBTQ+ activism is marginalized and small-scale, queer LGBTQ+ civil society is multivocal, heterogeneous and often conflictual. Since commencing this research, I have regularly been asked for advice by diplomats in South Africa, about whom to fund, which Prides to attend and about my knowledge of the local context for LGBTQ+ organizing. I have welcomed these requests and have often been able to help, but it does reveal the partial knowledge diplomats often have about local LGBTQ+ civil society and their limited time and resources to gain a sufficient understanding.

When some activist groups are chosen for support over others, certain identities, political orientations and strategies are also privileged. Groups deploying language and strategies drawing on models of activism that are predominant in Western countries, such as universal human rights discourse, public advocacy work and LGBTQ+ terminology, are more likely to be recognized and intelligible to Western diplomats, and to receive support and funding. Groups lacking the resources to network with Western actors, using vernacular terminologies or prioritizing questions that are not part of the Western LGBTQ+ 'toolbox', may have a harder time to get allies among Western diplomats. In Mumbai, an elite of high caste and financially privileged LGBTQ+ activists has reinforced long-standing caste divides. An Indian queer activist explained:

> These diplomatic partners privilege some people over others. Some of these organizations have become the who's who of queer movement in India and most of them are upper caste … If I give a proposal to the Canadian Embassy, I don't think my proposal will get accepted. What these people talk about is what LGBT rights in India are compatible with what these countries think of LGBT rights. So for example: marriage – caste is not an issue in the West. I don't think any of these issues would translate, the West wouldn't think of caste pitching in.

A UK diplomat in Shanghai suggested that there was a tension between local activists' priorities and what the UK government was willing to support:

> They were mainly focusing on throwing parties and doing lots of fun stuff, but because of the nature of our funding, obviously as a

government, we would want to have much more policy advocacy roles in the project ... So, we had a chat and then kind of helped structure the Pride a bit more in-depth and into more panel discussions, film events, or different, more diverse programmes instead of parties ... I'd like to think we actually helped shaping the Shanghai Pride in a way that going towards more substance instead of parties. I'm not against parties, it's just that the UK government can't be supporting parties ... we do want to do more advocacy, not discussions, but changing mind kind of events instead of film screenings.

While the argument that 'UK tax money can't be used to throw parties in China' may sound reasonable, the above quote also expresses a clear standard for what 'real' LGBTQ+ activism is, privileging public opinion shaping, visible advocacy work over activities aimed at strengthening the community, create safe spaces or make the every day more liveable for LGBTQ+ people. Western actors' support and funding of LGBTQ+ groups, under the banner of 'following the lead of local activists', may have the unintended consequence of increasing hierarchies and stratification among activist groups. Some activists' voices are amplified through Western support, and others' further marginalized and invisibilized. That reliance on international funding may reproduce hierarchies and elitism among civil society groups is well established in development research (Sakue-Collins, 2020). However, such dynamics may impact LGBTQ+ activism in specific ways, differently than, e.g. environmental or women's rights groups, especially when it comes to adopting Western identity categories and visibility strategies, at the risk of further marginalizing alternative subjectivities and forms of politics.

Balancing individual commitments vs policy consistency

As Jamie, the US diplomat in Cape Town quoted at the beginning of the chapter demonstrates, diplomats who themselves identify as LGBTQ+, or have been involved in LGBTQ+ activism at home, are more likely to prioritize, or be asked to prioritize, LGBTQ+ issues in their diplomatic capacities. Personal commitment can thus lead to a stronger and more visible emphasis on LGBTQ+ in certain places, something that blurs the boundaries between official and unofficial diplomacy, and can make LGBTQ+ diplomacy inconsistent (even within the same country) and fragile. The dependency on individual commitment was present even in cases where support for LGBTQ+ rights was clearly backed by official policy, such as Sweden's 'feminist foreign policy'.

At Mumbai Pride in 2019, staff from the UK consulate carried a large Rainbow Union Jack flag and the UK government's 'Love is Great' branded banners. This was the first time the UK consulate had been involved in India's largest Pride parade and was at the behest of a gay consular diplomat who had been posted to Mumbai before homosexuality was decriminalized. This was his first posting abroad and he arrived with his civil partner, who unlike heterosexual spouses did not have diplomatic immunity under Indian law. Stories circulated about LGBTQ+ diplomats and their partners being harassed, with them being followed and their phones tapped. The diplomat's partner started to feel unsafe and became convinced he was being followed. This led to the breakdown of the relationship and his now ex-partner returned to the UK. Participating in Mumbai Pride and celebrating the decriminalization of homosexuality in India was therefore borne out of deep personal commitment. However, despite the visible presence of the UK at Pride, as discussed above, the UK high commissioner had never raised the issue of LGBTQ+ rights formally with the Indian government because of the overriding diplomatic priority of UK-India trade relations.

The interrelationship between personal identity, beliefs and policy commitment is symbolized in the emergence of governmental 'Special Envoys' on LGBTQ+ rights. In 2021, the UK appointed Lord Herbert as the UK government's special envoy on LGBTQ+ rights. The creation of this post mirrored other LGBTQ+ 'special envoys' appointed by the United States, France and Italy. However, despite an office and a small team focused on LGBTQ+ rights in the FCDO, Herbert was not a government minister and was unsalaried. Speaking at an event hosted by the Baring Foundation in 2023, Herbert was notably out of step with his Conservative Party government colleagues when he denounced conversion therapy, transphobia and 'culture wars' discourses. Senior FCDO staff at the event commented in private afterwards that it was difficult to work in the areas of gender and LGBTQ+ advocacy, because although Herbert was personally committed, there was no high-level leadership or commitment to these issues.

In South Africa, the posting of LGBTQ+ UK diplomats and diplomats who had been involved in human rights and development led to a new desire to become involved in LGBTQ+ advocacy in the country. I had held a photography exhibition of images from Soweto Pride in London and wanted to hold it in South Africa. I sent an email enquiry to the Deputy High Commissioner just days after he had held a meeting asking his staff to make connections with LGBTQ+ activists in the country and he immediately replied saying he was interested in my offer. I worked with two mid-ranking diplomats and the GALA Queer Archive of South Africa to organize an exhibition and reception and we invited a range of grassroots activists, government officials and ministers, other diplomats and funders. This event led to meaningful impacts, the Forum for the Empowerment of Women had faced financial difficulties over the previous months, largely due to Johannesburg Municipality reneging on an agreement to support Soweto Pride, but having met them at the reception, diplomats from the European Union and Germany agreed to fund Soweto Pride, which they continue to do in 2024. Two weeks after the reception, the UK High Commission hired a coach and twenty-five diplomats from different embassies travelled from Pretoria to participate in Soweto Pride for the first time. Over the following years, activists from the Forum for the Empowerment of Women were invited to meet visiting UK government officials and other embassy events invited the activists to their LGBT advocacy events. In 2022, I obtained university funding to fly the organizers of Soweto and Ekurhuleni Prides to London, where they spoke from the stage of London Pride, marched in the Parade and spoke to the UK Parliament's All Parliamentary Group on Global LGBTQ+ Rights. The Forum for the Empowerment of Women had been in negotiation for years with Johannesburg Municipality to agree on a policy framework for LGBT rights in the city, to set up an LGBT consultative forum and to recognize Soweto Pride as a partner and guarantee funding. Returning from London, they arranged a meeting and showed the evidence of how seriously they had been taken and finally obtained the formal agreement.

Creating a forum for diplomats, officials, funders and grassroots activists demonstrates how meaningful diplomatic engagements can be for grassroots activism, but it also demonstrates their precarity. Apart from the fact I had shaped the engagement to deliver this outcome, the routine turnover of diplomatic staff and changes in government funding and political priorities make sustained diplomatic involvement in LGBTQ+ rights issues in South Africa vulnerable. These events took place in Pretoria and Johannesburg. In Cape Town, Jamie, the US diplomat, commented how she had never seen or encountered UK diplomatic staff at LGBTQ+ or any other human rights events and in 2024, they were not marching in the Pride parade. I heard that although there was a senior UK diplomat in Cape Town who was gay, he was 'only interested in partying, not the human rights stuff'. One of the diplomats I had been working with moved on to another posting and as with other diplomatic missions, changes in personnel, funding and foreign and development policies make ongoing involvement of the UK High Commission LGBTQ+ rights work in South Africa vulnerable. Without clear leadership and resources to support, engagement in LGBTQ+ advocacy work and support remains precarious and variable across time and context.

Conclusion

The platform for civil society and LGBTQ+ individuals that Pride provides makes it an 'easy' focus for LGBTQ+ diplomacy and venue for diplomats to participate in and support, but it is not always the right vehicle. Visibility can be counterproductive and dangerous for LGBTQ+ communities under certain circumstances, and even in less hostile environments there can be a complex local politics. Therefore, poorly judged visible interventions in LGBTQ+ advocacy by Western diplomats can put local activists at risk and feed into local narratives that LGBTQ+ identities are 'Western'. Choosing to participate in one Pride event rather than another can privilege one set of activists and issues over another, and as I have argued, there is a perception in some Global South contexts that Western embassies privilege groups that emphasize 'homonormative' issues such as same-sex marriage, rather than local issues such as intersections of caste and queerness. Financial accountability requirements and political norms can lead to shaping Pride events in ways that impact the ideological and cultural nature of those events, such as moving away from socially motivated parties, to more 'serious' kinds of activism, or policy discussions. Pride events can meaningfully engage with grassroots activists and issues, or they can be a one-day celebratory party for the privileged few. Engaging with LGBTQ+ grassroots across the year is therefore important.

Pride can be used by states to project a progressive, modern and liberal international image and to contrast with more conservative rivals, such as is the case for Taiwan vs China and Cuba vs the United States, but this can belie gaps in LGBTQ+ rights and a lack of other rights and freedoms. Similarly, international governments, from the United States, Canada to the United Kingdom, turn up to Pride parades with rainbow-branded national flags and pro-LGBTQ+ rights slogans, but these visual statements are not matched by financial commitments or the willingness to speak out when LGBTQ+ rights intersect with trade or security priorities. Queer activists are right to be suspicious of Global North states' reliability as allies and their reluctance to become involved in supporting intersectional queer social justice causes, rather than the easily recognizable 'heteronormative' legal goal of same-sex marriage. Nevertheless, diplomatic support for grassroots activism can make a meaningful difference to grassroots activists and community Pride events. Diplomatic partners can also provide more willing and amenable partners to Pride organizers than the corporations discussed in the previous chapter. Involvement can also help inform and shape both foreign and national policies as diplomats engage with local governments as well as their home government about LGBTQ+ rights. Nevertheless, the overall impression I gained of diplomatic involvement in Pride was just how haphazard it was, how premised on the commitment of individual diplomats and how there was a consistent lack of clear national leadership on LGBTQ+ issues, even when governments claimed otherwise. International LGBTQ+ rights commitments are not framed in 'homocapitalist' terms, rather they are part of Human Rights commitments, and remain easily dispensable and contingent on other, more mainstream, commitments to trade and security.

Chapter 6

RECLAIMING PRIDE: QUEER AND ALTERNATIVE PRIDE ORGANIZING

I didn't have to do very much, I just put out 2,000 little flyers that looked like Christian tracts that on the cover said, 'Jesus Loves Drag', and on the back had the drag prayer that I kind of took from a real Christian tract, only changing certain words. And inside – and we got like I think 7,000 to 8,000 people marching through the streets in what the *New York Times* referred to later in an article as, 'The most authentic of the Stonewall 25 events', because it was! We were illegal. We were pissing off the cops. We went the wrong way down a one-way street because I had walked the march route and somehow, I didn't notice that I was taking us down a one-way street. But we made it to the Stonewall Inn. There were impromptu fire dancers which was a tradition that carried on for about 10 years and we sang 'Somewhere Over the Rainbow' which is a tradition we still carry on to today.

– Brian Griffin on helping to organize the first New York Drag March in 1994 (interview with the author, 2019)

In 2019, hundreds of people in drag, fetish wear, and t-shirts with satirical political slogans, gathered for the Drag March in Tomkins Square park on the anniversary of the Stonewall Riots and the evening before the New York World Pride parade. There, the Sisters of Perpetual Indulgence performed a 'queer ceremony' and prayed for those lost to HIV and police violence and celebrated queer identity and sex. The Drag March had started in 1994, on the twenty-fifth anniversary of the Stonewall Riots. The organizers of New York Pride had announced that people dressed in drag or fetish wear would not be permitted to take part in the official Stonewall 25 Pride parade. During the controversy that followed, Gilbert Baker, a group of ACT UP activists and the 'drag nun' HIV and LGBTQ+ rights group, the Sisters of Perpetual Indulgence, decided to organize a Drag March the evening before the official

New York Pride March. Brian Griffin, involved in the first march and quoted above, recalled the irreverence and creativity of the first Drag March and how popular it was. In 2019, the Drag March began and thousands sang and paraded through the streets of lower Manhattan. At the front of the march were pets in pushchairs and a large banner with 'It's still just a Drag March. You may applaud!' People on sidewalks and from balconies laughed and cheered as we went by. Brian said that he considered the Drag March 'the canary in the coalmine' and at the first Drag March in 1994 he had been worried about police violence against the marchers, but now the relations with the police were good. At one point, a group of marchers in fetish wear posed for a photograph with a group of smiling New York Police. Brian and Kenneth W Mechler, aka Sister Hucklefaery Ken, told me that relations with the police, particularly the working-class and Latinx police, had improved over the years. Relations with Heritage of Pride, the organizers of New York Pride, were still tense though. When we arrived at the Stonewall Inn, the organizers of the Drag March were surprised to see Heritage of Pride had placed the World Pride stage close to the Inn, whereas they had been told it would be a street away. A small crowd by the stage were dwarfed by the thousands of Drag Marchers who had begun to sing Somewhere over the Rainbow. The speaker on the World Pride stage told them to be quiet and that they were being disrespectful. 'How dare a 20-something Pride official tell us that. She was being disrespectful to us!' said Sister Hucklefaery Ken afterwards. The Drag March's creative irreverence and joyfulness were queer protests and the official New York Pride/World Pride stage and the dry speeches demonstrated the anodyne and less popular, conformist politics of the main New York Pride events.

Pride parades are seldom the homogeneous, or the exclusive, platforms for the celebration of corporate diversity policies and 'homocapitalism'. Nor are organizers always able to entirely control what happens during the parade. Pride parades are also sites of controversy, protest and open contestation with queer activists subverting the efforts of the organizers to frame and control the event. As discussed in Chapter 3, at Mumbai Pride, the TISS Queer Collective had created queer spaces of queer critique at Mumbai Pride, but the police had targeted them the following year. In South Africa, the disruption of Johannesburg Pride by One in Nine and the Forum for the Empowerment of Women had led to 'alternative' Prides across the city. In Cuba, a group of LGBTQ+ activists held an unofficial march. The emergence of 'alternative' Pride events in the United States, the United Kingdom, South Africa, Cuba

6. Reclaiming Pride

Figure 16 New York Police with the Drag March.

and Hong Kong also reveals that queer activists, after trying to protest and engage with mainstream Pride organizers with few results, have increasingly chosen to organize their own Pride events. Focusing on these alternative Prides provides answers for Rao's (2015: 48) question of 'where will resistance to global homocapitalism come from?'. This chapter analyses activist efforts to 'reclaim', protest and queer Pride across the contexts discussed in the book. Chapter 4 explored how and why activists' critique 'mainstream' Pride events and how they seek to disrupt and transgress mainstream Prides. Alternative Queer Prides, include the Queer Liberation March, Dyke March and Drag March in New York; Soweto, Ekurhuleni and Khumbulani Prides in South Africa; Hong Kong Migrants Pride and also larger Prides organized by activists including Hong Kong Pride and Taiwan Pride. Issues raised by queer activists at Pride include the importance of framing Pride around broader questions of social justice, intersectionality, critiques of globalization, hostility to institutional involvement in Pride events, and also 'reclaiming' the 'queerness' of Pride from assimilatory and homonormative constructions of LGBTQ+ identities and lifestyles.

In 2019, for the first time, a Queer Liberation March took place a few streets from and shortly before the New York/World Pride parade. In the years leading up to World Pride in New York there had been protests by Black Lives Matter at Pride parades in the United States and Canada. In 2012, Toronto Pride was bitterly protested by queer activists after the Pride organizer, who had previously been on the board of Joburg Pride, and Toronto City Council banned the Queers Against Israeli Apartheid from marching in the parade (see Schulman, 2012a). This sparked years of protests about Toronto Pride's racism and the involvement of the police (Walcott, 2017). In the months leading up to World Pride in New York, weekly meetings were held in community centres at different venues across the city. At these meetings, queer activists from ACT UP, the Sisters of Perpetual Indulgence, the Drag March, Dyke March, Black Lives Matter and other community groups across New York discussed how to organize a Queer Liberation March. These meetings were not always easy, and activists told me that generational, class, gender and racial divisions could cause considerable conflict at them. Robert Baez, who was involved in the organization of the March, reflected that 'we tried to think about experiences that are outside of our own and that can sometimes be tricky. With people from different social locations – I mean, it's not easy either having really difficult conversations about the approaches, about how we include people who have usually felt marginalized by other movements'. Sister Hucklefaery Ken, a member of the Sisters of Perpetual Indulgence and ACT UP, told me that despite their disagreements with other, particularly younger, activists:

> I came out as a radical in a way with the Queer Liberation March. I came out as a socialist and a radical. Which was important to the sort of conservative upbringing I had had. I feel like the Queer Liberation March is the first social justice movement that has done anything to combat the fear and hate that we're being force-fed by our government. The alternative march was the result of years of tension between members of the Reclaim Pride Coalition and Heritage of Pride and a protest of the over policing of NYC Pride and the selling off of Pride to hundreds of corporate floats.

The Queer Liberation March's stated aims, as explained on the leaflets given out to marchers, was that it took place

> in our communities' tradition of resistance against police, state and societal oppression a tradition that is symbolized by the 1969 Stonewall Rebellion, which we remember and honour today. We march in protest of continued oppression against our communities

and others, locally, nationally and internationally, with Black trans women being subject to particular brutality and violence. We march to celebrate our communities and history, in solidarity with other groups and to demand social and economic justice worldwide – we March for Liberation.

Directly responding to the charge made by Sylvia Rivera in 1973 that New York Pride had forgotten precarious Black, trans and sex worker communities, the organizers of the Queer Liberation March pledged that all donations raised at the march would be given to 'black trans women and projects that are led by black trans women and trans people of colour'. The organization of the Queer Liberation March mirrored the grassroots community approach taken by the ACT UP activists in the 1980s and 1990s and this contrasted with the professionalized approach taken by Heritage of Pride when organizing New York Pride.

The organizers of the Queer Liberation March were not sure how many people would attend, particularly since the march clashed with the main World Pride parade happening almost at the same time. On the day the March exceeded the organizers expectations with approximately 45,000 people attending. Many of the same activists I had seen at the Drag March and would see at the Dyke March which took place in New York the following day were at the Queer Liberation March. The march became so large that the police stopped all traffic on 6th Avenue. Robert Baez recalled:

> Several people said that they were crying, like tears of joy and excitement. I certainly had an emotional moment, particularly when – because we started off with half the street, but then it got, there were so many people that the police had to allow us to expand and so there was this one moment where we took over the entire 6th Avenue and everybody was just yelling and screaming and chanting, 'Whose streets? Our streets'. And we were getting messages from people saying that they were so thankful that they came, that we organized this, that they came from all over the world. I met people from Australia, activists, and the people that I met from Australia specifically are HIV activists who wanted to come and be part of this moment. Because it was, it's a … hopefully it'll be a historical moment where people, where we're shifting the conversation around Pride and hopefully challenging many ideas. Some people were asking how can we start our own in our city?

The large banner at the front of the march proclaimed, 'We Resist'. Placards carried on the march included 'Capitalism = Death', 'Fund Schools not Prisons', 'The last thing LGBTQ+ people need is more US intervention', 'Fuck Guns', 'Medicare for all', 'Queer as in Fuck the Police', 'My Pride is not for sale', 'Fuck the Trump/Pence Fascist Regime', 'Zionism = Racism', 'Palestine is a Queer Issue – Boycott, Disinvest, Sanctions', 'Decriminalise Sex Work' 'Abolish ICE', 'Gentrification Destroys Gayborhoods' and 'A Gay Landlord is Still a Landlord'. Marchers chanted 'Whose streets, our streets', 'Off the Sidewalks and onto the Streets' and 'ACT UP! Fight Back!' At one point, the march passed a Mastercard World Pride advertisement on 6th Avenue, which stated, in rainbow colours, 'the street is now a statement'. This unintentionally captioned the Queer Liberation March's anti-capitalist and purpose which was, of course, not Mastercard's intended meaning of the slogan. As the march reached the top of 6th Avenue 45,000 marchers led down on the road to stage a silent mass 'die in' to commemorate deaths from AIDS, homophobic and transphobic violence, and due to lack of access to healthcare. It was an extraordinarily powerful moment.

World Pride, like many major Pride parades, now intends to be 'family friendly' and inoffensive to heterosexual society. As the marchers entered Central Park, the 'offensiveness' of the Queer Liberation March to some was evidenced by the appalled expressions on some of the onlookers already in the park. I saw one middle-aged woman hurry her family away. A younger, preppy, white man sat and held *The Economist* magazine in front of his face. This was to, presumably, obscure the march passing by. The woman sat next to him closely studied her mobile phone, so that she would also not look at the marchers. As discussed in Chapter 2, social movement scholars would consider this a 'failure' of messaging and desired impact on the audience, but from a queer perspective it was a success, because it had caused discomfort and disruption for its white, middle-class, heterosexual audience in Central Park. The large gathering area in Central Park had a stage with 'None of Us are Free until All of Us are Free!' emblazoned across it. The first speaker proclaimed: 'We are here today in Central Park because other people are not … We who are here today to share our art to remember our people. United in rage, seeding dreams for the future.' Art installations lined the edges of the park themed on the violence of settler land theft in the United States, racist and transphobic violence and memorializing deaths from AIDS. As explained in the introduction, I had regretfully left Central Park to watch the World Pride parade on 5th Avenue. The official parade had none of the energy, political protest or fun of the Queer Liberation March.

6. Reclaiming Pride

Queer Pride organizing in Asia

First organized in 2003, Taiwan Pride, held in central Taipei and close to the President's official residence, is the largest Pride event in Asia with an estimated attendance in 150,000 people marching. LGBTQ+ civil society groups had initially organized Taiwan Pride, primarily the Taiwan Tongzhi Hotline Association that runs numerous support services and advocacy campaigns for LGBTQ+ communities across Taiwan. The Tongzhi Hotline Association was still represented in the march and had a booth in the central meeting area, but a committee of volunteers now organizes Taiwan Pride. While Taiwan Pride is not organized in response to another 'mainstream' Pride in Taipei and as discussed in the previous chapter, it is used by the Taiwanese state to construct and project a progressive and Western international identity, it is very different to Prides I define as 'mainstream' in this book, such as New York Pride. This is because it is organized by volunteers, anyone can join its march route and its organizers have consciously sought to incorporate local LGBTQ+ struggles and marginalized issues and communities, such as indigenous LGBTQ+ groups and also BDSM communities, and not simply adopt homonormative Western LGBTQ+ discourses around same-sex marriage. The organizing committee have sought to limit the involvement and influence of corporate participants.

Taiwan Pride had been significantly politicized and had grown when it was joined by a new generation of LGBTQ+ activists following the Sunflower Student Movement protests had taken place in 2014. The Sunflower Movement had protested the long-standing ruling and pro-China conservative KMT party. The young protestors had broken into and occupied parliament. It was these protests that had helped propel President Tsai's DPP party into power and Tsai had committed herself to marriage equality in the election campaign. When I met with the organizers of Taiwan Pride in a small queer bookshop in Taipei, they explained that although the 2019 Pride had taken place a week before the referendum that questioned same-sex marriage and amid widespread frustration with President Tsai for delaying the implementation of same-sex marriage legislation, the committee had decided not to make same-sex marriage the main theme of the Pride parade. Rather, they chose 'Tell Your Story, Vote for Equality'. While this underscored the importance of the referendum, which also focused on sex and gender education in schools, but it allowed for people to bring to Pride the issues that mattered to them and did not restrict Pride to focus on same-sex marriage rights. Taiwan Pride refused official commercial sponsorship, but did allow a small number of commercial floats in the parade, including the social networking and dating apps Grindr, Hornet and Blued, a gay bar in Beijing, Citibank and GAP clothing. Uber offered free rides to the parade and a Pride stage, drinks stands and pop-up shops were at the 'gay district' of Taipei surrounding the 'Red House'. Commercial floats in the parade were far outnumbered by civil society groups, politicians, diplomats and individuals marching on the three routes across the city. Activists handed out leaflets advising attendees how to vote in the forthcoming elections and made political speeches from small floats. The three parade routes converged on a square and large stage in front of the president's official residence. Taiwan Pride, although large scale and as the organizing committee explained, the main and only outlet for LGBTQ+ politics and expression in the capital, maintained its queer grassroots connection by allowing anyone to join the parade, restricting commercial involvement and creating a platform that multiple groups and causes could participate in.

The open and participatory nature of the parades allowed for marginalized issues to be highlighted, particularly striking were issues related to the right to sex and sexual pleasure. This included a celebration of sex and sexuality in the face of the proposed conservative restrictions of Taiwan's progressive laws in the forthcoming referendum, which sought to limit discussion of sexual practices in schools and promote abstinence. Two women with lollipops covering their breasts carried placards with 'students need their orgasms too', 'kinky sex is a must' and 'not having sex isn't sex education. Let's deal with shame and talk about sex'. Just before the parade began, I came across a group of activists in wheelchairs and stood by them a man in a jockstrap carrying a sign which had written on it 'not establishing sex zones/red-light districts for sex work is against the constitution. Seven years have passed without the setting up of red-light districts. Let's establish a union for fighting against exploitation.' I spoke with Kong, who was carrying the sign. Kong explained that as a sex worker and gay porn actor, he was campaigning for the rights of sex workers and for the Taiwanese government to enact its legal obligation to set up zones for legalized sex work. The rest of the group were LGBTQ+ disability rights activists and were there to highlight the right of disabled LGBTQ+ to sex and to raise the visibility of disabled people in the broader LGBTQ+ community. Meeting with Kong and Vincent, one of the disability rights activists, a few days later, they explained that although their two issues were distinct, there were interconnections. They had met and made an alliance at Taiwan Pride a few years earlier, and following this established a pressure group called 'Hand Job' which campaigned for sex workers who offered services to LGBTQ+ disabled people and to make the right to sex for disabled people and the rights of sex workers more visible in Taiwan's LGBTQ+ rights landscape. Kong said:

> For me as a gay sex worker I have to say that 'hey you forgot this issue that's important for me'. It's difficult for this year because everyone is focusing on the marriage issue and prostitution and marriage is contradictory. Most married people don't want their husband to go with a prostitute, so these two issues are opposed to each other. So this is difficult for me, but these two issues are kind of connected to law and political issues so I try to state that.

Kong thought that many people assumed sex work is illegal in Taiwan, but it is only unlawful if conducted on city streets. The Taiwanese government had been instructed to create sex work zones in cities by the constitutional court, something they had yet to do. This is what he was campaigning for to happen at Taipei Pride. Vincent explained that he was often felt marginalized and overlooked in Taipei's gay bars because he uses a wheelchair and with many of Taiwan's LGBTQ+ advocacy groups focused on campaigning for same-sex marriage, it was easy to forget more marginal issues such as LGBTQ+ disabled people's rights. He was also concerned that if same-sex marriage laws were achieved, it would be easy to conclude that full equality for all LGBTQ+ people was achieved in Taiwan.

Kong is the most well-known and downloaded gay porn star in Taiwan and during the parade, many people wanted to have their picture taken with him. As they marched, Vincent and the other activists shouted 'disabled people have the right to fuck! We want the right to have and enjoy sex!' Vincent later recalled that behind them in the march was an LGBTQ+ Christian group, who initially looked shocked and uncomfortable with these chants, but as the march continued members of the Christian group started chatting with Vincent and Kong and thanked them for explaining the issues they were campaigning for. They explained that they had not considered these issues as LGBTQ+ rights issues before and that they had learned something new and important by attending Taiwan Pride. This is exactly the kind of visibility for marginalized groups and issues that Pride parades should enable. The open nature of Taiwan Pride meant that new connections could be made between causes and groups and the fluid and unregulated nature of the parade meant disparate LGBTQ+ groups could learn and become conscientized about marginalized issues such as sex work, sexual

Figure 17 Kong and Vincent at Taiwan Pride.

pleasure and disabled people's right to sex. Although Taiwan Pride is large scale and an 'official' Pride in Taipei, it is a queer Pride because of the nature of its voluntary organization and that people and groups can freely be involved and highlight their cause.

In Chapter 3, I discussed the class, racial and pro-democracy politics of Pride in Hong Kong. Unlike other LGBTQ+ advocacy events in the territory, Cantonese working-class activists organize Hong Kong Pride. While Hong Kong Pride has sometimes struggled for funding, in 2018, they did receive sponsorship from some of the major transnational corporations that operate in the territory, including Citibank, Standard Chartered and BNP Paribas. Despite the large corporate presence in the parade and at the afterparty in front of Hong Kong City Hall, where they had stalls giving out branded merchandize, there was a large contingency in the march from civil society and multiple issues including China's largest HIV+ advocacy and support group, student LGBTQ+ groups and most noticeably, activists from Hong Kong's pro-democracy and civil rights movement. When I met with Wylie Yeo and Johnson, two of the main organizers, they explained that they had not planned to originally hold a Pride march, and had been organizing International Day Against Homophobia (IDAHO – later International Day Against Homophobic, Biphobia and Transphobia IDAHOBIT) day events that focused on silent mourning and commemoration. These events were reasonably well attended, but Wylie noticed that people 'were very tense and they were very nervous, because for most of them, it was the first time in their lives that they were marching on the streets to support IDAHO and LGBT'. By 2007, Wylie recalled:

> The crowd became very delighted and very happy. They were singing on their own and they marched with rainbow flags and costumes on their own. This was not promoted by us; this was not designed by us. They turned it that way. And what they did in 2007, the IDAHO event showed us that they need a kind of Pride parade.

Wylie believed that this change was due to the growth and popularity of Taiwan Pride, which many LGBTQ+ people from Hong Kong attend, alongside other images of Pride on the TV and web. For Wylie though, the key moment to decide to organize a Pride event was having a drink with the pro-democracy activist and politician 'Long Hair' Leung Kwok-Hung. Wylie recalled that she had said to him:

> 'I didn't know how to move on in the Hong Kong LGBT movement.' And he, as an ally, he told me that he thought the LGBT people should stand up in public and then allies can support them and they'll know how to support them and they can find a way to support them ... I think for many allies or many potential allies in Hong Kong, they need some kind of visibility of LGBT people, so that they know that these are those people they are supporting. So, I think these were the reasons for me to have the Hong Kong Pride parade event.

As mentioned above, the pro-democracy parties and activists in Hong Kong were a large contingency in the parade and pro-democracy members of the Legislative Council, such as Eddie Chu, who stood at the halfway point of the parade with a megaphone shouting 'Hong Kong needs LGBT rights! Hong Kong needs democratic rights! LGBT people must be free! Hong Kong people must be free!' This intersection with political rights and broader human rights marked Hong Kong Pride as different from, for example, New York, or Johannesburg Pride, which primarily celebrate LGBTQ+ rights progress and avoid overt political statements or attacks on existing political elites. In the years that followed Hong Kong Pride in 2019, the pro-democracy politicians I had seen at the parade, including Nathan Law, Raymond Chan Chi-Chuen, Eddie Chu, Joshua Wong and 'Long Hair' Leung Kwok-Hung, are now in exile, or in prison due to Hong Kong's 'National Security Law' that criminalized pro-democracy activities. 'Pro-Beijing' politicians are split on LGBTQ+ rights issues, with veteran politician Regina Ip expressing pro-LGBTQ+ rights positions and has attended Hong Kong Pride in the past. Whereas others, such as Junios Ho, Vincent Cheng and Holden Chow, are outspoken critics of LGBTQ+ rights and argue they are Western identities, a threat to national security and a bridgehead for Hong Kong's enemies to agitate against China (Chan, 2019; Harris, 2023). Hong Kong Pride continues to take place, but the interconnections with broader political and human rights are now difficult to express without breaching Hong Kong's draconian legal framework.

Subaltern Pride: Hong Kong migrants Pride

Hong Kong Pride has links with many grassroots communities across the territory and had been involved with LGBTQ+ Migrant Domestic Worker (MDW) advocacy groups. MDWs are a common feature in middle-class Hong Kong homes and are allowed into the territory on a temporary residence permit that requires they live in their employers' property, and they must leave Hong Kong within two weeks if they lose their job. Coming mainly from the Philippines, Indonesia and Thailand, MDWs are marginalized, precarious and often maligned by broader society in Hong Kong (Chang and Groves, 2000; Constable, 2018; Lai, 2018). Invisibility is a key issue for MDWs, because as Enloe writes, MDWs 'slip out of sight so easily' (2014, 330). LGBTQ+ MDWs face further marginalization and prejudice within the migrant community itself. Being subject to gendered dress codes, isolated from other LGBTQ+ people in Hong Kong, and with no protection from being dismissed if suspected of being LGBTQ+, they face challenges that are entirely different to the professional LGBTQ+ immigrants in Hong Kong, who can apply for permanent residence after five years and whose multinational employers provide protections for LGBTQ+ staff. MDWs' only statutory day off is on Sunday, and Hong Kong Pride takes place on Saturday, so MDWs started to organize Hong Kong Migrants Pride the day after Hong Pride. I attended Hong Kong Migrants Pride in 2018, a few days after I had been to the Out Leadership Asia Summit, held at HSBC's headquarters in Hong Kong. An alliance of LGBTQ+ migrant domestic workers, MDW Trade Unions and advocacy groups held Hong Kong Migrant Pride in Central and marched in front of HSBC and beside and through the 'HSBC Community Festival' that was also being held that day. Every Sunday, thousands of MDWs gather in front and underneath HSBC's building and in the pavements, parks and beside the Central district's financial and government institutions and luxury shopping malls. Here, MDWs sit and socialize, eat, apply makeup, cut hair and relax on their day off.

In 2005, a trans MDW, Marrz Balaoro, was having a drink in a bar with a lesbian MDW friend. Another person in the bar started making homophobic and transphobic comments and a fight broke out. The bouncer in the bar also started to attack Marrz and his friend and the police were called. Marrz's friend arrived back at her employer's home in the early hours of the next morning with injuries and was sacked and deported from Hong Kong just over a week later. In 2006, Marrz established Filguys, a Transmen and Lesbians association for MDWs. At around the same time, the local LGBTQ+ activists who organize Hong Kong Pride, already aware of the differences between their struggles and privileged migrants had started to engage with MDW advocacy groups. Migrants Pride evolved after decades of transnational and local feminist organizing among migrant workers in Hong Kong. This organizing includes support and social groups, legal advice and also trade union organizing. MDW support groups, such as the Mission for Migrant Workers at Hong Kong's Anglican cathedral and MDW trade unions and advocacy groups, such as Gabriella Hong Kong, realized the distinctive challenges LGBTQ+ MDWs faced. Hong Kong Migrants Pride was organized by a coalition of these groups and aimed to challenge the absence of consideration about LGBTQ+ MDWs and make them visible as a distinct community in Hong Kong. Sheila Tebia-Bonifacio, chair of the MDW support group Gabriela Hong Kong, explained that Pride was a good platform to raise visibility and pursue a serious political purpose, but also 'we saw the need to make it fun, so it will reach more LGBT migrants'. Tebia-Bonifacio added:

> We are educating the people of Hong Kong that this is the plight of LGBT migrants and even though they are a minority they are part of Hong Kong and they play an important role in the lives of many Hong Kong families.

Equally, Tebia-Bonifacio was keen that the other 'elite' LGBT activist communities took notice of the issues LGBTQ+ MDWs face. MDW activists also became aware that participating in and being visible at other LGBTQ+ events, such as Hong Kong Pride, was difficult because MDWs can only take part on Sundays when they are not working.

In 2018, Hong Kong Migrants Pride march began in front of the City Hall with a few hundred MDW activists wearing t-shirts that were colour coordinated to represent the different colours of the rainbow. Carrying rainbow flags and banners, the march began with the slogan 'Pride, Freedom, Change' and walked through Statue Square, in front of HSBC headquarters and across the pavements and walkways besides the luxury shopping malls and hotels. The march coincided with HSBC's Community Festival, which had cordoned off many of the streets. As we walked, one of the participants in the Pride March said to me:

> HSBC is dominating all the streets with their Community Festival, and it shows what they think the community is, it isn't migrant domestic workers! We're all sat outside it … and Migrants Pride is taking place next to it and we're walking beside and through it.

The HSBC Community Festival's theme was 'harmony' and 'bringing people together'. The festival sought to highlight the groups and organizations HSBC supported in Hong Kong, none of which related to migrant domestic workers, gender or LGBTQ+ rights organizations. In contrast, Migrants Pride's march was disruptive with its colourful display and the marchers shouting and singing 'No to discrimination and social exclusion', 'We're here, we're queer and we want to say hello!' and 'Long live international solidarity!'. While Migrants Pride did not attack or criticize HSBC directly, its noisy disruptiveness and open queerness contrasted with the calm, harmonious and anodyne atmosphere of the Community Festival.

Hong Kong Migrants Pride March ended with a rally adjacent to HSBC, in front of the walkways and shops of a designer shopping mall. As retail assistants, security guards and shoppers looked on from the shops and walkways at the scene below, the Migrants Pride rally presented an arresting sight alongside the luxury and wealth on display. MDWs gathered in front of large banners that described migrant domestic work as 'modern day slavery', demanded labour rights such as 'humane accommodation and 11 hours uninterrupted rest' and 'dignity and freedom' for LGBT MDWs. Representatives from different national and community MDW groups made speeches in their languages and English about migrants' rights, LGBTQ+ rights and the exploitative labour policies in the Philippines, Indonesia and Hong Kong. Over the course of the afternoon, the women sang feminist songs about the importance of women's rights and development, danced and ran t-shirt printing and make-up workshops.

Migrants Pride also sought to directly contest and reveal the spatial, colonial and corporate power relations in Hong Kong. Shortly before the march, a group of MDWs held what was described by one of the organizers, Alma Quinto, as an art and activist 'guerrilla workshop' in Statue Square, which faces HSBC. This square contains the solitary statue of Sir Thomas Jackson, a founder of HSBC and a powerful figure in Hong Kong's colonial past. Quinto explained that few knew its history or reflect on the ongoing power relations it symbolizes. At the workshop, MDWs made small traditional Filipino dolls dressed in national costume and depicted with raised fists. Some made figures in gendered female dress, but others made trousers signifying their chosen pronouns, or trans identity. The figures were placed in front of Jackson's statue. Quinto explained that with these statues 'migrant workers create and write their own stories ... people can see them, can learn about the stories of these workers' and that this challenges the 'one dimensional' image MDWs have in Hong Kong.

MDWs articulated an alternative truth of (post)colonial and capitalist power relations and how these relations produce and depend on migrant domestic work. The guerrilla workshop questioned the regime of truth that constructed Hong Kong as a diverse 'global city' and corporations as empowering and inclusive of both migrant workers and LGBTQ+ employees. The small figures, with their fists

Figure 18 Hong Kong Migrants Pride 2018.

raised in defiance in front of the large statue of Jackson, highlighted the MDWs lack of power 'against this backdrop, this towering backdrop of colonial power and also male dominance'. As the participants placed their statues by Jackson and took photos raising their fists next to it, other MDWs came to ask what they were doing, as did the security guards from HSBC's headquarters. Quinto explained:

> No one questions the statue … and now we're putting up Filipino statues, but only for a very short time. It's transient because the life of domestic workers here is transient. We cannot be permanent. Sir Thomas Jackson is permanent.

Using feminist and queer activist practices, such as using art and crafts traditionally made by women and queering this through dress, the truth of Filipino LGBTQ+ MDWs lives was made defiantly visible in the same space as the nexus of Hong Kong's colonial, postcolonial and corporate power. The dolls' transience and scale symbolized the precarity and power of MDWs, but, as Quinto added, 'It was very symbolic of defiance … we conquered Statue Square!'

Empowering and politicizing LGBTQ+ MDWs, as well as the MDW community more broadly, was an important aim for the Pride March. This politicization presented LGBTQ+ rights in intersectional terms, combining sexuality with migrant rights and labour rights. Marrz Balaoro explained:

> For those who are still not aware of their rights then they are belittled … so it's important that they know their rights and campaign for them. You should understand that you are born differently and you should be open, you should also have this ability to cope with the situation [of LGBT experience in Hong Kong.

The central message of Migrants Pride, of the slogans, literature, songs, banners and speeches, was to articulate LGBTQ+ migrants' issues in intersectional terms with migrant, labour and LGBTQ+ rights combined with a critique of global capitalism. One MDW speaker explained to the rally, 'I couldn't be myself and proud at my old employers' homes because they would ask me why I dressed like a man wearing trousers. I felt very troubled because I knew if I came out to them, I might lose my job'. LGBTQ+ visibility and rights were combined with a broader critique of heteronormativity, exploitative labour practices, global inequality and demands for social justice. As the official leaflet for Migrants Pride explained, 'We are no different from our MDW sisters and brothers who suffer under racist, sexist and inhumane conditions.' This sought to disrupt discourses about Hong Kong as an international city and place of opportunity for migrants, and work as a fulfilling and safe place to be 'out' for LGBTQ+ migrants. Instead, it presented an alternative narrative that framed work and Hong Kong as exploitative and oppressive.

As they marched, different MDW campaign and support groups, including Gabriela and Filguys, carried banners protesting about plans to charge migrant workers in Hong Kong an additional insurance tax. A trans migrant sex worker group handed out leaflets explaining that migrant sex workers had the least rights of all groups in Hong Kong, with trans sex workers subject to abuse and deportation. Migrants Pride volunteers handed their leaflet to onlookers, explaining their purpose: 'March with Pride towards equality, justice and a world without discrimination and violence' the leaflet explained. 'We still have a lot of struggles to win as LGBT and as migrants ... migrants are forced to migrate because of poverty.' In Hong Kong, the government 'refuses to recognize domestic work as work' and MDWs faced unequal pay, precarious visa conditions and unfair working conditions. The leaflet outlined how LGBTQ+ migrants were vulnerable to becoming 'victims of domestic abuse, violence and discrimination'.

Migrants Pride used Pride as a platform for activism and articulated contrasting narratives of truth. Drawing from their 'subaltern knowledge' to name 'the system' and reveal 'new ways of seeing the world' (Cox and Fominaya, 2009), By talking about themselves, their experiences and their intersectional identities and needs, LGBTQ+ MDWs produced 'a knowledge of resistance and struggle' (Macleod and Durrheim, 2002, 42). Articulating the truth of LGBTQ+ MDWs lives is important because they can be obscured in broader narratives of LGBTQ+ rights struggles. For these reasons, Migrants Pride was an important platform to make visible LGBTQ+ MDWs, the truths of their lives and the 'complex web of local and international complicities that produce today's exploitation of domestic workers' (Enloe, 2014, 333). Migrants Pride's location and route were also symbolic, taking place next to HSBC, its Community Festival and at the heart of colonial and contemporary corporate power in Hong Kong.

Alternative Prides in South Africa

Queer activists who protest against mainstream Prides and/or organize alternative Prides essentially aim to 'reclaim' the political protest and transgressive roots of Pride, rather than being purely a celebratory party marking progress, or the achievement, of LGBTQ+ rights. In South Africa, these alternative Prides expressly sought to reclaim queer politics and continue the legacies of the radicalism of the South African Liberation Struggle. 'I think what Simon Nkoli was fighting for back in the days is what Soweto Pride is currently doing,' explained Jade Madingwane. Jade also believed that Soweto Pride was reclaiming the original political purposes of Pride:

> How do we protest, how do we educate, and how do we grasp that history of where Pride started, because we've lost it. Somewhere along the way, Pride has become a party. We've lost that ethical purpose. It's where we get to mourn and celebrate our lost loved ones.

Jade continued that for her the purpose of Soweto Pride was to raise awareness of LGBTQ+ people in the townships

> because people think being queer is a Western thing, it's un-African. So, for us, we are saying that we want to have a Pride in Soweto where we can celebrate our queer identities as people that reside in this area. Society, our elders, think that this was brought to us and it's not a black thing, for lack of a better word, it's not an African thing to be queer ... we want to raise that awareness for ourselves but also for the society, to say, 'We live in this township. We exist in this township. We are just as human as everyone else.'

On the morning of Soweto Pride in 2018, one of the organizers told the crowd gathering for the march:

> Feminism made this possible. We need to reclaim the streets. Who we want to fuck is political. We need to be in the townships. We need to be visible. We can't just campaign over gay issues. We have to campaign for free education. We have to be intersectional. We want social justice!

Around 150 people marched in Soweto, and although this was a fraction of the thousands who would eventually join the afterparty, I spoke with one person who had travelled overnight on a Greyhound bus from Durban to come to the march. She had seen Soweto Pride advertised on social media and thought 'I must go!'.

Apart from some white NGO staff and the two people who came with me, the only other white people in the parade were a gay couple who had travelled from the wealthy northern suburb of Sandton. They explained they wanted to be there to show solidarity with Black communities in South Africa and said it was frustrating how few white LGBTQ+ people took notice or bothered to attend Soweto Pride. The march progressed through the streets on the edge of Soweto singing, chanting and dancing. Jade Mandingwe explained the purpose of the march:

> It's not about modelling on the street. That is great, I'm not contesting that, but we are much angrier because of the violence that we experience within our own communities. Our anger is kind of justified because just being in Soweto on its own is dangerous for a woman, let alone an LGBTI identifying person. So, the difference there would then be that all around the world, I think, there are parades. Then Soweto Pride, because I know of Soweto Pride, we have like a march to say we are angry in these streets, and our anger is justified because you are not accepting of what we are doing. You are not accepting of our sexual orientation. You don't have to accept it but at least respect that I exist as a person. Maybe there is a difference in how we call our marches and parades because we are angrier because we live in a very violent society. Maybe other countries are not as violent as us. I'm not saying they're accepting on their end, but there's different ways of acceptance in every country, I guess, around identifying as an LGBTI person.

As we marched, Zandile Matsoeneng, who had helped organized on the first Soweto Prides, said to me: 'What is the face of a rape survivor? It's a black woman. And when you are black and you live in a township and you come out as a lesbian, then you are a number one target'. People in the march wore t-shirts with 'Stop the war on women's bodies' and carried placards with 'my body my choice my rights respect them', 'End heterosexual privilege equal rights for all' and 'Creating the communities we desire'. During the Soweto Pride march participants carried pictures of Black lesbians who had been murdered and staged a 'die in' to commemorate their deaths. Highlighting the reality of the threats and challenges of LGBTQ+ communities in Soweto and other townships across South Africa was at the heart of Soweto Pride's queer political purpose.

At the afterparty, which went on into the night, there were NGO and activist group stalls, representatives of the Gauteng government, LGBTQ+ and sexual health services, food and drink stalls, speeches and music. Jade explained that although the march was, for her, the main focus, the afterparty was also important for LGBTQ+ communities in the townships:

> The after-festivities where people are now able to celebrate as themselves. It's very hard to even go out in your local tavern as a queer person, with either your partner or your friends, because you are targets. So, at least, at Soweto Pride you have that advantage to hang around with your queer friends and to just chill in one space and have a good time, and you know that you can leave or you can stay for the after-party.

Zandile Matsoeneng told me that the social aspects of Soweto Pride were also important to her and her family:

> I take my whole family to Pride, and I come from a family of traditional healers where patriarchy is rife, and they get to see me in that space and they get to realise who I am in that space and in that moment. They've come to be so understanding that every year it becomes an annual thing. You can imagine how many families that are supportive of their kids that come to Soweto Pride.

As well as organizing Soweto Pride, FEW organizes numerous support and discussion groups about LGBTQ+ identity and issues across the year and seeks to offer support and advocacy for victims of homophobic attacks at police stations. FEW is also working on developing an app to report and document hate crimes, which as explained in the previous chapter, are statistics that are not currently collated by the South African police. FEW's work therefore continues across the year and extends beyond the day of Pride. Soweto Pride had combined serious political and social justice messages with a welcoming and fun afterparty, but one in which attendees could learn about other activist groups and causes, become conscietized and involved further if they wish. The social and partying aspects of Pride also mattered because there were no safe spaces for LGBTQ+ people to gather socially in townships and this too, helped raise visibility and understanding of LGBTQ+ people by friends and family who attended.

On the southeastern edges of Johannesburg is the sprawling municipality of Ekurhuleni, which includes the former white suburbs, and mining towns of Benoni, Boksburg and Brakpan and the Black townships of KwaThema, Daveyton and Wattville. In 2018, I visited Ntsupe Mohapi in the KwaThema home that she shared with her partner, Bontle, and her mother. Ntsupe had helped establish Ekurhuleni Pride in 2008 following the homophobic sexual assault and murder of the former football player, lesbian activist and KwaThema resident, Eudy Simelane. Ntsupe explained that Pride was organized

> just to create awareness around the township, around the KwaThema township. So, we organized our first Pride. It was just a walk. The theme was Walk Against Hate because it was the first time it was happening in KwaThema and we were so shocked. So, we wanted the community to be aware that it was not just this one particular person; there are many of us in the community.

Attendees at the walk told Ntsupe that there were many challenges and issues facing LGBTQ+ people in KwaThema. Following Pride, Ntsupe established the Ekurhuleni Pride Organizing Committee (EPOC).

> [W]e realized that there were so many challenges that our community was facing at that time. So, we started an organization because now we realized that people don't know about themselves, the diversity. There are a lot of misconceptions, and the community doesn't have information, they don't know where to go. There was no information like materials. Everything was in Johannesburg and nothing in Ekurhuleni.

A small room at the back of Ntsupe's house served as the office for EPOC and contained literature on being Christian and LGBT and literature about support services in the local area. On the wall were pictures of Ntsupe and Bontle at Ekurhuleni Pride, but also of other lesbians. Bontle explained:

> This is our memory wall ... some of them died of natural causes, but many of the lesbians in the pictures were murdered because of their sexual orientation. Women are less than men. If you're a black woman, you are even less, and if you're a black lesbian woman you are basically nothing in this country.

Ntsupe explained that as well as offering information and support to LGBTQ+ people from her home, she encourages people to think of it as a social space in an area where there are none for LGBTQ+ people. The LGBTQ+ people she has met at Ekurhuleni Pride are welcome to come and spend time and socialize. Ekurhuleni Pride has managed to get funding from the local municipality. This funding covers the cost of sound equipment, a marquee and hire of a local park, but not any staff costs. Ntsupe is unwaged and EPOC is staffed by volunteers, many of who are also unwaged. Given the scale of violence directed at Black lesbians living in townships and the personal risk Ntsupe and the other activists from EPOC were taking, I was deeply struck by how courageous this activism was and the political and social significance of the visibility she and EPOC sought to bring to LGBTQ+ issues in such spaces of danger.

The location of Ekurhuleni Pride changes each year and some years an area where there has been a recent homophobic attack is chosen. In 2022, I attended Ekurhuleni Pride held in township of Wattville, on the edge of Benoni. Ntsupe commented that for her, the purpose of Ekurhuleni Pride

> means not only one thing. It's political in the way that we're challenging the government, we're challenging the powers in our community, political power. We're saying, "We're here, we're saying, 'these are our challenges. Fix this. Help us with this'. And also, it's about the LGBTI person. It's about our diversity. It's about showcasing who we are and telling the community that we are different, although we are all homosexuals but we are different, we're not the same. And also to give out information to the community. I think it's awareness. I think when we march and we have our posters up we are saying something to the community.
>
> I think it's that one-day where we can share our lives with the community. I think for me, also, it's important to invite them because we cannot have Pride on our own, just to be with us from morning to late. And also see what Pride is all about. And also give their input because what we do normally, before the Pride, in certain townships, we talk with the stakeholders of the township, the ward councillors. And we find out what people think Pride is, what is it that they want to see.

Like FEW, Ntsupe stressed that EPOC sought do activism and engagement across the year and not just on the day of Pride. In the past they had held community dialogues about LGBTQ+ issues and were discussing doing a 'door-to-door campaign'.

[G]o inside the houses, talk to the families, tell them about us, about homosexuality, find out about what they know, leave pamphlets. I think just reaching out to people, because we believe if people have more information about homosexuality, it will reduce the rates of hate crimes and hate speech. Because we've found through our community dialogues that people lack information, or they're misinformed about what homosexuality is.

The Ekurhuleni Pride march attracted hundreds of attendees and marched through most of the streets of the township. As the colourful and noisy march went by singing, shouting slogans and dancing, I noticed residents peering over walls and around corners of gates at the march. A group of African LGBTQ+ asylum seekers in South Africa had marched in the parade and held a rainbow flag with 'Refugees Welcome', referring to the high levels of xenophobic hostility to asylum seekers in South Africa, and the difficulties of claiming LGBT asylum in the country. As we reached the park in the centre of Wattville, where the NGO, government, services and food stalls were, some residents approached me, assuming that as one of the only two white people there, we must have arranged the event. I explained what was happening and the residents stayed and talked with the organizers and other attendees. At the afterparty venue, there was a 'memorial tree' where people were writing messages to LGBTQ+ who had died in the previous year. A sex workers rights group had a stall and were wearing t-shirts with 'this is what a sex worker looks like' on them. A photographer from the *Benoni City Times* took photos and they appeared on the front page of the next edition of the newspaper. Ekurhuleni Pride was organized to raise visibility, educate, create safe spaces in places in danger and foster a sense of community and belonging where otherwise this would be difficult to achieve.

Conclusion

The organization of alternative or 'Reclaim' Pride marches has arisen because of sustained criticism and protest at mainstream Pride parades about racism, classism, and the causes and communities Pride includes or ignores or excludes. The organization of alternative Pride marches have also been in response to the specific restrictions of mainstream Prides, such as the imposition of dress codes and the desire to 'straighten' Pride and exclude sexual and other LGBTQ+ subcultures.

The professionalization and commercialization of Pride have also caused tensions, and often very conflictual relationships between Pride organizers and queer activists, leading to queer activists organizing their own Pride events. The alternative Pride events draw from histories or queer and radical activism which in New York includes ACT UP and the Sisters of Perpetual Indulgence; in Hong Kong pro-democracy and feminist trade union and global justice activism; in Taipei youth pro-democracy activism and in South Africa the Liberation Struggle and women's and queer activism that emerged out of it. While these activist legacies draw from broader social justice movements, they also relate to the early LGBTQ+ activists involved in the Stonewall Riots and the first Pride marches, and they harness and emphasize emotions of anger and protest to a much greater degree than contemporary mainstream Prides. Mainstream Pride parades often fulfil the 'happy smiling face' (Ahmed, 2012) of diversity politics that does not confront or offend commercial institutions and broader society. Queer Prides from New York to Soweto are often an incongruous, confronting and uncomfortable sight for onlookers, even if they continue to embody a joyful, creative energy and their after events being welcoming spaces for local communities.

The fact that queer Prides do not seek to police and restrict who participates in the parade, apart from commercial institutions, the police and political parties, and that the organizing communities are either voluntary, or staffed by NGO workers whose main purpose is not just organizing the Pride event, but campaigning for broader social justice, also means these Pride events are 'alternative' to mainstream Prides. During the political march and at the after social after event, there is the opportunity to see and learn about marginalized causes, communities and rights issues, to make connections and become involved in activism. These opportunities are also often either limited, or non-existent in commercial Pride parades, particularly if such parades simply celebrate rights won and are populated by corporate floats. The alternative Pride events discussed in this chapter demonstrate that Pride can be a useful platform for radical and queer activism, for alternative community building and for forging future activist, social justice struggles, but that for this to happen activists have to draw from broader queer and radical activist histories and practices than from just Pride alone.

Chapter 7

CONCLUSION: HOMOCAPITALISM AND THE QUEER POLITICS OF PRIDE

> Pride holds people's lives in it. And when you organize a thing like that, you think about everyone else. You cannot be thinking about yourself and your own. Pride belongs to the people. It does not belong to the 5 people that are going to organize it.
>
> – Mpumi Mathabela, One in Nine Campaign, Johannesburg (interview with the author, 2018)

Mpumi Mathabela reflected on the ownership of Pride while considering the organizer of 2012 Joburg Pride's angry response towards the Black protestors who were disrupting what the organizer considered to be her Pride parade. The organizer shouting 'get off my route' at the protestors from the window of her gold Mercedes car vividly illustrated this. With mainstream Prides in towns and cities becoming large-scale, logistically complex and expensive enterprises, the 'ownership' of Pride has become controversial and contested. The gentrified model of Pride is logistically complex and expensive. Large-scale Prides with orchestrated parades, require negotiations with and conditions from financial and official stakeholders, permit permissions, tickets, barriers, security personnel, and bars and food outlets that prohibit self-made picnics. Many Pride organizers uncritically accept the necessity of this and as has been documented in this book, will argue that their queer critics are naïve, that their hands are effectively tied and that they are, by necessity, beholden to government and corporate partners. While these 'choices' made by Pride organizers may, to varying degrees, be borne out of financial and legal necessities, they do fundamentally change the nature of the Pride event, the people included or excluded, the communities that are highlighted or overlooked and the issues and causes that are considered important, or irrelevant. As Mpumi Mathabela's comment implies, tightly controlled Pride events organized by a small number of people are likely to conform to and evoke the world views and tastes of the organizers themselves, and with the professionalization of LGBTQ+ activism, this is likely to be a white, middle-class, gentrified and male worldview.

'Alternative' Prides, whether the Queer Liberation March, Drag and Dyke Marches in New York, Hong Kong Migrants Pride, or a Pride that is 'alternative' to the 'mainstream' Pride in the city or region, such as Soweto and Ekurhuleni Prides in the Johannesburg region, do not take an exclusive approach to organizing Pride. These queer Prides draw from the intersectional grassroots community organizing approaches of previous generations of radical activism, most notably ACT UP for the New York Queer Liberation March and also the women's grassroots organizing in the South African Liberation Struggle in the cases of Soweto and Ekurhuleni Prides. Hong Kong Migrants Pride combines the feminist anti-globalization, social justice activism and grassroots and transnational trade union organizing among migrant domestic workers in the territory. Volunteers who draw from community activism-based approaches can organize even large-scale Pride events, such as Taiwan Pride. These grassroots and community-based Prides allow for a multiplicity of individuals, groups, causes and issues to freely participate. 'Alternative' Prides still combine the social and fun aspects of 'mainstream' Prides, with afterparties, food stalls and music events, but what distinguishes them from 'mainstream' Prides is that organizers consider the march and the issues it raises to be of central importance and the afterparty includes speeches, and stalls representative of activist and community groups and services. This means that even casual attendees can become informed and drawn into activism if they wish to be. Furthermore, all the 'alternative' Pride organizers featured in this book continue to organize campaign and hold events throughout the year. Queer Prides are more than for just one day.

While researching this book and thinking about the mainstream Pride events I attended, I was consistently struck by not just the often joylessness of these events, but also the frequent disorganization of gentrified 'mainstream' Pride events. I found the official World Pride parade in New York interminably dull, with long gaps between each contingent in the march. It is difficult to get excited about seeing IBM, EY or the Israeli embassy marching past, and especially so when you are standing behind a barrier and watching a parade that lasts for many hours. It was incongruous to hear the marshals shouting 'Happy Pride' in such circumstances. The World Pride Human Rights conference was disorganized and as became clear over the months and years of my research, included a small elite of LGBTQ+ diversity professionals and

7. Conclusion

Figure 19 Silent 'Die In', Soweto Pride, 2018.

Figure 20 Jade Madingwane, Forum for the Empowerment of Women and organizer of Soweto Pride.

celebrities, many of whom I would see time and again at other LGBTQ+ international events and some of whom, as one of my informants laconically observed, jumped from one organization to another 'failing up' the LGBTQ+ NGO ladder. I wondered why the 'career queers' who were responsible for these events seemed so distant and disinterested in the grassroots queer activists and issues they claimed to speak and act on behalf of. I believe Sarah Schulman's (2012b) identification of the bland mediocrity that characterizes social, cultural, economic and political gentrification helps explain why gentrified Pride events were often so exclusive and unsatisfactory for those not in the 'in group'.

Pride is a pre-eminent location for witnessing the gentrification of queer culture, in the policing of bodily appearance and dress, the downplaying and 'straightening' of the celebration of sex and sexuality, in the neatly printed signs and banners of corporate and other institutional marchers in the parade, by the conflation of business practice and human rights advocacy, and in the plethora of glamorized VIP and ticketed events focused on consumption and the communication of aspirational and moneyed 'lifestyles'. In Chapter 2, I located queerness in the realm of the aesthetic, the artistic and the subcultural. Muñoz is one of the many queer theorists who has drawn from the radical subcultures of New York, London and elsewhere in the 1970s, '80s and '90s and wrote 'often we can glimpse the worlds proposed and promised by queerness in the realm of the aesthetic ... queer aesthetics map future social relations' (Muñoz, 2019: 1). Along with Shulman (2012b) and many queer cultural producers, Muñoz sees the 'ossifying effects' and 'denigration of politics' inherent in the co-optation and representation of queerness in contemporary popular culture (Muñoz, 2019: 22). The boundaries between queer subcultures and gentrified mainstream culture are porous and co-optation of that which was once weird, radical and outside the mainstream for commercial gain is common. Pride organizers, academic and other commentators on Pride, who do not adopt a curious and critical perspective on Pride's intersectional location between queer sub-cultures and capitalist co-option, serve to obscure and aid that co-option.

I continue to think about the lack of success I had in trying to connect the South African (and other) queer Black grassroots activists I had met with the InterPride organizers of the World Pride Human Rights Conference in Copenhagen. The theme of the 2021 World Pride Human Rights Conference in Copenhagen was 'You are Included', but none of the grassroots activists from South Africa had been invited to participate, even though they had applied, and I had spoken to the

7. Conclusion

organizer of the conference several times to try and get them included. Grassroots queer organizers continue to be often overlooked in reports produced by LGBTQ+ international agencies and in funding decisions by international donors. I think this is because of the same gentrified logics that underpin the exclusion and lack of interest given to marginalized queer communities across broader society. When re-reading Schulman's *The Gentrification of the Mind*, an anecdote about John Kelly, a radical underground gay artist from 1970s and 1980s Manhattan, whose performances would often 'channel' the folk singer Joni Mitchell resonated with my thoughts about the reasons for why queer grassroots voices are so often absent from Pride and LGBTQ+ spaces. Despite Kelly's long association with Mitchell's work and his pedigree as a queer subcultural artist from the 1970s and 1980s, he had not been included in a Joni Mitchell tribute album produced in the 2000s. When interviewed by the *New Yorker* magazine, Kelly was asked why 'he did not want' to be part of a recent Joni Mitchell tribute album. 'I wasn't invited,' Kelly replied. Schulman continues:

> It was such an amazing moment. The *New Yorker* reporter, who by definition has power and access, projected that this important senior artist would have the same. She assumed that he had 'made it'. And that the only reason he was not being included would be because of his own refusal. She projected power onto this gay experimental artist that he cannot possibly have because of his cultural position. I would have understood from the first second that of course he was excluded, that inclusion in the Joni Mitchell tribute album was not based on talent, understanding, merit, or having something to say. But this reporter, believing that things are different than they actually are, believed that he was now normal.
> (Schulman, 2012b: 85)

The parallel to this example is Pride and the assumptions that it is automatically inclusive of LGBTQ+ communities and that it will inevitably highlight the realities of LGBTQ+ lives and the causes that are important to them. Pride, like much of contemporary culture, politics and society, is often gentrified and exclusionary. As this book has argued, there is a dislocation and disassociation between gentrified 'career queers', Pride organizers and queer grassroots, even in the Global South. Prescriptive rules on dress and appearance at Pride parades also reveal this disassociation and discomfort with the reality of difference, subcultural lifestyles and identities, poverty and precarity.

Schulman's explication of the 'gentrified', educated and wealthy residents of contemporary Manhattan identifies that they have suburban values that are premised in whiteness and a disidentification with those who are different or marginalized, with an attendant disinterest in adopting critical perspectives on social relations, and a deference to authority. Yet, they do like the idea of the radical queerness of Manhattan's subcultural past and craft aspirational lifestyles that draw from these subcultures, even though they are entirely disinterested in the realities of those pasts and would be uncomfortable with, or disdainful of, the queer, immigrant, working-class communities that populated those subcultures. I believe Schulman's analysis of these gentrified new progressive elites underpins the reasons for the exclusion and lack of consideration of marginalized LGBTQ+ people by gentrified 'career queers' (Rodriguez, 2022).

Much of the existing academic and popular literature on Pride is positive and celebrates its political, social and cultural effects. As I have argued in this book, I believe that there are several reasons for this. The first is the dependence on the social movement, or contentious politics, studies approach that over-simplifies and overstates Pride as being a social movement, assuming it has a political rationale, goals and that it consistently uses protest. Yet Pride can be no more than a day-long festival with entirely commercial aims, or a celebratory event with no protest involved. Also, defining Pride as a transnational social movement, where modes of behaviour and political meanings are transmitted and translated across the world overstates Pride as an organized and connected transnational movement. It is rather like defining and analysing weddings as a transnational social movement on the premise that many wedding ceremonies and rituals draw from those developed in European courtly society in the eighteenth and nineteenth centuries. Weddings, like many Pride parades and afterparties, can appear to have the same dress and rituals, but have no political or social function beyond the event itself and the opportunities for consumption that they afford.

While Pride often involves a parade, it does not always do this, according to whether the organizers want a protest focused march or are legally prohibited from holding a parade or march. The widespread and transnational use of the rainbow to identify Pride and LGBTQ+ identities is as much, and possibly more, to do with the ease of the free commercial application of the rainbow for these purposes, than from an expression of Pride as a transnational political or social movement. Claiming Pride is like a 'May Day parade' or a 'civil religion' with rituals and modes of dress is not only a simplifying overstatement, but also reveals the epistemological whiteness and privileged global locations of the authors who make such claims. In many areas of the world, Pride's emphasis on collective and individual 'coming out' is not applicable because of the social, legal and physical risks that this would entail. Sweeping, catch-all statements about Pride in transnational terms should be avoided. The purpose, performance and desired impacts of Pride have been controversial and contested in many contexts, and were contested in the United States almost immediately after Pride became phenomenon in the early 1970s. Choosing to overlook, or minimize, these controversies does a disservice to the queer activists who have struggled and continue to fight for Pride to highlight precarity, marginalization and campaign for social justice.

Shifts in late-capitalism that ostensibly include celebrate and advocate for LGBTQ+ communities and rights are most visibly evident at Pride parades and by the ubiquitous marketing opportunities afforded by rainbow branding during 'Pride Month'. The commercial involvement in and celebration of Pride have created complex dilemmas and controversies for queer activists, LGBTQ+ employees and academics alike. The simultaneous framing of ethical human rights problems and the 'business sense' of commercial actors' involvement in these problems as a positive good emerged in the 1970s and 1980s. These shifts follow a long trajectory of capitalism adapting to incorporate socio-political challenges and global financial changes. These included the relative financial decline of Europe and North America and a desire to appeal to new markets in East and South Asia, alongside adapting to the challenge of the women's and Black rights movements, changes in employment law, and seeking to neutralize and sidestep specific social justice activist campaigns that targeted business activities, particularly those opposing US and other Western companies operating in apartheid-era South Africa.

In the case of Western business operations in South Africa, the voluntary Sullivan codes and the apparent commitment to non-racist and ethical business standards, in what was otherwise a racist and oppressive context, defined apartheid as a local problem at once outside the responsibility of international companies who operated in country, but also a local problem that was most effectively mediated and resolved by the engagement of international companies as ethical and egalitarian actors in that context. Many of these companies' trade with the country not only helped South Africa present itself as a bastion of Western civilization, but they also directly ensured the operation of apartheid and the military repression of those who struggled against it. The Sullivan codes split the international anti-apartheid movement and continue to be upheld as a model of ethical business leadership, despite the evidence pointing to international business ideological, financial and operational underpinning of white minority rule. While one international socio-political-economic problem is not the same as another, particularly across time and space, the example of the 'business sense' of ethical corporate involvement in apartheid-South Africa illuminates the adroit shifts of capitalism and business strategy to maximize profit and sidestep challenge from activists when operating in morally and ethically problematic contexts. The lineage of business as ethical actors and agents of positive social and political change resonates throughout contemporary 'homocapitalist' discourses that frame homophobia as a local cultural 'problem' that Global North businesses can intervene and act as a constructive and positive arbiter for change. This, like for apartheid, obscures the structural and intersectional dynamics of homophobia, the role transnational business plays in keeping some countries poor and others rich, some communities educated and others not, and underpins the authoritarian populist leaders where homophobia is part and parcel of the regime. LGBTQ+ 'beneficiaries' of homocapitalism, whether they be professional employees in an LGBTQ+ staff group in London, Hong Kong or Johannesburg, can have genuine intentions and have benefitted in financial and other ways by their participation, but the corporate framing of LGBTQ+ Pride and identities in this way obscures and discriminates against those who are not, or cannot, participate as professional employees in those contexts.

The ostensible embrace of Pride and LGBTQ+ rights by many transnational corporations and governments, particularly in the Global North, has created opportunities and dilemmas for LGBTQ+ activists. I agree with Moreau and Currier (2018) that activists in the Global South face a 'queer dilemma' when faced with limited, or no local financial resources, and that corporate or diplomatic involvement and support for Pride can provide a vital lifeline. Similarly, corporate employees and diplomats can be well intentioned and have personal and political convictions that propel them to become involved. I am sympathetic to Atshan's (2020) criticisms of the queer critique of 'pinkwashing' espoused from academics from the convenience of the Global North, critiques that can be too purist and isolate grassroots queer activists even further. However, I would point to the paucity of funding for LGBTQ+ causes and activism of any kind in corporate and government budgets, and to the precarious and vicarious nature

7. Conclusion

of this funding. Businesses are very reluctant to openly challenge homophobic legislation in the territories they operate in and quick to drop LGBTQ+ Pride branding and commitments when targeted by homophobic critics in all contexts. National governments have also proven to be capricious when maintaining, already shallow, commitments to LGBTQ+ international advocacy and funding. While leveraging support for grassroots LGBTQ+ activism and Pride is sometimes possible and can make a positive difference, it does not evidence the inherently positive role international business and governments' play, nor is it a reliable defence in the face of the backlash against LGBTQ+ rights.

Figure 21 Queer Liberation March, New York, 2019.

We live within and are constrained by capitalism, many of us find the developments and shifts in contemporary capitalism alluring and rewarding. I can understand why corporate employees who are engaged in LGBTQ+ Staff committees march in Pride parades, even though I choose not to do so myself for ethical reasons. Like some of my students, many people sometimes struggle to understand queer, feminist and critical race critiques of 'post-feminist' consumption (McRobbie, 2008) and 'diversity politics' (Ahmed, 2012) and wonder why queer, and other commentators, are criticizing what is ostensibly progressive and supportive developments. I believe that the sanguine academic accounts of Pride are also, in part, the result of academics' enmeshment with neoliberal capitalist discourses and the gentrification of higher education. This is not just because of an individual embeddedness within capitalism, but also the pressures to publish in quantity, the reduction of time and resources to conduct sustained ethnographic research, particularly if it involves costly and sustained international fieldwork, and a gentrified lack of curiosity and intellectual commitment to challenge and disrupt. I believe academic researchers, like artists, have a duty to be forever curious about what appears to be otherwise self-evident, to tell the truth of things as we see it and to, as Skeggs (2007) advocates, to continually think 'in whose interests' do we research and write for. For researchers of Pride, we have duty to consider who is not included, why this is and to be honest about whether Pride events are truly representative of the precarious and complex lives LGBTQ+ communities live in the contexts we study. We should also always go further than just accepting at face value the accounts of Pride we are presented with by organizers and attendees and think about the motivations these actors may have and the ideological effects of Pride as a platform for activism, consumption, marketing and institutional diversity politics.

I began this project intrigued by whether queer critics' accounts of Pride in the Global North are replicated elsewhere and whether Pride has a useful utility in LGBTQ+ activism and community building internationally. I found that there are queer critiques that are replicated across the world, with the spaces and places Pride takes place, the communities included and excluded, the messages and politics allowed and disabled and the involvement of commercial institutions, becoming common points of tension. Pride is also a prime location where local socio-political divisions are refracted and exacerbated in the sharpest of terms: becoming a flashpoint for racial tensions in South Africa, political and caste tension in India and between global elites and the globally and locally marginalized and exploited in Hong Kong. Despite many problematic 'mainstream' Prides that misrepresent and mislead participants and spectators alike about truths of LGBTQ+ lives. Pride can and does serve as a useful platform for activism, community building, celebration, mourning and political protest. Queer Prides draw from the grassroots, participatory and community-based radicalism of movements such as ACT UP, which itself drew from feminist, anti-racist and anti-capitalist movements. There are parallels in other radical grassroots movements, such as the South African Liberation Struggle. Queer Prides are flexible, inclusive, large and small scale, fun and serious, sometimes chaotic, but also meaningful and impactful. By including and representing the truth of LGBTQ+ lives and deaths, and relating these to the social, economic and political struggles of other marginalized groups, they communicate the reality of things and enable attendees and observers to become aware, and more involved as activists if they want to be. I was deeply inspired by the courageousness and commitment of the queer activists across the contexts I studied and encourage anyone reading this book to become more aware of, engaged in their work and to support them. Pride should indeed belong to the people, but because of homocapitalism, all too often it does not.

REFERENCES

AFP (2016) 'HSBC's "Disgusting" Rainbow Lion Statues "Trample Family Values", Anti-Gay Groups Claim', *Hong Kong Free Press HKFP*. Available at: https://hongkongfp.com/2016/12/06/hsbcs-disgusting-rainbow-lion-statues-trample-family-values-anti-gay-groups-claim/ (Accessed: 26 May 2020).

Ahmed, S. (2006) *Queer Phenomenology: Orientations, Objects, Others*. Durham, NC: Duke University Press.

Ahmed, S. (2012) *On Being Included: Racism and Diversity in Institutional Life*. Durham, NC: Duke University Press Books.

Ammaturo, F.R. (2016) 'Spaces of Pride: A Visual Ethnography of Gay Pride Parades in Italy and the United Kingdom', *Social Movement Studies*, 15(1), pp. 19–40.

Arnold, M. (2023) 'German Top Court Strikes down €60bn Off-Budget Climate Fund'. Available at: https://www.ft.com/content/e36830bf-0fb4-4878-944c-0bf9088478d2 (Accessed: 7 May 2024).

Atshan, S. (2020) *Queer Palestine and the Empire of Critique*. Redwood, CA: Stanford University Press.

Ayoub, P.M. and Stoeckl, K. (2024) *The Global Fight against LGBTI Rights: How Transnational Conservative Networks Target Sexual and Gender Minorities*. New York, NY: New York University Press.

Ayoub, P.M., Page, D. and Whitt, S. (2021) 'Pride amid Prejudice: The Influence of LGBT+ Rights Activism in a Socially Conservative Society', *American Political Science Review*, 115(2), pp. 467–85.

Bancroft, A. (2012) 'Leigh Bowery: Queer in Fashion, Queer in Art', *Sexualities*, 15(1), pp. 68–79.

Beetar, M. (2016) 'Intersectional (Un)Belongings: Lived Experiences of Xenophobia and Homophobia', *Agenda*, 30(1), pp. 96–103.

Bell, D. and Binnie, J. (2000) *The Sexual Citizen: Queer Politics and Beyond*. Cambridge: Polity Press.

Bell, D. and Valentine, G. (1995) *Mapping Desire: Geographies of Sexualities*. 1st edn. London: Routledge.

Berlant, L. (2011) *Cruel Optimism*. Durham, NC: Duke University Press.

Berlant, L. and Freeman, E. (1992) 'Queer Nationality', *Boundary 2*, 19(1), pp. 149–80.

Bernot, A. and Davies, S.E. (2024) 'The "Fish Tank": Social Sorting of LGBTQ+ Activists in China', *International Feminist Journal of Politics*, 26(2), pp. 351–74.

Bernot, A., Yang, F. and Davies, S.E. (2024) 'The Glowing Fireflies': Invisible Activism under China's Queer Necropolitics', *Convergence: The*

International Journal of Research into New Media Technologies [Online First]. https://doi.org/10.1177/13548565241288466.

Bevington, D. and Dixon, C. (2005) 'Movement-Relevant Theory: Rethinking Social Movement Scholarship and Activism', *Social Movement Studies*, 4(3), pp. 185–208.

Blee, K.M. (1993) 'Evidence, Empathy, and Ethics: Lessons from Oral Histories of the Klan', *The Journal of American History*, 80(2), pp. 596–606.

Boston, N. and Duyvendak, J.W. (2015) 'People of Color Mobilization in LGBT Movements in the Netherlands and the United States', in D. Paternotte and M. Tremblay (eds) *The Ashgate Research Companion to Lesbian and Gay Activism*. 1st edn. Farnham: Routledge, pp. 135–48.

Bourdieu, P. (1992) *The Logic of Practice*. Cambridge: Polity Press.

Brown, G. (2007) 'Mutinous Eruptions: Autonomous Spaces of Radical Queer Activism', *Environment and Planning A: Economy and Space*, 39(11), pp. 2685–98.

Brown, G. (2015) 'Queer Movement', in D. Paternotte and M. Tremblay (eds) *Ashgate Companion to Lesbian and Gay Activism*. Farnham: Ashgate, pp. 73–86.

Brown, S. and Swiss, L. (2017) 'Canada's Feminist International Assistance Policy: Bold Statement or Feminist Fig Leaf?', in K. Graham and A. Maslove (eds) *How Ottawa Spends 2017–2018*. Ottawa: School of Public Policy and Administration, Calrelton University, pp. 117–31.

Browne, K. (2007) 'A Party with Politics? (Re)making LGBTQ Pride Spaces in Dublin and Brighton', *Social & Cultural Geography*, 8(1), pp. 63–87.

Browne, K. and Nash, C.J. (2014) 'Resisting LGBT Rights Where "We Have Won": Canada and Great Britain', *Journal of Human Rights*, 13(3), pp. 322–36.

Bruce, K.M. (2016) *Pride Parades: How a Parade Changed the World*. New York, NY: New York University Press.

Burack, C. (2018) *Because We Are Human: Contesting US Support for Gender and Sexuality Human Rights Abroad*. Albany, NY: State University of New York Press.

Burchiellaro, O. (2023) *The Gentrification of Queer Activism: Diversity Politics and the Promise of Inclusion in London*. Bristol: University of Bristol Press.

BusinessTech (2019) *This Is the Average Salary in South Africa*, *BusinessTech*. Available at: https://businesstech.co.za/news/wealth/307088/this-is-the-average-salary-in-south-africa/ (Accessed: 20 September 2019).

Butler, J. (1999) *Gender Trouble: Feminism and the Subversion of Identity*. 2nd edn. New York, NY; London: Routledge.

Butler, J. (2002) 'Is Kinship Always Already Heterosexual?', *Differences*, 13(1), pp. 14–44.

Butler, J. (2010) *Frames of War: When Is Life Grievable?* London; New York, NY: Verso.

Camminga, B. (2019) *Transgender Refugees and the Imagined South Africa: Bodies over Borders and Borders over Bodies*. Basingstoke: Palgrave Macmillan.

Chan, H. (2019) 'Hong Kong's Equal Opportunities Watchdog Swaps One Anti-Gay Member for Another', *Hong Kong Free Press*. Available at: https://hongkongfp.com/2019/04/27/hong-kongs-equal-opportunities-watchdog-swaps-one-anti-gay-member-another/ (Accessed: 23 March 2025).

Chancel, L, Piketty, T., Saez, E. and Zucman, G. (2021) *World Inequality Report 2022*. Paris: Paris School of Economics. Available at: https://wir2022.wid.world/www-site/uploads/2023/03/D_FINAL_WIL_RIM_RAPPORT_2303.pdf (Accessed: 16 March 2025).

Chang, K.A. and Groves, J.M. (2000) 'Neither "Saints" nor "Prostitutes": Sexual Discourse in the Filipina Domestic Worker Community in Hong Kong', *Women's Studies International Forum*, 23(1), pp. 73–87.

Chisholm, A. (2022) *The Gendered and Colonial Lives of Gurkhas in Private Security: From Military to Market*. 1st edn. Edinburgh: Edinburgh University Press.

Choudry, A. and Kapoor, D. (eds) (2012) 'Introduction: NGOization: Complicity, Contradictions and Prospects', in *NGO-ization: Complicity, Contradictions and Prospects*. London: Zed Books, pp. 1–22.

Christensen, J.F., Just, S.N. and Schwarzkopf, S. (2024) 'Productive Tensions of Corporate Pride Partnerships: Towards a Relational Ethics of Constitutive Impurity', *Journal of Business Ethics* [Preprint]. Available at: https://doi.org/10.1007/s10551-024-05813-w.

City of Cape Town. (2023) *Census 2022: Cape Town Profile*. Cape Town: City of Cape Town. Available at: https://resource.capetown.gov.za/documentcentre/Documents/City%20research%20reports%20and%20review/2022_Census_Cape_Town_profile.pdf.

Constable, N. (2018) *Maid to Order in Hong Kong: Stories of Migrant Workers*. 2nd edn. Ithaca, NY: Cornell University Press.

Conway, D. (2009) 'Queering Apartheid: The National Party's 1987 "Gay Rights" Election Campaign in Hillbrow', *Journal of Southern African Studies*, 35(4), pp. 849–63.

Conway, D. (2014) 'Struggles for Citizenship in South Africa', in E. Isin and P, Nyers (eds) *Routledge Handbook of Global Citizenship Studies*. London: Routledge, pp. 240–9.

Conway, D. (2016) 'Shades of White Complicity: The End Conscription Campaign and the Politics of White Liberal Ignorance in South Africa', in Robin Dunford, A. Afxentiou, and M. Neu (eds) *Exploring Complicity: Concept, Cases and Critique*. London and New York, NY: Rowman & Littlefield Publishers, pp. 133–56.

Conway, D. (2022) 'Whose Lifestyle Matters at Johannesburg Pride? The Lifestylisation of LGBTQ+ Identities and the Gentrification of Activism', *Sociology*, 56(1), pp. 148–65.

Conway, D. (2023) 'The Politics of Truth at LGBTQ+ Pride: Contesting Corporate Pride and Revealing Marginalized Lives at Hong Kong Migrants Pride', *International Feminist Journal of Politics*, 25(4), pp. 734–56.

Conway, D. (2024) 'Conceptualising Queer Activist Critiques of Pride in the Two-Thirds World: Queer Activism and Alternative Pride Organizing in South Africa, Mumbai, Hong Kong and Shanghai', *Sexualities* [Online First]. https://doi.org/10.1177/13634607241248898.

Conway, D. and Leonard, P. (2014) *Migration, Space and Transnational Identities: The British in South Africa*. Basingstoke: Palgrave Macmillan.

Coopoo, S. (2023) 'Opinion: Queer Bodies Are Still Crime Scenes' *MambaOnline – Gay South Africa online*. Available at: https://www.mamba.lgbt/2023/08/22/opinion-queer-bodies-are-still-crime-scenes/ (Accessed: 9 December 2024).

Cox, L. and Fominaya, C.F. (2009) 'Movement Knowledge: What Do We Know, How Do We Create Knowledge and What Do We Do with It?', *Interface*, 1(1), pp. 1–20.

Currier, A. (2011) 'Representing Gender and Sexual Dissidence in Southern Africa', *Qualitative Sociology*, 34(3), pp. 463–81.

Danewid, I. (2023) *Resisting Racial Capitalism: An Antipolitical Theory of Refusal*. Cambridge: University of Cambridge Press.

De Waal, S. and Manion, A. (eds) (2006) *Pride: Protest and Celebration*. Johannesburg: Jacana Media.

DeBarros, L. (2016) 'Shocking Scale of LGBT Discrimination in South Africa Revealed', *MambaOnline – Gay South Africa online*. Available at: http://www.mambaonline.com/2016/11/29/shocking-scale-lgbt-discrimination-south-africa-revealed/ (Accessed: 16 December 2018).

Delatolla, A. (2020) 'Sexuality as a Standard of Civilization: Historicizing (Homo)Colonial Intersections of Race, Gender, and Class', *International Studies Quarterly*, 64(1), pp. 148–58.

Dlungwana, P, S. Allen and Y. Nakamori (eds). (2024) *Zanele Muholi*. London: Tate Publishing.

Dreyfus, H. and Rabinow, P. (1982) *Michel Foucault: Beyond Structuralism and Hermeneutics*. Chicago, IL: University of Chicago Press.

Duggan, L. (2004) *The Twilight of Equality: Neoliberalism, Cultural Politics, and the Attack on Democracy*. Boston, MA: Beacon Press.

Eisenbach, D. (2006) *Gay Power: An American Revolution*: New York, NY: Carroll & Graf.

Encarnación, O.G. (2016) 'The Troubled Rise of Gay Rights Diplomacy', *Current History*, 115(777), pp. 17–22.

Eng, D. (2010) *The Feeling of Kinship: Queer Liberalism and the Racialization of Intimacy*. Durham, NC: Duke University Press.

Enguix, B. (2009) 'Identities, Sexualities and Commemorations: Pride Parades, Public Space and Sexual Dissidence'. Available at: https://www.semanticscholar.org/paper/Identities%2C-Sexualities-and-Commemorations%3A-Pride-Enguix/01b9233ce9c65e99b5ffe19f152d74bdfacee935 (Accessed: 20 July 2023).

Enloe, C. (2004) *The Curious Feminist: Searching for Women in a New Age of Empire*. Berkeley, CA: University of California Press.

Enloe, C. (2014) *Bananas, Beaches and Bases: Making Feminist Sense of International Politics*. 2nd edn. Berkeley, CA: University of California Press.

Eschle, C. and Maiguishca, B. (2009) *Making Feminist Sense of the Global Justice Movement*. Lanham, MD: Rowman & Littlefield Publishers.

Estes, N. (2023) *Our History Is the Future: Standing Rock versus the Dakota Access Pipeline, and the Long Tradition of Indigenous Resistance*. London and New York, NY: Verso Books.

Fairclough, P.N. (1995) *Critical Discourse Analysis: The Critical Study of Language*. Harlow: Longman.

Fletcher, J. (2016) 'Born Free, Killed by Hate', 7 April. Available at: https://www.bbc.com/news/magazine-35967725 (Accessed: 16 December 2018).

Foucault, M. (1980) *Power/Knowledge: Selected Interviews and Other Writings 1972–1977*. Brighton: Harvester Press.

Foucault, M. (1998) *The History of Sexuality: 1: The Will to Knowledge: The Will to Knowledge*. Translated by R. Hurley. London: Penguin.

Foucault, M. (2001) 'Truth and Power', in J.D. Faubion (ed), R. Hurley (trans.) *Power: The Essential Works of Foucault, 1954–1984, Vol. 3*. 1st edn. New York, NY: The New Press, pp. 111–33.

Foundation, T.B. and Out, G. (2023) *The UK LGBTIQI International Giving Report*. London: The Baring Foundation.

Fox, D. (2024) 'John Lewis Pulls LGBTQ+ Photo Exhibition "for the Safety and Protection" of Staff', *Attitude*. Available at: https://www.attitude.co.uk/news/john-lewis-pulls-lgbtq-photo-exhibition-for-the-safety-and-protection-of-staff-460082/ (Accessed: 28 August 2024).

Franke, K. (2012) 'Dating the State: The Moral Hazards of Winning Gay Rights', *Columbia Human Rights Law Review*, 44, pp. 1–46.

Gamson, J. (1995) 'Must Identity Movements Self-Destruct? A Queer Dilemma', *Social Problems*, 42(3), pp. 390–407.

Gan, J. (2007) '"Still at the Back of the Bus": Sylvia Rivera's Struggle', *Centro Journal*, XIX(1), pp. 124–39.

Gevisser, M. and Cameron, E. (eds) (1994) *Defiant Desire: Gay and Lesbian Lives in South Africa*. Johannesburg: Ravan Press.

Glass, D. (2020) *United Queerdom: From the Legends of the Gay Liberation Front to the Queers of Tomorrow*. London: Bloomsbury Academic.

Global Philanthropy Project (2024) *Global Resources Report: Government and Philanthropic Support for Lesbian, Gay, Bisexual, Transgender and Intersex Communities 2021/2022*. Global Philanthropy Project. Available at: https://globalresourcesreport.org/wp-content/uploads/2024/06/GRR_2021-2022_WEB-Spread-Colour_EN.pdf (Accessed: 16 March 2025).

Green, M. and Stevenson, N.J. (2024) *Outlaws: Fashion Renegades of Leigh Bowery's 1980s London*. London: Scala Arts & Heritage Publishers.

Grewal, K. (2012) 'Reclaiming the Voice of the "Third World Woman" but What Do We Do When We Don't Like What She Has to Say? The Tricky Case of Ayaan Hirsi Ali', *Interventions*, 14(4), pp. 569–90.

References

Guerandi, G.R. (2022) 'Inclusivity Debate Still Ruffling South African Pride's "Elite" Feather Boas', *Daily Maverick*, 1 March. Available at: https://www.dailymaverick.co.za/article/2022-03-01-inclusivity-debate-still-ruffling-south-african-prides-elite-feather-boas/ (Accessed: 10 December 2024).

Halberstam, J. (2011) *The Queer Art of Failure*. Illustrated edn. Durham, NC: Duke University Press.

Harris, P. (2023) 'Defence of Equal Rights for Hong Kong's Gay Citizens Dovetails with China's Human Rights Playbook', *Hong Kong Free Press*, 17 December. Available at: https://hongkongfp.com/2023/12/17/denial-of-equal-rights-for-hong-kongs-gay-citizens-dovetails-with-chinas-human-rights-playbook/ (Accessed: 25 March 2025).

Harrisberg, K. (2021) 'Fear Breeds Bravery as LGBT+ South Africans Resist "War on Queerness"', *Reuters*, 13 May. Available at: https://www.reuters.com/article/world/fear-breeds-bravery-as-lgbt-safricans-resist-war-on-queerness-idUSKBN2CU0QA/ (Accessed: 9 December 2024).

Henry, M.G. (2003) '"Where Are You Really From?": Representation, Identity and Power in the Fieldwork Experiences of a South Asian Diasporic', *Qualitative Research*, 3(2), pp. 229–42.

Hewlett, S.A. and Sears, T. (2024) 'Why Companies Must Recommit to the Fight for LGBTQ+ Rights', *Harvard Business Review*, 7 May. Available at: https://hbr.org/2024/05/why-companies-must-recommit-to-the-fight-for-lgbtq-rights (Accessed: 28 August 2024).

Highleyman, L. (2002) 'Radical Queers or Queer Radicals? Queer Activism and the Global Justice Movement', in B. Shephard and R. Hayduck (eds) *That's Revolting!: Queer Strategies for Resisting Assimilation*. New York, NY: Soft Skull Press, pp. 100–20.

Hoad, N. (1999) 'Between the White Man's Burden and the White Man's Disease: Tracking Lesbian and Gay Human Rights in Southern Africa', *GLQ: A Journal of Lesbian and Gay Studies*, 5(4), pp. 559–84.

Hokowhitu, B. et al. (eds) (2020) *Routledge Handbook of Critical Indigenous Studies*. London, New York, NY: Routledge.

Holmes, A. (2017) 'Normalizing Queer Spaces: Have Pride Parades Lost Their Political Touch?', *Journal of Political Studies*, 20 (February), pp. 34–56.

Hooper, C. (2001) *Manly States: Masculinities, International Relations, and Gender Politics*. New York, NY: Columbia University Press.

Igual, R. (2015) 'Cape Town Pride to Change Controversial 2016 Theme', *MambaOnline – Gay South Africa online*, 3 December. Available at: https://www.mambaonline.com/2015/12/03/cape-town-pride-change-controversial-2016-theme/ (Accessed: 12 December 2024).

Jackson & Jackson (2023) *Kaleidoscope Diversity Trust Audited Financial Statement 31 March 2023*. London: Charity Commission for England and Wales. Available at: https://register-of-charities.charitycommission.gov.uk/en/charity-search?p_p_id=uk_gov_ccew_onereg_charitydetails_web_portlet_CharityDetailsPortlet&p_p_lifecycle=2&p_p_state=maximized&p_p_mode=view&p_p_resource_id=%2Faccounts-resource&p_p_cacheability=cacheLevelPage&_

uk_gov_ccew_onereg_charitydetails_web_portlet_CharityDetailsPortlet_objectiveId=A14536325&_uk_gov_ccew_onereg_charitydetails_web_portlet_CharityDetailsPortlet_priv_r_p_mvcRenderCommandName=%2Faccounts-and-annual-returns&_uk_gov_ccew_onereg_charitydetails_web_portlet_CharityDetailsPortlet_priv_r_p_organisationNumber=5024230 (Accessed: 16 March 2025).

Johannesburg People's Pride (2013) 'Our Manifesto', 10 June. Available at: https://peoplespride.blogspot.com/p/pride-movement-of-protest-celebration.html

Johnston, L. (2005) *Queering Tourism: Paradoxical Performances of Gay Pride Parades*. London: Routledge.

Judge, M. (2017) *Blackwashing Homophobia: Violence and the Politics of Sexuality, Gender and Race*. New York, NY: Routledge.

Kao, Y.-C. (2024) 'The Coloniality of Queer Theory: The Effects of "Homonormativity" on Transnational Taiwan's Path to Equality', *Sexualities*, 27(1–2), pp. 136–53.

Kates, S.M. and Belk, R.W. (2001) 'The Meanings of Lesbian and Gay Pride Day: Resistance through Consumption and Resistance to Consumption', *Journal of Contemporary Ethnography*, 30(4), pp. 392–429.

Khambay, A. and Dorey, K. (2018) *Engaging with LGBT+ Advocates: A Guide for UK Officials Working Abroad*. London: Stonewall. Available at: https://www.stonewall.org.uk/resources/engaging-lgbt-advocates (Accessed: 20 March 2025).

Khomami, N. (2018) 'Stonewall Withdraws from Pride in London over "Lack of Diversity"', *The Guardian*, 23 February. Available at: https://www.theguardian.com/world/2018/feb/23/stonewall-withdraws-from-pride-in-london-diversity-uk-black-pride (Accessed: 9 December 2024).

Kirk, E.J. (2017) *Cuba's Gay Revolution: Normalizing Sexual Diversity through a Health-Based Approach*. Lanham, MD: Lexington Books.

Kong, T. (2011) *Chinese Male Homosexualities: Memba, Tongzhi and Golden Boys*. London: Routledge.

Kong, T.S.K. (2019) 'Transnational Queer Sociological Analysis of Sexual Identity and Civic-Political Activism in Hong Kong, Taiwan and Mainland China', *The British Journal of Sociology*, 70(5), pp. 1904–25.

Kong, T.S.K. (2023) *Sexuality and the Rise of China: The Post-1990s Gay Generation in Hong Kong, Taiwan, and Mainland China*. Durham, NC: Duke University Press.

Kulpa, R. (2014) 'Western Leveraged Pedagogy of Central and Eastern Europe: Discourses of Homophobia, Tolerance, and Nationhood', *Gender, Place & Culture*, 21(4), pp. 431–48.

Lai, F.Y. (2018) 'Migrant and Lesbian Activism in Hong Kong: A Critical Review of Grassroots Politics', *Asian Anthropology*, 17(2), pp. 135–50.

Langlois, A.J. (2022) *Sexuality and Gender Diversity Rights in Southeast Asia*. Cambridge: Cambridge University Press.

Larson, Z. (2020) 'Sullivan Principles: South Africa, Apartheid, and Globalization', *Diplomatic Hiostory*, 44(3), pp. 479–503.

Lemke, T. (2001) '"The Birth of Bio-Politics": Michel Foucault's Lecture at the Collège De France on Neo-Liberal Governmentality', *Economy and Society*, 30(2), pp. 190–207.

Lewis, C., Chandra, S. and Markwell, K. (2023) 'Exploring Queer People of Colour's Perceptions of Pride in Sydney', *Tourism Geographies*, 26(3), pp. 520–39.

Liu, P. (2023) *The Specter of Materialism: Queer Theory and Marxism in the Age of the Beijing Consensus*. Durham, NC: Duke University Press.

Lopes Heimer, R. dos V. (2020) 'Homonationalist/Orientalist Negotiations: The UK Approach to Queer Asylum Claims', *Sexuality & Culture*, 24(1), pp. 174–96.

Lowery, W. (2017) *They Can't Kill Us All: The Story of Black Lives Matter*. London: Penguin.

Macleod, C. and Durrheim, K. (2002) 'Foucauldian Feminism: The Implications of Governmentality', *Journal for the Theory of Social Behaviour*, 32(1), pp. 41–60.

Maiguashca, B. (2011) 'Looking beyond the Spectacle: Social Movement Theory, Feminist Anti-globalization Activism and the Praxis of Principled Pragmatism', *Globalizations*, 8(4), pp. 535–49.

Markwell, K. and Waitt, G. (2009) 'Festivals, Space and Sexuality: Gay Pride in Australia', *Tourism Geographies*, 11(2), pp. 143–68.

Martin, J. (2017) ''Woke' Whiteness at Johannesburg Pride Events', unpublished MA Thesis, University of the Witwatersrand.

Matebeni, Z. (2018) 'Ihlazo: Pride and the Politics of Race and Space in Johannesburg and Cape Town', *Critical African Studies*, 10(3), pp. 315–28.

Mbembe, A. (2019) *Necropolitics*. Durham, NC: Duke University Press.

McAdam, D., Tarrow, S. and Tilly, C. (2001) *Dynamics of Contention*. Cambridge: Cambridge University Press.

McCartan, A. and Nash, C.J. (2022) 'Creating Queer Safe Space: Relational Space-Making at a Grassroots LGBT Pride Event in Scotland', *Gender, Place & Culture*, 30(6), pp. 770–90.

McRobbie, A. (2008) *The Aftermath of Feminism: Gender, Culture and Social Change*. London: Sage Publications.

Milani, T.M. (2015) 'Sexual Cityzenship: Discourses, Spaces and Bodies at Joburg Pride 2012', *Journal of Language and Politics*, 14(3), pp. 431–54.

Miller, D. (1997) *Capitalism: An Ethnographic Approach*. Oxford: Berg.

Mills, Charles W. (2007) 'White Ignorance', in S. Sullivan and N. Tuana (eds) *Race and Epistemologies of Ignorance*. Albany, NY: State University of New York Press, pp. 11–38.

Mohanty, C.T. (2003) '"Under Western Eyes" Revisited: Feminist Solidarity through Anticapitalist Struggles', *Signs*, 28(2), pp. 499–535.

Mohdin, A. and Correspondent, A.M.C. affairs (2021) 'Entire Pride in London Advisory Board Resigns Citing "Hostile Environment"', *The Guardian*, 18 March. Available at: https://www.theguardian.com/world/2021/mar/18/entire-pride-in-london-advisory-board-resigns-bullying-claims (Accessed: 9 December 2024).

Moran, F. (2025) *Leigh Bowery*. London: Tate Publishing.
Moreau, J. (2017) '"Homophobia Hurts": Mourning as Resistance to Violence in South Africa', *Journal of Lesbian Studies*, 21(2), pp. 204–18.
Moreau, J. and Currier, A. (2018) 'Queer Dilemmas: LGBT Activism and International Funding', in C.L. Mason (ed) *Routledge Handbook of Queer Development Studies*. London: Routledge, pp. 222–38.
Morris, M. (2017) *LGBT Community Still Faces High Levels of Violence – Report*, News24. Available at: https://www.news24.com/Analysis/lgbt-community-still-faces-high-levels-of-violence-report-20171204 (Accessed: 16 December 2018).
Muñoz, J.E. (2019) *Cruising Utopia: The Then and There of Queer Futurity*. New York, 2nd edn. NY: New York University Press.
Murray, C. (2025) 'LGBTQ Pride Organizing in NYC, San Francisco and More Saying Corporate Sponsors Are Scaling Back This Year', *Forbes*. https://www.forbes.com/sites/conormurray/2025/03/18/san-francisco-pride-says-sponsors-bailed-this-year-as-support-for-pride-appears-to-dwindle-across-country/ (Accessed: 21/3/2025).
Murray, D.A.B. (2014) 'Real Queer: "Authentic" LGBT Refugee Claimants and Homonationalism in the Canadian Refugee System', *Anthropologica*, 56(1), pp. 21–32.
Nai-Chia, C. and Fell, D. (2021) 'Tongzhi Diplomacy and the Queer Case of Taiwan', in M. Thornton, R. Ash, and D. Fell (eds) *Taiwan's Economic and Diplomatic Challenges and Opportunities*. London: Routledge, pp. 194–214.
Ndabeni, K. (2018) '"White" Joburg Gay Pride Bashed as Frivolous', *TimesLIVE*, 23 October. Available at: https://www.timeslive.co.za/sunday-times/news/2016-10-23-white-joburg-gay-pride-bashed-as-frivolous/ (Accessed: 9 December 2024).
Neumann, I.B. (2012) *At Home with the Diplomats: Inside a European Foreign Ministry*. Ithaca, NY: Cornell University Press.
Nogueira, M.B.B. (2017) 'The Promotion of LGBT Rights as International Human Rights Norms: Explaining Brazil's Diplomatic Leadership', *Global Governance*, 23(4), pp. 545–63.
Olouch, A. and Tabengwa, M. (2017) 'LGBT Visibility: A Double-Edged Sword', in ILGA, *State Sponsored Homophobia 2017: A World Survey of Sexual Orientation Laws*. Geneva: ILGA, pp. 150–5.
O'Reilly, K. (2008) *Key Concepts in Ethnography*. London: Sage Publications.
Othen-Reeves, R. (2020) 'Leading the Way: The Role of Global Britain in Safeguarding the Rights of the Global LGBTI+ Community', *The Baring Foundation*. Available at: https://baringfoundation.org.uk/resource/leading-the-way-the-role-of-global-britain-in-safeguarding-the-rights-of-the-global-lgbti-community/ (Accessed: 7 May 2024).
Other Foundation (2024) *Size Matters: How Big Is the LGBTI Market in South Africa and What Economic Influence Does It Have?* Johannesburg: The Other Foundation. Available at: https://theotherfoundation.org/size-matters/ (Accessed: 21 March 2025).

References

Outright International (2021) *Pride around the World*. New York, NY: Outright International.

Parisi, L. (2020) 'Canada's New Feminist International Assistance Policy: Business as Usual?', *Foreign Policy Analysis*, 16(2), pp. 163–80.

Paternotte, D. (2014) *LGBT Activism and the Making of Europe: A Rainbow*. Basingstoke: Palgrave Macmillan.

Peterson, A., Wahlström, M. and Wennerhag, M. (2018) *Pride Parades and LGBT Movements: Political Participation in an International Comparative Perspective*. London: Routledge.

Power, E.M. (2004) 'Toward Understanding in Postmodern Interview Analysis: Interpreting the Contradictory Remarks of a Research Participant', *Qualitative Health Research*, 14(6), pp. 858–65.

Press-Barnathan, G. and Lutz, N. (2020) 'The Multilevel Identity Politics of the 2019 Eurovision Song Contest', *International Affairs*, 96(3), pp. 729–48.

Puar, J.K. (2002) 'Circuits of Queer Mobility: Tourism, Travel, and Globalization', *GLQ: A Journal of Lesbian and Gay Studies*, 8(1), pp. 101–37.

Puar, J.K. (2017) *Terrorist Assemblages*. Durham, NC: Duke University Press Books.

Rahman, M. (2014) 'Queer Rights and the Triangulation of Western Exceptionalism', *Journal of Human Rights*, 13(3), pp. 274–89.

Rainer, E., Ayoub, P., Mclain, K. and Chen, K. (2021) *Guide to Inclusion of LGBTI People in Development and Foreign Policy*. New York, NY: Outright International. Available at: https://outrightinternational.org/sites/default/files/2023-04/GuideToInclusionRevised_Revised_OutrightInternational_4.pdf (Accessed: 10 December 2024).

Rainer, E.C. (2021) *From Pariah to Priority: How LGBTI Rights Became a Pillar of American and Swedish Foreign Policy*. Albany, NY: State University of New York Press.

Rao, R. (2014) 'The Locations of Homophobia', *London Review of International Law*, 2(2), pp. 169–99. Available at: https://doi.org/10.1093/lril/lru010.

Rao, R. (2015) 'Rahul Rao: Global Homocapitalism / Radical Philosophy', *Radical Philosophy*. Available at: https://www.radicalphilosophy.com/article/global-homocapitalism (Accessed: 28 February 2019).

Rao, R. (2020) *Out of Time: The Queer Politics of Postcoloniality*. Oxford: Oxford University Press.

Rao, R. (2024) 'Is the Homo in Homocapitalism the Caste in Caste Capitalism and the Racial in Racial Capitalism?', *South Atlantic Quarterly*, 123(1), pp. 79–103.

Rodriguez, S.M. (2018) *The Economies of Queer Inclusion: Transnational Organizing for LGBTI Rights in Uganda*. Durham, NC: Duke University Press.

Rodriguez, S.M. (2022) *The Economies of Queer Inclusion: Transnational Organizing for LGBTI Rights in Uganda*. Lanham, MD: Lexington Books.

Rooke, A. (2009) 'Queer in the Field: On Emotions, Temporality, and Performativity in Ethnography', *Journal of Lesbian Studies*, 13(2), pp. 149–60.

Rossdale, C. (2019) *Resisting Militarism: Direct Action and the Politics of Subversion*. Edinburgh: University of Edinburgh Press.

Rossi, A. (2020) 'The Rainbow Flag between Protection and Monopolization: Iconic Heroine or Damsel in Distress?', *Journal of Intellectual Property Law & Practice*, 15(9), pp. 727–37.

Rowbotham, S. (1993) *Women in Movement: Feminism and Social Action*. London: Routledge.

Roy, S. (2022) *Changing the Subject: Feminist and Queer Politics in Neoliberal India*. Durham, NC: Duke University Press.

Rushbrook, D. (2002) 'Cities, Queer Space, and the Cosmopolitan Tourist', *GLQ: A Journal of Lesbian and Gay Studies*, 8(1), pp. 183–206.

Sakue-Collins, Y. (2020) '(Un)Doing Development: A Postcolonial Enquiry of the Agenda and Agency of NGOs in Africa', *Third World Quarterly*, 42(5), pp. 976–95.

Santos, A. (2012) *Social Movements and Sexual Citizenship in Southern Europe*. Basingstoke: Palgrave Macmillan.

Saunders, C. (2022) 'Contentious Politics: Politics as Claims Making', in R. Ballard and C. Barnett (eds) *The Routledge Handbook of Social Change*. London: Routledge, pp. 315–25.

Schulman, S. (2012a) *Israel/Palestine and the Queer International*. Durham, NC: Duke University Press.

Schulman, S. (2012b) *The Gentrification of the Mind: Witness to a Lost Imagination*. Berkeley, CA: University of California Press.

Schulman, S. (2013) *The Gentrification of the Mind: Witness to a Lost Imagination*. Berkeley, CA: University of California Press.

Schulman, S. (2021) *Let the Record Show: A Political History of ACT UP, New York, 1987–1993*. New York, NY: Farrar, Straus and Giroux.

Scott, J. (2013) 'The Distance between Death and Marriage', *International Feminist Journal of Politics*, 15(4), pp. 534–51.

Scott, L. (2017) 'Disrupting Johannesburg Pride: Gender, Race, and Class in the LGBTI Movement in South Africa', *Agenda*, 31(1), pp. 42–9.

Sender, K. (2006) 'Queens for a Day: Queer Eye for the Straight Guy and the Neoliberal Project', *Critical Studies in Media Communication*, 23(2), pp. 131–51.

Shelver, C. (2012) 'LGBT Activists Disrupt Joburg Gay Parade 2012.wmv', *YouTube*, 7 October. Available at: https://www.youtube.com/watch?v=Hnxip-T_Hnw (Accessed: 9 December 2024).

Sherman Heyl, B. (2007) 'Ethnographic Interviewing', in P. Atkinson et al. (eds) *Handbook of Ethnography*. Los Angeles, CA; London: SAGE Publications, pp. 369–81.

Siddiqi, D.M. (2019) 'Exceptional Sexuality in a Time of Terror: "Muslim" Subjects and Dissenting/Unmournable Bodies', *South Asia Multidisciplinary Academic Journal* [Preprint] (20). Available at: https://doi.org/10.4000/samaj.5069.

Skeggs, B. (2007) 'Feminist Ethnography', in P. Atkinson et al. (eds) *Handbook of Ethnography*. London: Sage Publications, pp. 426–42.

Slootmaeckers, K. (2017) 'The Litmus Test of Pride: Analysing the Emergence of the Belgrade "Ghost" Pride in the Context of EU Accession', *East European Politics*, 33(4), pp. 517–35.

Statman, J.M. and Ansell, A.E. (2000) 'Rise and Fall of the Makgoba a Case Study of Symbolic', *Politikon*, 27(2), pp. 277–95.

Stein, A. and Plummer, K. (1994) '"I Can't Even Think Straight" "Queer" Theory and the Missing Sexual Revolution in Sociology', *Sociological Theory*, 12(2), pp. 178–87.

Steyn, M. (2001) *Whiteness Just Isn't What It Used to Be: White Identity in a Changing South Africa*. Albany, NY: State University of New York Press.

Stonewall International (2012) 'Engaging the UK Government (English)'. Stonewall. Available at: https://www.stonewall.org.uk/resources/engaging-uk-government-english (Accessed: 6 August 2020).

Suen, Y.T. (2019) 'Sexual Minority Expatriates as Agent of Change? How Foreign Same-Sex Couples Won the Recognition of Same-Sex Relationship for Immigration Purposes in Hong Kong', *Journal of Ethnic and Migration Studies*, 47(13), pp. 1–18.

Svensson, J., Edenborg, E. and Strand, C. (2024) 'We Are Queer and the Struggle Is Here! Visibility at the Intersection of LGBT+ Rights, Postcoloniality, and Development Cooperation in Uganda', *Sexualities* [Online First]. Available at: https://doi.org/10.1177/13634607241232556.

'Taiwan (PRC) | HIV Justice Network' (no date). Available at: https://www.hivjustice.net/country/tw/ (Accessed: 7 May 2024).

Tarrow, S. (1998) *Power in Movement: Social Movements and Contentious Politics*. Cambridge: Cambridge University Press.

Tatchell, P. (2019) 'Pride Has Sold Its Soul to Rainbow-Branded Capitalism | Peter Tatchell', *The Guardian*, 28 June. Available at: https://www.theguardian.com/commentisfree/2019/jun/28/pride-rainbow-branded-capitalism-stonewall-lgbt (Accessed: 19 July 2019).

Taylor, V. (1998) 'Feminist Methodology in Social Movements Research', *Qualitative Sociology*, 21(4), pp. 357–79.

Taylor, V. and Dyke, N.V. (2004) '"Get up, Stand up": Tactical Repertoires of Social Movements', in D. Snow, S. Soule and H. Kriesi (eds), *The Blackwell Companion to Social Movements*. Oxford: Blackwell, pp. 262–93.

The Guardian (2024) 'Target Pride Merchandise Only Available at Select Stores after Rightwing Backlash' | *Retail Industry* | *The Guardian*. Available at: https://www.theguardian.com/business/article/2024/may/11/target-pride-merchandise-backlash (Accessed: 28 August 2024).

The Wire (2020) 'The Wire: The Wire News India, Latest News, News from India, Politics, External Affairs' Science, Economics, Gender and Culture', 4 February. Available at: https://thewire.in/law/mumbai-sedition-sharjeel-imam (Accessed: 10 December 2024).

Thebus, S. (2024) 'Homeless Evictions and Fires: Sea Point, Castle "Tent Cities" Burn', *IOL*, 23 February. Available at: https://www.iol.co.za/capeargus/news/homeless-evictions-and-fires-sea-point-castle-tent-cities-burn-ffff50c6-04ee-4842-b4af-156ce3b1ac6a (Accessed: 10 December 2024).

Tian, I.L. (2020) 'Perverse Politics, Postsocialist Radicality: Queer Marxism in China', *QED: A Journal in GLBTQ Worldmaking*, 7(2), pp. 48–68.

Tilley, S. (2025) *Leigh Bowery: The Life and Times of an Icon*. 2nd edn. London: Thames and Hudson.

Toole, B. (2021) 'What Lies Beneath: The Epistemic Roots of White Supremacy', in E. Edenberg and M. Hannon (eds) *Political Epistemology*. Oxford: Oxford University Press, pp. 76–94.

Tramps! (2022). Low End.

Turok, I., Scheba, A. and Visagie, J. (2020) 'Cape Town: A City Still Divided by Race and Class'. SLHC Research Summary 01. GCRF Centre for Sustainable, Healthy and Learning Cities and Neighbourhoods (SHLC): University of Glasgow. Available at: https://www.centreforsustainablecities.ac.uk/wp-content/uploads/2020/10/SHLC_Research_Summary_CAPETOWN.pdf

UK Black Pride (no date) *UK Black Pride*. Available at: https://www.ukblackpride.org.uk (Accessed: 9 December 2024).

Upadhyay, N. (2020) 'Hindu Nation and Its Queers: Caste, Islamophobia, and De/coloniality in India', *Interventions International Journal of Postcolonial Studies*, 22(4), pp. 464–80.

USAID (2023) *LGBTQI+ Inclusive Development Policy*. USAID. Available at: https://www.usaid.gov/sites/default/files/2023-07/USAID_LGBTQI-Inclusive-Development-Policy_August-2023_1.pdf.

Van Niekerk, G. (2017) *Queer Communities Boycott 'Pink-washed' Johannesburg Pride*, HuffPost UK. Available at: https://www.huffingtonpost.co.uk/2017/10/24/queer-communities-boycott-pink-washed-johannesburg-pride_a_23253841/ (Accessed: 17 June 2020).

Waites, M. (2024) 'The International Politics of Development for LGBT+ Inclusion: How the UK's Johnson Government Used Crisis as a Political Opportunity', *International Politics* [Online First]. https://doi.org/10.1057/s41311-024-00612-6.

Walcott, R. (2017) 'Black Lives Matter, Police and Pride: Toronto Activists Spark a Movement,' *The Conversation*. Available at: http://theconversation.com/black-lives-matter-police-and-pride-toronto-activists-spark-a-movement-79089 (Accessed: 20 July 2023).

Ward, J. (2003) 'Producing `Pride' in West Hollywood: A Queer Cultural Capital for Queers with Cultural Capital', *Sexualities*, 6(1), pp. 65–94.

Ward, J. (2008) *Respectably Queer: Diversity Culture in LGBT Activist Organizations*. Nashville, TN: Vanderbilt University Press.

Westwood, V. (2016) *Get a Life: The Diaries of Vivienne Westwood*. London: Serpent's Tail.

Williams, J.R. (2008) 'Spatial Transversals: Gender, Race, Class, and Gay Tourism in Cape Town, South Africa', *Race, Gender & Class*, 15(1/2), pp. 58–78.

Yu, D. and Nackerdien, M.F. (2019) 'South Africa's Informal Sector: Why People Get Stuck in Precarious Jobs,' *The Conversation*. Available at: http://theconversation.com/south-africas-informal-sector-why-people-get-stuck-in-precarious-jobs-113401 (Accessed: 30 September 2019).

INDEX

affect and emotional politics
 anger and grassroots activism 42, 53, 123, 132, 159, 164
 happiness and deradicalization 23, 27, 46, 94, 126
 queer joy and event organizing 28, 35, 54, 112, 142, 151
Ahmed, Sara
 corporate and institutional rhetoric 8–9, 21–2, 27, 53–4, 89–90
 visibility politics and representation 41, 92–3, 174
AIDS Coalition to Unleash Power (ACT UP)
 activism, protests, visibility campaigns 11–12, 20, 35–6, 57, 144–6
 legacy and global influence 164, 166, 175
 radical queer activism and organizing model 26–7, 39–41
 visibility and media tactics 42, 44, 141
Ally, Kaye
 capitalism and corporate sponsorship 67–68, 90–1, 106
 on human rights and Johannesburg Pride 70–1
 Soweto Pride critique 17
alternative Prides 3, 22, 42, 108, 113, 141–6, 166
 Drag March (New York) 30, 85, 141–5
 Dyke March (New York) 85, 143–5
 Khumbulani Pride (Cape Town) 61, 72–4, 143
 organizing events 60, 110, 163–4
 as political protest 157–8
 Pride Uganda 4, 10, 117, 126
 Trans Pride 3, 78
Anohni
 queer subculture and artistic resistance 24
art and artistic performance
 activist performance and queer protest 15–16, 23–4, 42–4, 123
 photographic exhibitions 16–17, 63, 137–8
 queer aesthetics and visual culture 47–8, 84–5, 94, 142
 symbolism and branding 20, 48, 54–5
assimilation politics
 impact on Pride and LGBTQ+ movements 46–7, 120
 intersection with homonormativity 49–50
Ayoub, Phillip M. 27–8, 33

Baker, Gilbert
 rainbow flag and corporate symbolism 20, 54–5, 94, 128
Bhuptani, Ankit
 on corporate engagement 105
 on politicization of Pride 77–80
Black Lives Matter
 as critical race theory 39
 disruptions of Pride events 2, 60, 143–4
Bowery, Leigh 43
Browne, Kath 28–9, 32, 37
Burchiellaro, Olimpia
 co-optation of LGBTQ+ activism 41–3, 56–7, 90, 111–12
 neoliberalism and pinkwashing 16, 46, 48–50

Butler, Judith
 grievability and visibility politics 11, 39–40
 norms, power, and depoliticization 42, 51, 79

Cameron, Edwin 62
Canada
 national branding with Pride events 119–22, 126, 139
 rainbow diplomacy 118, 133, 143–4
Cape Town Pride
 corporate sponsorship debates 90
 and queer representation 115–16, 133
 racial and class tensions 61, 71–8, 81
capitalism
 branding and globalization 20–1, 34, 53, 56–7, 83, 156
 co-optation of Pride 2, 8–9, 11–12, 58, 68, 171–2
 neoliberalism and diversity politics 87, 93
 homocapitalism critiques by LGBTQ+ 4–5, 27, 48–51, 55, 89, 142–3
 as social injustice 33, 41, 112–13, 174–5
capitalist governmentality
 corporate sponsorship and institutional control 21, 55, 58, 82
 corporatization of Pride organizing 27, 32, 42–3, 50–1
 governance policies and Pride branding 85, 155, 168
 state-corporate alignment in Pride diplomacy 123–5, 129–30
career queers
 gentrification 58, 169–70
 NGO-ization 22, 51–2, 80, 107–8
 professionalization of activism 10, 87, 109–10
Castro Espín, Mariela
 CENESEX and Cuban LGBTQ+ advocacy 123, 128–9
 Conga march in Havana 14
China
 and the British Council 128
 corporate involvement in Pride events 150, 152
 LGBTQ+ rights and state repression 89, 130–1, 136, 147
 Shanghai Pride 5, 31, 95–8
class inequalities
 career queers and privilege 10, 26, 39, 45–7, 64, 106
 intersection with gender 9, 33, 54, 105
 intersection with race 14–17, 20, 67–8, 71, 89, 98
 within Pride events 29, 57, 61, 74
class privilege
 access to and exclusion from Pride 9–10, 14–15, 32–3, 66–7
 corporate Pride and elite dominance 68–9, 74–6
 gentrification and spatial displacement 26–7, 38–9, 42–3
 institutional advocacy and marginalization 98–9, 113, 142
 intersection with gender in Pride participation 146, 150, 152, 166, 170
 visibility gaps and representation in media 51, 54, 79–80
commodification 44, 102
contentious politics 13, 20, 26, 33–5, 57, 61, 170
corporate Pride participation
 corporate sponsorship debates 90–1, 106
 diversity marketing and contradictions 87–8, 112–13

IBM's activism claims 93–4
rainbow branding and critique 88, 94–5
state alignment and rainbow diplomacy 21–2, 123–4, 129–30
World Pride commercialization critiques 85–6
corporate social responsibility
diversity marketing and contradictions 87–8, 91–4, 112
state alignment and rainbow diplomacy 21–2, 123–5, 129
corporate sponsorship 4, 47, 49, 90, 110–11
Cuba
grassroots LGBTQ+ organizing in Cuba 14, 123–4, 128–9, 134, 142–3

depoliticization of activism
corporate and state involvement in Pride 22, 113
impacts on grassroots organizing 48, 143–4
Ditsie, Beverly Palesa 62, 67
diversity politics
Ahmed's critique 8–9, 27, 86, 89–90, 174
corporate appropriation and branding 53–4, 100–1, 112–13
and LGBTQ+ rights 41
state-sponsored diversity initiatives 20–2, 55, 87, 142, 164
Duggan, Lisa
homonormativity concept 46–51

Ekurhuleni Pride
grassroots alternative organizing 24, 63, 83, 160–3, 166
Ekurhuleni Pride Organizing Committee (EPOC) 161–2
Embassy involvement in Pride events 123–4, 126–8, 130–1
Enloe, Cynthia
feminist curiosity and activism 19–20, 152
European Union (EU)
LGBTQ+ diplomacy in Taiwan 126–7, 130, 134
and Pride 10, 28, 119–20, 128, 138
EuroPride
NGO-ization and Pride governance 10, 33, 52, 107
exclusionary practices
LGBTQ+ spaces and Pride events 60–1, 71, 75, 166
marginalization of intersectional identities 38–9, 75, 106, 113, 166

feminism
intersection with LGBTQ+ activism 9–10, 158
post-feminism and commercialization 8–9
Forum for the Empowerment of Women, the (FEW) 12, 44, 66, 109, 138, 160
Foucault, Michel
LGBTQ+ visibility and state power 49–50, 55–6
framework of truth 26–7

gentrification
displacement of queer communities 26–7, 38–9, 42–3, 57–8
impact on queer space and radical culture 45–6, 169–70
New York subcultural spaces 35–6, 39–40, 44–5
grassroots Pride, case studies
Drag March (New York) 30, 85, 141–6
Dyke March (New York) 85, 143–5

Index

Ekurhuleni Pride 22, 25, 166
Havana Pride (unofficial) 123
Hong Kong Migrants Pride
   155–6, 166
Khumbulani Pride (Cape Town)
   61, 72–4, 143
Reclaim Pride March 57, 85
Soweto Pride 12, 17, 44, 65,
   109–10, 137–8
Taiwan Pride 132, 147–51
UK Black Pride 3, 22
grassroots Pride organizing
   community-based activism and
      organizing 60–1, 107, 157–8
   decentralized and volunteer-led
      models 163–4
   distinctions from corporatized
      Pride events 61, 166
   global grassroots alternatives
      123, 132, 166

Hindu nationalism 18, 20, 77–81, 105
Homocapitalism
   corporate co-optation and Pride
      8–9, 21–2, 41, 55, 105–6, 142
   global expansion and critique 20,
      86, 94, 109, 132–4, 143
   intersection with neoliberalism
      and capitalism 4–5, 12, 53–4,
      58, 88–9
   rainbow capitalism 16, 27,
      111–12
   state alignment 22, 120
   theoretical development of the
      term 48–50, 125, 172–3
Homocolonialism 120, 132
homonationalism
   state alignment with LGBTQ+
      agendas 22, 120
homonormativity
   assimilation and neoliberal
      LGBTQ+ identities 46–7, 49–50
   depoliticization critique 46, 58
   intersection with
      homocapitalism 4–5, 9, 12

Hong Kong
   activist responses 5, 31, 129
   corporate involvement in Pride
      events 5, 31, 95–8
   state responses to LGBTQ+
      organizing 127–8, 130–1
Hong Kong Migrants Pride
   activism for migrant workers'
      rights 14–15, 22, 35, 55
   Gabriela Hong Kong 153
   grassroots LGBTQ+ organizing
      5, 129
   international solidarity and
      recognition 155–7, 166
   visibility, precarity, and exclusion
      98–9, 143, 152–4
Hong Kong Pink Dot
   alternative to Pride politics 98–9,
      129
   corporate-sponsored LGBTQ+
      visibility event 100, 104
Hong Kong Pink Season
   alternative to grassroots activism
      98–9, 129
   cultural agenda and lifestyle
      branding 104
Hong Kong Pride 14, 98–100, 103–4,
   110–11, 150–4
Hoyle, David 23–4, 44
HSBC
   corporate sponsorship
      controversies 9, 16, 99–103,
      152–7
   see also Hong Kong; Hong Kong
      Migrants Pride; Hong Kong
      Pride

IBM
   corporate diversity campaigns
      90–3, 100
inclusion policies
   corporate diversity rhetoric
      86–7
   critiques from queer activists
      89–90

India
  corporate and state involvement 77–8, 80–1, 105–6
  Hindu-Nationalist BJP Party 77–8, 80
  LGBTQ+ activism 59, 174
  Mumbai Pride critiques of TISS 79–81, 135, 137
  visibility politics and media narratives 14, 68, 125
International Lesbian and Gay Association (ILGA)
  global LGBTQ+ advocacy 10, 52, 107–8
  ILGA World Conference 16, 72, 108
InterPride
  global Pride influence 10, 13, 33, 51–2, 107–8, 168
intersectionality
  grassroots versus elite activism 29, 51–2, 106–8, 144
  marginalization within Pride 15–17, 45–7, 66–7, 79
  race, class, gender exclusions 9, 38, 42–3, 64, 98
  see also class privilege; feminism; visibility politics

Johannesburg People's Pride
  activist-led, intersectional Pride event 59, 66
  Johannesburg Pride critique 61, 81–2
Johannesburg Pride
  controversy over space and ownership 61–2, 65–6, 69–70, 74–6, 110
  Ally's role and related controversies 67–8, 90, 106–7
  Lifestyle Conference 47, 70
  racial and class tensions 57, 81, 165
Johnson, Marsha P.
  radical activism and Pride critiques 32–3

LGBTQ+ activism
  intersectional approaches 35–6, 89
  professionalized advocacy 11, 107–9
  protesting state involvement in Pride 124–6
LGBTQ+ consumer markets
  corporate targeting and pink capitalism 47, 49, 51
LGBTQ+ media coverage
  corporate-sponsored content 40, 46–8, 84, 91
  digital platforms and social media 65–8, 100–2, 110–11
  global campaigns and branding 13, 123, 127–8
  representation and critique 29–30, 34, 42–3, 72, 158
LGBTQ+ rights
  activism professionalization 9–10, 80, 107
  backlash and reversals 120–1, 123
  global progress narratives 14, 46
  intersection with Pride organizing and critique 22–4, 57, 109
  state diplomacy and international image-making 115, 128–9
lifestylization
  commercialization of Pride 21, 47, 50, 65, 83–9, 105–7
London
  queer subcultures and histories of activism 11–13, 59–60, 83, 99, 137–8
London Pride
  corporate sponsorship and NGO-ization 16–17, 83
  criticisms and activist responses 35
  diplomatic participation and state presence 59, 138
  early mentions and event description 12–13, 30–1

Madingwane, Jade
  organizing Pride events 65, 109
  South African Pride events critique 67–8, 158
Mathabela, Mpumi
  activism and Johannesburg Pride critique 64–7
  homocapitalism critique 83, 106–7
  intersectionality and grassroots organizing 22, 165
Matsoeneng, Zandile
  Johannesburg Pride critique 1, 67, 159–60
migrants' rights and Pride
  grassroots migrant-led Pride organizing 152–4
  international recognition and solidarity networks 155–7, 166
  intersection with LGBTQ+ activism 14–15, 22, 35
  precarity and visibility in Pride 55, 98–9, 143
Mohapi, Ntsupe
  challenges facing LGBTQ+ people 161–2
meaning of Pride 12, 23
Mumbai Pride
  corporate and nationalist politics 14, 18, 20, 77–81, 137
  exclusion and class privilege 105–6, 125, 142
  queer and grassroots resistance 59
Muñoz, José Esteban
  queer aesthetics and radical futures 42–3, 168

national identity
  case studies in branding with Pride 128–9, 132–3, 154–5, 173
  construction through Pride events 27–8, 118, 120, 128–33, 147
  LGBTQ+ inclusion as state soft power 29, 81
  NGO and consular partnerships in Pride diplomacy 119, 123–4
  Pride in diplomatic image-making 21–2, 75, 105
  state sponsorship and international visibility 90, 116–18
neoliberalism
  co-optation of LGBTQ+ activism 8, 11, 45–6, 50, 53, 87
  diversity politics and depoliticization 45–8, 53, 86
  homocapitalism dynamics 12, 93, 103, 174
  institutional control of LGBTQ+ activism 87, 112
New York
  alternative Pride organizing 2–3, 11–12, 22, 24–5
  community memory and organizing histories 20, 57, 68–9, 93
  cultural visibility and queer performance 108–9, 111, 143–5, 147, 151, 164, 166–8
  gentrification and loss of queer spaces 35–6, 39–40
  Queer Liberation March 26–7, 30
  radical queer activism and Stonewall legacy 6, 13–15, 84–5, 141–2
  urban displacement and Pride geography 43, 48, 52–3
  see also alternative Prides; Queer Liberation March (New York); World Pride
NGO-ization of activism
  LGBTQ+ advocacy 9–10, 80, 107, 135

One in Nine Campaign
  Johannesburg Pride 2012 critique 65–6, 83, 165

Out & Equal
  corporate LGBTQ+ inclusion 5, 49, 96–7
  Out and Equal Asia Conference 15
Out Leadership
  corporate LGBTQ+ advocacy 15–16, 49, 99–100, 152
Out Leadership Asia Summit 15, 99–100

pink capitalism
  commodification of Pride events 47, 68–9, 102
  corporate targeting of LGBTQ+ markets 4, 105, 128–9
pinkwashing
  state and corporate tactics 13–14, 27, 128–9, 172
  use in corporate and diplomatic strategies 3–4, 115
politics of truth
  Foucauldian knowledge production 26, 55–7
  in Pride narratives 38–41
precarity
  economic and labour insecurity 21, 33, 169
  LGBTQ+ marginalization 9, 26, 86, 156
  racialized precarity and intersectionality 22, 38
  visibility politics and grievable lives 39, 171
Pride
  commercialization and branding 6, 9, 47–8, 55–6, 92–4, 104
  corporations and elite participation 21, 68–9, 95–6, 105–6, 164
  existing literature critique 10–11, 22–3, 27, 33–5, 144–5
  governance and state alignment 120–1, 123–4, 128–33
  grassroots critiques and activist refusals 3, 42–3, 85–6, 143–5
  as protest and visibility platform 2–3, 39–41, 57–8, 60
  racial and class exclusions 9–10, 14–15, 61–2, 70, 75–7, 80–1
  urban gentrification and spatial politics 44–6, 64–5, 71–2, 168
  visibility politics and public image 86–7, 94, 103, 169–70

queer activism
  anti-capitalist critiques 26–7, 40–2, 46
  grassroots models and ACT UP 11–12, 20, 144–6
  intersection with Pride politics 57–8, 164
  reclamation of Pride 3, 143
Queer Eye for the Straight Guy 9, 47
Queer Liberation March (New York)
  grassroots, alternative Pride 3, 6, 143–6, 166
queer subculture 43–5, 168
queer theory 15–16, 20, 35, 42

rainbow branding
  branding by global consumer companies 48, 85–6
  corporate appropriation of LGBTQ+ symbols 5, 20–2, 83
  state and NGO deployment in diplomacy 128–30, 132–3, 171
rainbow branding, case studies
  Absolut 55, 94–5
  British Airways 55, 84
  Cape Town Pride (sponsorship costs) 90
  IBM 90–3
  John Lewis (UK) 4
  Starbucks 112
  Target (US) 4
  T-Mobile 84–5
rainbow diplomacy
  corporate–state partnerships in LGBTQ+ advocacy 115–17

Israeli LGBTQ+ image strategy 128–30
national image-making and soft power 118–19, 132–3
pride sponsorships and diplomatic branding 120–2
in Taiwan's national identity 129–134

Rao, Rahul
capitalism, queerness, and global power 42–3, 48, 93, 98
development of homocapitalism theory 18, 49, 53, 89, 143
state power and LGBTQ+ diplomacy 108, 112, 121
see also depoliticization of activism; homocapitalism; pink capitalism

Reclaim Pride (New York)
anti-corporate organizing 11, 22, 57, 113

regime of truth
Foucauldian regime of truth 26, 155
political and social confrontations 55–6, 86

respectability politics
grassroots activist responses 42
intersection with homonormativity and exclusion 3, 144–5

Rivera, Sylvia
legacy in queer radical politics 145
Stonewall activism and trans resistance 32–3, 85

Rodriguez, S. M.
queer politics critique 10, 31
grassroots queer activism in Uganda 51–2
NGO-ization and career queers critiques 9, 80, 87

Rooke, Alison 15–16

Roy, Srila
neoliberalism 50–1, 53

RuPaul's Drag Race 9

Schulman, Sarah
ACT UP and activist resistance 11–12, 39–40
co-optation and neoliberal respectability 46–8, 83, 107
gentrification of the mind 26–7, 41–5, 168–70
queer politics 35, 120, 128

Shanghai Pride
diplomatic partnerships 127, 135–6
organizing under state repression 5, 31, 95–8, 103

Sisters of Perpetual Indulgence
Drag March participation 144, 164
queer performance and ceremonial protest 141–2

social movement theory
and analyzing Pride 6–7, 33–4, 146, 170
feminist and queer theoretical responses 19–20, 35–6, 93
mainstream LGBTQ+ activism critique 26–7, 52

South Africa
access and spatial politics in Pride 70–1, 71–3, 75–7, 79–81
African National Congress (ANC) 62, 75
community representation and LGBTQ+ organizing 113, 133, 135
corporate and state involvement in Pride events 83, 86, 89–92, 94
Democratic Alliance (DA) 71–7
diplomatic partnerships and global support 106–10
early Pride activism and resistance 16–18, 24, 44, 52
race, class, and intersectionality in Pride 20–2, 60–1, 66–7
regional activism and Pride leadership 137–9, 142–3, 157–60

Soweto Pride
  alternative Pride and grassroots organizing 12, 17, 44, 61, 65–6
  community-led Pride responses 137–8, 158–60
  intersectionality and activist critique 75, 83, 109–10
state involvement in Pride
  state co-optation critique 120–2, 126–7, 171–2
  national branding and diplomatic image strategies 116–20, 123–4
  state sponsorship of Pride events 89–91, 106, 115–16
Stonewall Riots
  origins of radical LGBTQ+ resistance 6, 11–12, 14, 32
  symbolic legacy and commodification 40, 84–5, 141–5, 164
Stonewall UK
  LGBTQ+ advocacy and global networking 40, 59, 107, 119, 122, 141–5
Sullivan Code
  corporate social responsibility 91–2, 171–2
Sweden
  national branding through Pride 21, 119, 123
  rainbow diplomacy and state image-making 115, 118, 127, 133–4, 136

Taiwan
  Democratic Progressive Party (DPP) 147
  EU diplomatic involvement in LGBTQ+ rights 126–8
  Kuomintang (political party) (KMT) 147
  LGBTQ+ sovereignty and political visibility 106, 125
  participation in global LGBTQ+ movements 5, 21, 74, 100–1
  Pride, identity, and national diplomacy 130–2, 134, 139
Taiwan (Taipei) Pride
  inclusive, volunteer-led organizing 147–8
  large-scale grassroots event 143, 147
  limited corporate participation 148
  visibility and national identity 22, 126, 130–1, 149–51, 166
Tel Aviv Pride 128–9
Tata Institute of Social Sciences (TISS) Queer Collective
  Godrej India Cultural Lab critique 142
  Mumbai Pride critique 59, 78–81, 105–6
trans inclusion and exclusion at Pride events
  corporate Pride and tokenism 84–5, 115, 129, 144–5
  New York and Dyke March debates 24–5, 32
  South African Pride events 71–3, 78, 157
transnational LGBTQ+ politics
  diplomatic contradictions in LGBTQ+ rights 10–11, 119–20, 126–7
  NGO-ization and Pride governance 116, 130–1
  Pride and global solidarity claims 20, 26, 33, 35
  state power and international identity 147, 166, 170–1
transnational marketing
  advertising and consumer identity politics 99, 101, 105

corporate branding and
LGBTQ+ markets 9, 49, 52,
94–6
rainbow branding for global
Pride appeal 86, 90, 103
state-led marketing through
diplomacy 125, 130–1, 150,
153, 172
truth
alternative truths 38, 44, 155
art and truth 94–5, 137–8
importance and representational
stakes 54–5, 128

United Kingdom (UK)
corporate visibility and branding
4, 54–5, 86, 94, 106, 108
foreign policy and LGBTQ+
rights 118–19, 122–3
historical and national context
18, 21, 117–18, 126, 135–9
intersectional alternative Pride
events 3, 35, 59
Pride diplomacy and branding
119–21, 125
United Nations (UN)
international rights discourse 10,
52, 120, 122
and Taiwan 130
United States (US)
Black-led and grassroots political
resistance 39, 51, 60, 144–5,
171
commercialization of LGBTQ+
movements 4–5, 37–8, 60,
83–9, 95, 164
corporate sponsorship and
rainbow branding 47, 98, 106,
115
LGBTQ+ cultural exports and
global visibility 16, 117, 126,
146
Pride diplomacy and foreign
policy 118–19, 133, 137, 139

radical queer activism and Pride
protest 22–4, 28, 30

violence
against LGBTQ+ communities
31, 60–2, 71–2, 159
against trans communities and
activists 85, 151
homophobic and gender-based
44, 63–6, 73–5, 78, 110,
162
New York Queer Liberation
March 143–6
resulting from capitalism
49–50
state and police violence 3,
141–2, 145
TISS Queer Collective
experiences in Mumbai
105–6
visibility politics
branding and inclusion optics 64,
70, 89, 95, 160
cultural representation 135–6,
139, 151–3, 162–3
grievability and ungrievable
lives 39
institutional critiques of visibility
9, 11, 31, 33, 35
intersection with precarity 21,
38, 169
limitations and exclusions 27–8,
57–8, 126–8, 148–9
Pride as LGBTQ+ visibility
platform 15, 60, 86, 145

Ward, Jane
mainstream LGBTQ+ critiques
10–11, 34, 47–8, 51
queer whiteness and exclusion
60, 106
state and corporate alignment
critiques 98
Westwood, Vivienne 43–4

World Pride
    commercialization and elitism critiques 6, 12–14, 25–6, 40, 109
    corporate sponsorship and branding 72, 84–5, 93, 146
    New York events 6, 12–14, 25–6, 40, 84–6, 130–1, 141–4
    Rome events 30

World Pride Human Rights Conference
    access inequality and depoliticization 52, 91, 93
    corporate-led agenda and critique 72, 108–9
    diplomatic discourse and global LGBTQ+ rights 16, 166–9

www.ingramcontent.com/pod-product-compliance
Ingram Content Group UK Ltd.
Pitfield, Milton Keynes, MK11 3LW, UK
UKHW021845190226
468211UK00005B/66